Understanding the Consumer

Understanding the Consumer

Isabelle Szmigin

SAGE Publications

London • Thousand Oaks • New Delhi

SAGE Publications Ltd
6 Bonhill Street
London EC2A 4PU

SAGE Publications Inc
2455 Teller Road
Thousand Oaks, California 91320

SAGE Publications India Pvt Ltd
B-42, Panchsheel Enclave
Post Box 4109
New Delhi – 100 017

British Library Cataloguing in Publication data

A catalogue record for this book is available from the British
Library

ISBN 0 7619 4700 0
ISBN 0 7619 4701 9 (pbk)

Library of Congress Control Number available

Typeset by Mayhew Typesetting, Rhayader, Powys
Printed and bound in Great Britain by Athenaeum Press, Gateshead

Contents

Acknowledgements

There are a few people who really helped me with this book. Gerald Goodhardt first introduced me to the study of consumer behaviour. Peter Clark encouraged me to start writing and others helped me to finish. Marylyn Carrigan gave me moral support throughout. Jan, Alex and Nick just knew I would do it.

Introduction

for consumption is not the site of social division, inequity and poverty nor the focus of affluent, conspicuous and rapturous style cultures; rather it is both and all of these, though not necessarily equally, and its significance in either respect varies from time to time and from culture to culture. (Edwards, 2000: 31)

Marketing in advanced Western societies is at a crossroads. It must find new relevance grounded in an understanding of postmodern consumers and their behaviour or continue down a road which leads to both theorists and practitioners being seen as little more than the used car salesmen of business schools. For years marketing has been the new kid on the block. It has been tolerated as the business discipline without discipline, given the imperative of consumption and in recognition of the freedom needed in marketing to furnish creativity. There has clearly been much creativity but also much snake oil, the vocation for sharks and wise guys. Its ethical qualities have frequently been compared, and not always favourably, with politicians, journalists and other disreputable or even notorious groups of charlatans. A recent BBC television programme entitled *The Century of the Self* highlighted some of the techniques shared by politicians and marketers. The focus group, for example, was examined as a tool for identifying people's inner desires and finding ways for them to express their individuality through consumption. The programme argued that the technique originally developed by psychoanalysts proved as useful for getting Labour in the UK, and the Democrats in the USA back into power, as it had been for getting people to buy washing powder and chocolates. It was a technique aimed at identifying what people really wanted. Superficially, perhaps this might appear a positive development. Moulding goods and services to people's inner desires and supplying them with what they want at a price are essentially what capitalism and politics in Western societies are about. But the relationship between producer and consumer, just as with government and citizen, has never been so simple;

people do not shout out from the streets, 'This is what I want, give it to me' – they choose from a circumscribed range of options supplied to them by the manufacturers and suppliers, just as with government. We develop ideas, products, and services and then we show them to consumers and ask, which of these would you really like? To do this, suppliers clearly need 'to know' their potential customers, and the focus group, among other techniques, some of which will be examined in this book, has been a useful tool. Awareness of marketing's problems has been acknowledged. Holt (2002) has suggested that in the first few decades of the twentieth century, two principles were at work, one focused on the economics of marketing using branding to establish the legitimacy and prestige of a business and present the brand's value proposition to the market, while the other was closer to what he refers to as 'P.T. Barnum hucksterism' (2002: 80) that saw consumers as dupes who would buy inflated claims. While Holt charts the changes from this either functional or charlatan mode to today's use of branding as a 'cultural resource' (ibid.: 87) which allows a form of expressive culture, he emphasizes that brands and, by inference, marketing can no longer hide their commercial motivations. Consumption as expressive culture is perhaps where postmodern consumers have arrived but it can be argued that they still maintain many of the concerns of earlier consumers related to economic utility and not being cheated by the P.T. Barnums of the twenty-first century. Knowing what consumers want and what their motivations and concerns are, seems to be an obvious first staging post in developing appropriate responses for the discipline.

Knowing consumers leads to communicating with them as that is the marketers' route to using what they have learnt from their research. This is a fundamental building block of relationships, whether producer to consumer or government to citizen. Back in the 1970s Wells made the following insightful remark regarding marketing, communication and the consumer, 'Almost all of marketing is communication; marketers are most effective when they know their audiences' (1975: 197). But communication also has come under increased scrutiny. How we should communicate, when and to whom, are questions worth considering as not only being relevant to business and creative decisions but also ethical and moral ones. Monbiot (2000), for example, has criticized advertisers for treating children as 'consumers in training', highlighting the growing trend in advertising agencies for special children's divisions because, as one executive he cites said, 'Children are much easier to reach with advertising. They pick up on it fast and quite often we can exploit that relationship and get them pestering their parents' (quoted in Monbiot, 2000: 338). Marketers are criticized for the techniques they use and the promises they make. Companies are supporting schools, hospitals and universities and ensuring that their brands are well communicated as part of the relationship they develop. Marketing has been criticized for being responsible for the increase in social comparison, competitive consumption and the need to keep up, to have the latest and the best consumer goods. The competitive process of keeping up with others is determined, some say, largely by the drive for more and more consumption for which marketing is responsible.

While, on the one hand, marketing and the techniques employed by marketing are now under increased scrutiny, more and more young people flock to university to enrol in Business Studies degrees, Masters in Marketing and many other courses which teach a wide range of subjects both in and around the core of the subject. Marketing for students can be interesting, useful, fun even, especially when it is about communications in the form of advertisements. Students often warm to marketing because they recognize themselves as consumers. But marketing is also largely about techniques. It is about understanding the interrelationships of the marketing mix, recognizing the importance of strategy and planning, the seeing through of ideas to fruition, and, crucial to consumer behaviour, about trying to understand the consumer. It is the central theme of this book that, in a postmodern society, consumer behaviour has changed fundamentally and that marketing theory and practice in the devising and application of technique have not kept up. Fundamental, often implicit assumptions, such as regarding consumers as passive members of stable market segments, continue to influence both thinking and practice despite the rhetoric of understanding and catering to diversity. In the past marketing has attempted to control rather than embrace consumer complexity by devising neat typologies. These and other structures are breaking down as we fail to engage in understanding what drives individual behaviour in postmodern consumption.

That is not to say that consumers and consumption have not been and do not continue to be of great interest. Indeed, as Schroeder points out, 'The consumer is a hot topic in many fields right now, from literary studies to anthropology to history. What once seemed beneath the gaze of humanities scholars has emerged as a central site of analysis' (2000: 384). But the consumer is still in some strange way peripheral to marketing. Marketing has a job to do and that job involves and includes the consumer. An understanding of the consumer may seem an obvious necessity, a foundation even for marketing but the problem of the individual is a real one and one that has, as Schroeder points out, been subsumed 'under the rubric of target markets – groups of consumers that share a relevant demographic, psychological or psychographic characteristic, or variable' (ibid.: 385). Marketing management has responded to the difficulty of the unruly, irrational, and often changeable individual through aggregation.

At the same time, marketing in business schools, while teaching consumer behaviour through a range of content-similar textbooks, seems to be acknowledging its existence and contribution but resists its complexities and contradictions. For the theory and practice of marketing to move on, it is both an intellectual and practical imperative that the complexity of postmodern society and the consumer in that society is embraced.

In effect, modern marketing pays only lip service to the consumer and this is nowhere more evident than in the current dominant paradigm of relationship marketing. Relationship marketing in its current form is not an adequate response to the complexity of the postmodern world. Rather, it is little more than a mechanism to avoid complexity. This is not to deny the fundamental importance of relationships. There is no point in throwing the baby out with the bathwater. Indeed, this book argues that relationships more broadly considered play a central role in both the theory and practice of marketing. However, the theory and practice of relationship marketing have been seriously deficient in their failure to grasp the nettle of trying to understand the consumer.

What does this mean in practice? What is the point of this criticism if consumers continue to shop, buy new products and use their loyalty cards? First, it is quite simply essential to the theory and functions of marketing that it incorporates a critical and continual dialogue with consumers and consumer society. This is not going to happen through resorting only to the textbooks on technique for our information and knowledge. We need more than ever before to develop a critical and reflexive literature in marketing, to show that this is not only a managerial tool but also a way and means of examining at least a part of the world. This has a practical side as well. After all, it was Kotler who said that markets change faster than marketing and inevitably it is the consumers that make the markets. As we observe the traditional approaches to market segmentation and consumer typology breaking down, it is not enough to divide and rule, to segregate and aggregate. Consumers more than ever know what is being done to them, not only are they not fooled by the targeted admail that falls on their doorsteps or comes through their computers, they know the game well enough to play with it and even to undermine it if they so wish. The trouble, as Edwards says, is that there is no consistency to how they decide to play this particular game, 'However, the consumer is perhaps neither the victim or dupe of some capitalist conspiracy nor merely a pleasure-seeking and frivolous individualist, but a fellow conspirer in the world of advertising, sniggering one minute and taking it all too seriously the next' (Edwards, 2000: 76). We can no longer be confident in the tools of marketing practice, we need to read and understand the subtleties of consumers. Next we need more than ever to know how consumers respond to and identify with the goods they buy.

Once we recognize that for all but the most basic necessities, we need to go beyond the functional attributes of products which relate to use value, this inevitably leads us to engage with sign value, and the consumption of symbols, not products. This is perhaps where postmodern marketing and indeed criticism of marketing have taken us to – that we no longer purchase, consume and use things for the functional, utilitarian purposes but rather for how they speak to us, what they say about us to our fellows and how they make us feel about ourselves – how brands in particular define us as human beings. But is it really as simple as this? Can the use of goods to signal to others be the end point of the postmodern consumer? This is surely unlikely. This book will argue that, while an understanding of the implications of the consumption of symbols is critical, we also need to understand use values as important to demarcating usage and perception in responses to marketing in the form of resistance, alternative consumption approaches and downshifting. A considerable proportion of this book is devoted to the question of innovation and, in particular, consumers' approaches to the adoption of innovations. While for some the notion of innovation reeks of functional and positivist notions of going forward, onward and upward, it is an essential component to marketing thinking as it has been the adoption of things, services, ideas, concepts that is the fuel to the fire of business success. As such, innovation remains central to economic growth in postmodern society and represents perhaps the major challenge to marketing today. In particular, the dangers of failing to understand the implications of innovation in the consumption of symbols are emphasized, together with the necessity of drawing on a rich synthesis of material on consumer behaviour.

In order to formulate what should be a deeper fusion of thinking we will look beyond the confines of business literature. In examining consumers we should seek to understand the psychological, economic, social and cultural drivers behind postmodern complexity to widen the debate and allow room for argument. This, while a challenge, is one that is never better resourced than with literature from these areas. The richness and variety of sources are evidenced in just a few examples, Giddens and Lury in sociology, Miller in anthropology, Schor in economics, Belk in consumer research, and commentators such as Klein, Schlosser and Monbiot taking the marketing society to task. By means of these and many others in such fields, this book is deliberately eclectic. It aims to examine the consumer from a range of different perspectives and to reach out to readers of diverse backgrounds with a view to drawing them in through their own current understanding of consumers. The discussion of issues is aimed both at attacking unconscious preconceptions while ensuring that they are discussed and challenged. This is not a book attacking marketing but it is one that is critical of current practice in the sense that it suggests re-examining the principles marketers use and the way they go about things. While drawing on marketing and innovation literature, it seeks to go beyond this and inform the discussion from sources that should help to develop the discipline beyond the current position, into new and more critical avenues. Therefore a key feature of this book is that while it refers to much marketing practice and theory both historical and current, it also looks to a broader range in both the social sciences and humanities. For those readers coming to this book from disciplines outside of business, it will attempt to connect the areas of marketing covered here, in particular, relationships, consumers and innovation, to other realms of critical analysis. It is likely that some will be embarking on MSc courses in Marketing having read a first degree in the humanities perhaps, others may be taking more specialized courses in Marketing Ethics, Marketing in Society, or Consumerism. It is also intended to add to critical thinking in general on the nature of consumers and how they behave, it does not intend to replicate or add to the abundance of interesting textbooks in this area but it should add another dimension to analysis and understanding of consumers.

Overview of the Book

Chapter 1 critically examines marketing practice in one current form, that of relationship marketing. It looks carefully at what relationship marketing offers the consumer and supplier and attempts to understand why it is practised. In particular, it focuses upon the power relations and the reasons why a consumer would wish to maintain a long-term relationship with a company. Through a critical analysis of particular cases, it asserts that this form of marketing is seriously limited in what it offers the consumer. The final part of this first chapter focuses on the notion of risk and risk reduction which has been often cited as a reason why consumers might want to maintain long-term relationships, to find security in a wild marketplace. However, it concludes that consumers, while requiring to be informed appropriately, are well able to face up to the risks the commercial world presents. Chapter 2 looks deeper into the postmodern marketplace, first by focusing on the nature of the product and brand, its life cycle and cultural orientation, and how changes and innovations in products are directly related to consumers and new lifestyles. It distinguishes between the proliferation of new things and the development of meaningful innovations. It concludes by recommending that marketing needs to understand the paths of products through time and consumers' shifting relations with goods and their meanings to them. Chapter 3 continues the theme of the changing nature of goods on their paths, but now introduces the complexity of relationships between goods and the ever-changing consumer. The chapter argues that goods are used, consumed and understood in many different ways by consumers, making successful classification of consumers a difficult and a possibly fruitless objective. Chapter 4 outlines how the marketplace is changing and how consumers are becoming more active participants within it. Consumers readily fight back at perceived injustices, but they also act creatively, developing ways of doing things unanticipated by suppliers. The chapter warns that this is just the tip of the iceberg, consumers have adopted the Internet as a tool to combat injustice, to complain and to put their own points across to millions of others.

The second part of the book begins in Chapter 5 with a detailed examination of the role of innovation for today's company and consumer. It looks at the history of innovation research in marketing and its applicability to today's marketplace. In particular, this chapter highlights the complexity of what an innovation is to consumers today and focuses on the key differences between symbolic and functional in the innovation context. The discussion of innovation is continued in Chapter 6, which takes issue with simple linear notions of how consumers adopt over time. The complexity of the marketplace is such that it is increasingly difficult to make generalizations and neat categories of innovative behaviour based on notions of who adopts first. A comparison is made between the functional approach to diffusion and one that is built on the social consequences of innovation. This is followed in Chapter 7 by a detailed look at creativity in individuals as displayed by their innovative behaviour. It both considers some existing views on this creativity and introduces a major conclusion of the book that much innovation in marketing thinking will involve a realignment of production and consumption both by consumers and the companies that serve them. Chapter 8 then takes a critical look at some current creative consumer responses, examining the nature of both conspicuous consumption and downshifting before moving on to a more detailed look at how consumers are beginning to reconceptualize their own consumption, what is here termed 'reconsumption', which involves a closer alignment in thinking between the nature of production and consumption. This progression is completed in the final chapter which examines the historical precedent for reflecting on the nature of consumption in broader terms and in particular revisiting the importance of the production process. It is argued that increasingly marketing will need to have a more subtle conceptualization of consumers, their motives and responses and within this rethinking, the re-emergence of the importance of how, where and why goods are produced and consumed will be critical. It is hoped that this book will introduce a broader scope to thinking about consumers within the context of marketing and business and will also act as a bridge between critical works on the consumer society and business school functional thinking to open up a more inclusive future.

Chapter 1

The Consumer-oriented Approach to Marketing

we are faced with a profusion of minor choices and a dearth of major choices. We can enter a superstore and choose between twenty different brands of margarine, but many of us have no choice but to enter the superstore. Were we to tell the corporations dominating some sectors that, dissatisfied with their services, we shall take our custom elsewhere, they would ask us which planet we had in mind. (Monbiot, 2000: 16)

Introduction

This chapter will review the increasing importance of consumer behaviour to marketing management. It will highlight how consumers became more sophisticated in their purchasing and consumption behaviour towards the close of the twentieth century. Marketing management's response has been to advocate a shift from product or sales orientation towards greater customer focus. In practice this has led to the development of what has become known as relationship marketing. The chapter looks at the rise of relationship marketing and what it has sought to achieve. It suggests that as, presently practised, it has failed strategically because it still takes a passive view of the consumer and has never been nested in an understanding of their social context and evolving goals. Rather, the consumer needs to be understood as a more complex, sophisticated entity able and willing to manage their own 'relationships' who is far from passive in the marketing process and who has actively responded to relationship marketing.

The Marketing Choice – Relationship, what Relationship?

As consumers we probably face more choices than we do as citizens or even people. We may have no more than a handful of political parties to choose from, the choice of school to send our children to is likely to be numbered in single digits and, in many countries, there may be limited or even no choice at all when it comes to using other public services such as libraries and hospitals. However, in daily consumption of food and goods the situation is very different, with a vast array of new products and brands sitting on supermarket shelves. The nature of the choices we make has changed in a postmodern world and during our lifetime we will see even more of these choices changing. One response to the surfeit of choices available to the consumer has been the development of relationship marketing, where companies, brands and services engage with us in long-term partnerships in the hope that they will get to know us better and respond to our needs in an ongoing and mutually beneficial way, or at least that is the rhetoric. If we are positively involved with a company we will stay with them and be ready and able to receive new offers, product line extensions and other innovations. The key element of positive involvement is trust. Once you have a base of customers who trust you, the risk involved to the business in the introduction of innovations is mitigated to some degree, as its customers put their trust in the business meeting their needs.

Early proponents of relationship marketing identified its usefulness primarily in the services and business-to-business sectors, and then in the mid-1990s Sheth and Parvatiyar directly linked relationship marketing to consumer behaviour. Critical to their argument explaining why consumers would want to engage in relationships was the idea that reducing choice helped to simplify buying and consuming, which they described as 'tasks'. In particular, the transaction and search costs involved in choice were minimized, benefiting those consumers who were increasingly income-rich but time-poor. They suggested that the willingness and ability of consumers and businesses to engage in this form of marketing should be mutually beneficial, 'unless either consumers or marketers abuse the mutual interdependence and cooperation' (1995: 255). Clearly, in a competitive market, success should depend on demonstrating to the consumer that the relationship is mutually beneficial. This could fail either because there was some advantage to a business, possibly albeit in the short term, in ignoring this or alternatively simply because of a failure to identify the nature of benefits sought by the consumer. As we shall discuss later, there are a number of arguments that have been made against the usefulness of the relationship marketing paradigm, but we will begin with just a couple that relate directly to the notion of a creative consumer. First, one needs to examine whether the relationship is balanced in terms of equity, is the consumer getting as much out of it as the supplier? Second, do consumers always view shopping and consuming as a task? If not, the variety given to them by a range of transactions with different suppliers may be more beneficial than one or two long-term relationships.

The other day I was struck by the what now seems like the ubiquitous relationship metaphor (O'Malley and Tynan, 1999) and its emptiness for consumers. In the post I had just received a renewal reminder for a well-known fashion magazine for which I have had a subscription for the past five years (at least). Yet again it reminded me of how much I would lose out if I did not take up their wonderful opportunity to remain in the front line of fashion by reading their magazine and I would even gain a little financial advantage if, as they suggested, I took out a two-year subscription. I had, I suppose a relationship of some kind with them. How did I feel then when out of my latest copy of the same magazine a card dropped, offering much more advantageous rates for a one- and two-year subscription but with the proviso 'This offer is limited to new subscribers'? I felt that all this relationship held out to me was empty promises. They saw me as a sucker whom they assumed didn't know how to add up.

If there is to be any meaning in the relationship metaphor, then there has to be an exchange of value. For this to happen, building business may conflict with a short-term focus on profit. A company's technical advice would tell them that a new consumer is much more responsive to price than an existing consumer. Or, as an economist might put it, the price elasticity of demand is lower for existing consumers, making it profitable to separate the old and new as market segments. However, this approach ignores the fact that we are in a relationship where trust is an element and this strategy undermines it. Consumers aren't dumb; they understand the way the world works.

Given the widespread use of the metaphor, it is worth considering some of the more emotive meanings around the notion of 'relationship' in a marketing context. The analogy which was often used by marketing academics (Hunt and Morgan, 1995; Levitt, 1983) was the deeply personal one of marriage. Marriage implies exclusivity, longevity, and fidelity. Social psychologists who distinguish between personal and social relationships (Radley, 1996) warn of the dangers of generalizing from one to another. We do things and act in ways in one sphere that might be unacceptable in another. Social relationships at work are often necessary without being desired, with the motives and rewards being closely linked to the needs of the parties involved. Personal relationships may depend to a greater degree on the individual, psychological and emotional make-up of the parties than do social relationships. Distinctions such as these lead to the question of whether such exclusive metaphors as marriage hold up? Indeed, the metaphor has been criticized for failing to deliver in terms of the number and nature of the parties involved, the attendant costs and benefits and timescale of the relationship (Tynan, 1997). More than this, it needs to be re-examined from the point of view of consumers and how they conceptualize the relationships in which they willingly participate or just find themselves. A brief examination of the work of Thibaut and Kelley (1959) on comparison levels helps to understand how people operate their relationships. Thibaut and Kelley said that every relationship is embedded in a network of other relationships, both actual and possible. Each party uses their own experience and expectations to compare outcomes within the relationship against some minimum level they would find acceptable (the comparison level) and against the outcomes available from alternative relationships (the alternatives comparison level). It is the perceived balance of rewards and costs of a given relationship against these two comparison levels which determines a person's satisfaction with a relationship. Different consumers will of course perceive the balance between rewards and costs differently but the key is that they do perceive actual and potential benefits on the basis of what provides value for them.

So what's wrong with relationship marketing? And can it offer consumers anything that they will perceive as value such that they are motivated to reduce the number of associations with companies they hold? The rhetoric of marketing in recent years has been that companies will achieve their profit and other objectives by satisfying (even delighting) customers (Houston, 1986), and exceeding their competition at so doing. The modern marketing definition has been framed in absolute focus on the customer, such as this from Jobber, 'The achievement of corporate goals through meeting and exceeding customer needs better than the competition' (1998: 4). Note that mutual benefit is clearly central. It was this kind of consumer-centric thinking which suggested the feasibility of a form of marketing now known as relationship marketing, although as previously noted, its actual evolution owes more to services and business-to-business marketing where the nature of the offering lent itself easily to a longer-term association, than to relationships between businesses and individual consumers.

After analysing the work of various authors in this area, Peterson (1995) concluded that an individual customer–seller relationship needed both parties to benefit over some length of time. If the consumer is to gain, then there clearly should be something in it for him or her: additional value of some kind. The questions which need further investigation are, what kind of value? How much? In what circumstances will customers embark upon a commercial relationship? And also what do they require to maintain that relationship over time? As noted above, Sheth and Parvatiyar (1995) developed an efficiency approach. This involves what might seem like a contradictory notion of value in such terms. They concluded that, 'the fundamental axiom of relationship marketing is, or should be, that consumers like to reduce choices by engaging in an ongoing loyalty relationship with marketers' (1995: 256). Consumers, they said, engage in relationships with suppliers because this facilitates efficiency in their decision-making, helping them reduce their information processing requirements, achieving more cognitive consistency in their decisions and potentially reducing the perceived risks associated with future choices. They also suggested that brand loyalty is a form of relationship that a consumer has with a supplier's products and symbols. Such a basis for forming a relationship is essentially functional and implies that consumers choose in a sense to make life simpler, a way of easier navigation of the everyday shopping routines. While not disputing that these motives may precede relationship choices, Peterson (1995) suggests that such a theory leaves out the affective dimension of relationships which might explain why some do survive over a longer term and others do not. This affective, attitudinal aspect is essentially about how the two parties get on with one another, after all, you want to have a relationship with someone you like. The relationship may break down or not lead very far, not for any functional or efficiency reason, but simply because the two sides cannot develop the appropriate rapport.

A quite contrary argument to Sheth and Parvatiyar's efficiency argument was put forward by Weinberger who suggested that not all consumers want their world managed so efficiently, 'The idea that we can manage our world is uniquely twentieth century and chiefly American' (2000: 40). There is, he says, tremendous advantages to believing that life can be managed; it avoids risk, it provides smoothness and, particularly important from the point of view of relationship marketing, it creates 'discretionary attention'. So in a managed world you can have discretionary attention because the risks have been mitigated and for organizations it may be better for consumers to be managed. If consumers are prepared to forgo choices in light of the benefits that may accrue to them through a relationship, then this is an opportunity that no organization which thinks it can win the relationship prize is likely to turn down.

The Balance of Power

However, in considering the future of relationship marketing, there are a number of issues which need to be addressed from the consumer's perspective. First, despite my earlier example, the idea of developing a relationship between producer and consumer may have an inherent appeal and sense of fair play and, indeed as Sheth and Parvatiyar (1995) point out, in some situations, this may be the preferred choice. But let us examine what is really happening in these relationships in a little more detail. What has become apparent in the last few years is that many consumers have come to realize that relationship marketing is too often about the relationship that the producer wants and very little about the relationship that the consumer requires. When the balance of power lies in the hands of the producer, there is little the consumer can do other than refuse to respond to calls for further and deeper relationships, although depending on the choices available in the marketplace this may be more or less difficult. Even when consumers expressly exclude themselves from a relationship, the producer can still ignore their customers' wishes.

Just the other day the mail brought a magazine from Boots, the UK high street chemist, with the following letter attached:

> When you joined the Advantage Card scheme you expressed a preference not to receive mail from us. However, we thought you might like to know that as a result, you're missing out on *Boots Health and Beauty*, a fabulous magazine mailed to our most valued Advantage Card holders. As you'll see, it's packed with inspirational features on beauty, health and wellbeing, and keeps you up to date with the very best new products and expert advice. Every issue contains exclusive offers, plus a personalized voucher giving you extra Advantage Card points. We'd like to give you the chance to enjoy future issues and other relevant offers from Boots especially for you. To receive your personal copy of the next issue, due out in September, just tick the box below, and return this letter to us in the envelope provided. (Boots promotional material)

So not only has this company rejected my idea of a 'just friends' relationship by trying to take it deeper, and at the same time effectively turning down my request for privacy, and potentially making me feel bullied, but also they aim to entice me with flattery, being one of their most valued card holders, they care about me, I am better than the rest and will receive relevant offers that apparently the good people at Boots have been designing especially for me. Of course there is an unwritten implication that perhaps they care less about some of their other customers.

An example which highlights the different sides of the buyer–seller relationship is that of British Telecom. British Telecom (BT) is the leading supplier of domestic and business telephone systems in the UK. If your domestic supply is provided by BT, you may be telephoned at home and offered additional services. Their latest money saving offer is another service, selling me something that they have devised, but on every occasion when I have listened to the well-rehearsed sales patter and asked for some minor adjustments to suit my particular circumstances, they have been flummoxed. They do not know the answer, cannot help, no, that's not possible. Maybe they cannot personalize their relationship to that degree, but now look at the opposite side of the relationship. When my telephone breaks down, I call them, I do not get to speak to someone straight away but have to enter a long protracted series of recorded messages and pressings of buttons before I finally speak to a human voice. I am only allowed to talk to this person for a limited amount of time because (as one phone operator told me himself) they are required to process a certain number of people per hour. When the technician comes to fix the phone, he does not contact me beforehand to tell me when he is arriving and is upset when I am annoyed at his arrival at a time inconvenient to me. Maybe the consumer is being manipulated, encouraged to think there is a relationship when actually there is none. Recently a business person told me their latest BT encounter and elaborated what they thought was going on:

> I wanted to get in touch with BT because an interesting offer had come through on my phone bill. I went through all the press number 1 for this, number 2 for that and so on, finally, I found the line I needed, then another recorded voice came on saying that all their operators were busy, would I leave my name and address, etc., spelling any difficult words. So I did and then when I put the phone down I thought to myself, there was never going to be anybody taking my call. This wasn't because they were all busy, it was just a ruse to make it look like someone would take the call.

Whether his perception of what was happening was correct, the impression he was left with was one of frustration. These examples are all indicative of a failure to consider the reaction of the consumer to being treated as passive. They understand that the relationship is one-way, more about market segmentation and cross-selling, than building trust.

Of course phone relationships aren't all bad. Take Boden, for example, a leading UK clothing retailer that operates primarily by mail order. During sale time, when the phone lines are busy, a different message is played to the caller every few minutes. It is the voice of the owner, Johnny Boden, explaining precisely why you are waiting. For example, he explains that all sale catalogues are sent out at the same time as this seems fairer but does mean there can be hold-ups in the sale days; he says how many operators are working at any one time, and he even apologizes after you have been waiting some time. The main thing is that eventually an operator takes your call, and you do feel it is has been worth waiting, even if they have run out of the item you wanted. It's a more honest relationship that attempts to build loyalty by recognizing that active consumers will accept a reasonable explanation.

While these anecdotal examples reveal something of the frustration that a customer may feel with relationship marketing, the academic literature has further analysed some of the problems with relationship marketing in practice. In 1998 Fournier et al. published a paper precisely concerned with the potential premature death of relationship marketing. They had identified that a key problem for the future of relationship marketing was that relationships involve give and take. Relationships require at least two supposedly willing participants coming together in some mutually beneficial exchange over time, and while it appears to come as a surprise to some organizations, consumers may not be as keen to have such long-term relationships as the suppliers are. Just as Weinberger (2000) suggested, some people just do not want a relationship of any kind from tins of baked beans, through to the supermarket they visit most frequently and the bank where their monthly salary is deposited. What they prefer is a series of suitable transactions or at least the access to choice, even if they do not opt for a different supplier each time they shop. Others (Peterson, 1995) have pointed out that the evidence suggests reducing consumer choice is typically met with resistance. Consumers may enter into what appear to be relationships, but they may have many motives for so doing. The result may be a short- or long-term reduction of choice, which may or may not be important to them.

One-Way or Two-Way Loyalty

If companies want to have a relationship with their customers, if they expect loyalty, the passing on of information and repeat purchasing, then they have to operate by the same rules. Too often our loyalty is assumed in an almost offhand way from the voice telling us every few seconds that our call is valued while allowing us to run up a huge phone bill and wasting our time with no idea of when someone will respond, to the continuing request for the same set of personal information from companies to whom we have already given it. Often, with on-line Internet dealings, it is only through the process of giving information again that we are allowed to continue the transaction, so again the relationship is not really a relationship at all, but a series of discrete transactions. Now that relationship marketing is being followed by so-called customer relationship management, the breakdown of the personal is even greater. While there is talk of the so-called 'segment of one' where marketers will know what each customer wants and be able to tailor their offerings to them, this is patently not the case, people change and information about past purchasing may have little to do with future intentions. Fournier et al. highlighted one customer's experience with a catalogue company:

> Each year around the holidays, it sends out a reminder to its customers, telling them what they ordered the year before and for whom. The problem is, several years ago I ordered presents for the physicians who took care of my mother when she was hospitalized for an emergency medical condition. And each year now, the company reminds me of that awful time. I even called the company and explained that I don't generally buy presents for the people on that list. I told them why, and I asked for those names to be deleted. The operator was nice enough on the phone and said that the names would be taken off my list. But this fall, there they were again. (1998: 46)

This aspect of one-way relationships is common, and not necessarily all bad. Clearly, there are times when to be told as, say Amazon does, which other books or CDs were bought by the people who bought the same book as you, can be useful. It might also be a bit of a shock, and make you question your selections and what they say about you. This discussion raises the important issue of choice between customization and personalization. If we use the distinction suggested by Nunes and Kambil (2001), customization lets a customer identify and specify his or her preferences. The example they cite is MyYahoo at Yahoo.com which allows users to instruct the site to regularly display certain preferences, share prices, weather, search profiles, favourites, etc. Personalization, on the other hand, does not ask for explicit user instructions, rather, it uses the patterns of customers' choices and/or demographics to develop its profile of the customer. Amazon is an example of a company using the latter approach. The assumption, Nunes and Kambil suggest, is that time-pressed, information-overloaded consumers would appreciate such a service, but their research showed that in fact relatively few people saw any benefits in this form of personalization. They set up an experiment where they described two on-line grocers, one allowing customization, the other making personalized recommendations, only 6 per cent of their respondents said they would prefer the personalized site. What most customers wanted was more control in the relationship.

But there is another aspect to this one-way issue, which is to do with what the customer is actually getting from the relationship. It is the company and not the customer who sets the ground rules and parameters and makes changes to the nature of relationship. Store loyalty cards are perhaps the best example of this. A loyalty card scheme asks the customer to provide details about themselves and their household on a form. The details provided are integrated into the retailer's computer system and when the user presents his or her card at the till, the electronic strip attached to the card will collect data including what was purchased, how much was spent and when. The consumer receives points, the number and value of which are decided by the retailer and then totalled at a period of time specified by the retailer. Often the reward to the consumer is in the form of money-off coupons, often with a specified time by which they must be spent and also sometimes indicating certain products and brands on which they can redeem the coupons. The benefits to the retailer are huge and are largely derived from the amount and type of information that the card can potentially collect. Consumer profiles can be established and the organization's most profitable customers targeted. The marketing spend can be more efficiently allocated. The benefits to the consumer are less clear-cut. Essentially the relationship boils down to money-off vouchers, but these are usually temporally and category-defined by the company. Tesco's first mail-out of this kind involved a link with Coca-Cola that meant that all recipients received Coca-Cola money-off vouchers. For some this apparent disregard of the information so readily provided seemed bizarre. One customer remarked that 'he had never drunk the product in his life, and as he was 85 years old was very unlikely to start now' (Peck et al., 1997: 86). Despite such initial hiccups, the hype in relationship terms is huge. By using these cards, a company like Tesco in the UK is supposedly able to communicate through money-off coupons and quarterly magazines to create one-to-one relationships with their customers (Lovelock et al., 1999). But it could be argued that Tesco is still pursuing old-fashioned, demographic segmentation; certainly it has different mail shots for different ages and family types but little more personalization than this. According to Ziliani (2000), the Tesco data has been segmented into twelve customer groups, a typical cluster scheme, where a few customer groups are outlined according to the demographic information disclosed at the time of request, for example, students, singles, families with children, etc.

The example of Tesco's relationship with consumers highlights the importance of other relationships for the firm. It may well be that the development of a working relationship with Coca-Cola, as discussed above, is where a good deal of the real value in the loyalty cards, demo-graphic segmentation and money-off coupons really lies. This has been well documented in TV programmes such as *Branded* (BBC2) which showed how Heinz used the demographic details of consumers supplied to them by supermarkets to target specific promotions to particular cus-tomer segments. Schlosser (2001) has also discovered that many of the really successful relationships are between producer and producer, rather than producer and consumer. For example, he tells how the competition for young customers has led to alliances between those producers most interested in them, fast food chains and toy companies, as well as sports leagues and Hollywood studios.

> Burger King has sold chicken nuggets shaped like Teletubbies. McDonald's now has its own line of children's videos starring Ronald McDonald, *The Wacky Adventures of Ronald McDonald* is being produced by Klasky-Csupo, the company that makes *Rugrats* and *The Simpsons*. The videos feature the McDonald-land characters and sell for $3.49. (Schlosser, 2001: 48)

It is not difficult to identify the motivation for these linkages and alliances as McDonald's have clearly spelt out, 'We see this as a great opportunity,' a McDonald's executive said in a press release, 'to create a more mean-ingful relationship between Ronald and kids.' (ibid.: 48). Parents around the world, pestered for the videos and toys which are regularly advertised on the television might not be so sure as to just what kind of meaning such a relationship has for their children. One thing is certain – these alliances involve large sums of money. Schlosser reports that in the mid-1990s Walt Disney and McDonald's signed a ten-year global marketing agreement which probably brought in Disney anything between $25 to $45 million in additional advertising for a film. A spokesperson for McDonald's revealed just what the implications of such an alliance would be when he said, 'It's about their theme parks, their next movie, their characters, their videos . . . It's bigger than a hamburger. It's about the integration of our two brands, long-term' (ibid.: 49). There is also perhaps a more sinister aspect to the growth in these alliances as they move into schools and colleges to influence the taste of children with a view to forming relationships at an early age. Companies who help to pay for equipment in schools or colleges expect visibility and exclusivity. While it may help educational establishments facing continued cutbacks, children have no choice in attending school and then have to see the ads or consume the goods, again with no choice. For some, this is a very important way of expanding a market. As Schlosser (2001) points out, the adult market for soft drinks in the USA is stagnant, so the obvious route is to sell more to children.

What companies do not want customers to do is to play them at their own game. There are a number of issues that revolve around whether the relationship is worthwhile and which relationships are better for the company. It would be a mistake for every customer to believe their relationship is as valued as someone else's, clearly, it is not. The loyalty of some customers is more valuable than others. When Tesco launched the Clubcard in 1995, it had already segmented its customers into 'new', 'infrequent' and 'loyal' with whatever implications there may be for the future of the relationship with the different groups. While loyalty clearly has some value, Knox and Denison (2000) found that shoppers locate proportionally more of their grocery expenditure into their first choice store. The fact that most customers tend to have more than one loyalty card contradicts the whole notion of loyalty. The problem is, simply put, every organization wants to have a 'relationship' with the customer, hence more loyalty cards are available, more loyalty cards means less loyalty, the circle goes round and round. Passingham (1998) studied households with a weekly shopping expenditure of over £150 and found that about 17 per cent of these held three grocery loyalty cards. The irony of the loyalty card was well put in a letter to *The Times* in 1998, 'Sir, I have accumulated nine loyalty cards from various stores and supermarkets, does this make me more loyal or less? Dr. J. Burscough'. The consumer's potential for multiple relationships was also identified by Peterson (1995) when he pointed out that those who travel frequently tend to have simultaneous relationships with airlines, hotels and rental car agencies. There is no need for them to be limited other than by their own desires and personal constraints as there are few contractual restrictions that preclude engaging in relationships with many organizations at any one time.

Clearly, there are some transactions that are better done with one supplier, either because they get to know you and your needs, or because there is some kind of value implied in staying with the supplier over a length of time, but generally these relationships are embedded in the nature of the offering. Therefore, while one would prefer to go the same dentist and hairdresser, have the same electrician and builder to come and fix things in your house, you may be less concerned about which shop you buy your groceries, shoes or cosmetics from. The nature of some services is such that you need to be tied into a kind of relationship for them to have value; the nature of a car breakdown facility is such that one is inevitably tied in over a period, although one can change year on year. Much of this, however, is to do with the way the market works, rather than the character of the service itself. Even here you have the choice of accepting the risk that your car may break down and you will have to pay for a tow-away truck, or take less risk and have the reassurance of belonging to a breakdown service which will help out if and when car does break down.

Relationships taking the Risk out of Consumption

As mentioned earlier, an argument for the uptake of relationships by the consumer is the reduction of risk. What risk actually means for consumers is important to consider both in terms of their willingness or ability to be creative in their consumption and in relation to their need to maintain long-term relationships as a form of risk reduction. The perceived risk a consumer feels in a choice situation is generally described as being dependent on the uncertainty present in the information he or she has and the likely consequences of the purchase (Foxall, Goldsmith and Brown, 1998). Clearly for lots of daily consumer decisions there is likely to be very little risk involved and we may act or make decisions with little or no thought to the consequences. Increasingly though, we have more information available to us even in relation to the purchase of daily commodities and, if anything, this can be unsettling as the information may imply increased risk or be contradictory.

There is perhaps a perception that we are becoming in many ways less willing to take risks. The term 'nanny state' has come to signify nations unable and unwilling to take the risks involved in basic choices, but are we really so incapable of weighing up risks, costs and benefits and coming to decisions as consumers? It may be one of the major stumbling blocks in understanding consumers today that their abilities to evaluate the pros and cons of different consumption situations has been underestimated. As a result companies and governments have also underrated consumer creativity; the ability of people to innovate, initiate, and change the relationships with producers to better meet their needs. There will of course always be the need for protection for the weak and vulnerable, and for basic rules of engagement. The eight guidelines for consumer protection developed by the United Nations in the 1980s, outlined below, do not appear unreasonable in terms of a relationship between supplier and buyer. Possibly the most contentious in reality are items like the right to safety and the right to a healthy environment. It is often difficult for producers as well as consumers to be all knowing in terms of what is safe and what is not. Knowledge is built upon experience and as we know from issues such as Creutzfeldt-Jakob disease (CJD), foot and mouth disease, genetically modified food and cloning, our knowledge evolves even as we consume.

The United Nations Guidelines for Consumer Protection

1   The right to satisfaction of basic needs – To have access to basic, essential goods and services: adequate food, clothing, shelter, health care, education, public utilities, water and sanitation.

2   The right to safety – To be protected against products, production processes and services which are hazardous to health or life.

3   The right to be informed – To be given the facts needed to make an informed choice, and to be protected against dishonest or misleading advertising and labelling.

4   The right to choose – To be able to select from a range of products and services, offered at competitive prices with an assurance of satisfactory quality.

5   The right to be heard – To have consumer interests represented in the making and execution of government policy, and in the development of products and services.

6   The right to redress – To receive a fair settlement of just claims, including compensation for misrepresentation, shoddy goods or unsatisfactory services.

7   The right to consumer education – To acquire knowledge and skills needed to make informed, confident choices about goods and services, while being aware of basic consumer rights and responsibilities and how to act on them.

8   The right to a healthy environment – To live and work in an environment which is non-threatening to the well-being of present and future generations.

Consumers can and will respond as they see fit to scares, worries and opportunities. Whether or not their response is appropriate or 'right' is of course difficult for any of us to know, unless in every decision available there is always a right and a wrong choice. The notion of perceptual risk implies something different from objective risk (Mitchell and Boustani, 1993). Indeed, we have to question whether objective risk exists other than in probabilities that may change as knowledge itself changes. The safety or reassurance of this kind of closure, I would suggest, no longer exists for consumers. As Lawson says,

> Truth, in the sense of the possibility of a correct description of
> an independent reality, has had a good innings, but its time is
> over. It is not, however, the abandonment of truth in itself
> which is of concern, but the threat to meaning with which it
> is accompanied. It is as if we have fallen into an Alice in
> Wonderland rabbit-hole that has no beginning and no end.
> (2001: XV)

While Lawson in this quotation was referring to a change in the way we
see our world beyond just the way we behave as consumers, its implications for consumer behaviour are no less important. Nanny state or no
nanny state, consumers will operate in a way they see fit, given the
information they have and dependent on the risks they see – the result
may not always be what one might expect. Consider the following two
stories both concerned with goods that might be said to have a perceived
and objective, if not easily quantifiable, risk. Both the beef-on-the-bone
issue and the combined contraceptive pill involved a relationship between
legislators, essentially the government, commercial suppliers and
consumers. These were issues of well-being and consumer protection as
identified by the UN and of consumer choice.

Beef-on-the-bone

The Spongiform Encephalopathy Advisory Committee was set up by the
government as an independent committee of leading experts to provide
scientific advice with regard to Bovine Spongiform Encephalopathy (BSE)
and the safety of British meat. From 1988 a series of policies and legislation ensured inspection of animals for slaughter by veterinary surgeons,
the slaughter and diagnosis of any cattle suspected of suffering from BSE,
and the prohibition of sale of beef for human consumption that came
from cattle over 30 months old. Then in 1997 the Committee released
information showing that experimentally infected cows had developed
BSE infectivity in the dorsal root ganglia and possibly also the bone
marrow. This information was made public and the government also
warned consumers of this risk. Following a consultation process which
included the food industry and consumer organizations, the Beef Bones
Regulations 1997 came into force. The Regulations controlled the sale, use
and disposal of beef bones from cattle aged over six months at slaughter
which were de-boned in Great Britain. According to the Department for
Environment, Food and Rural Affairs (DEFRA), 'Their purpose was to

protect public health and to help maintain confidence in beef and beef products' (www.defra.gov.uk). The resultant uproar included a march to 10 Downing Street by butchers, representatives of the meat industry and consumers protesting against what they saw was a ban based on evidence that there was a slight chance that a person could catch CJD. The cattle farmers even presented a rib of beef to the Prime Minister. The protestors were particularly disturbed by the probabilities involved as beef-on-the bone accounted for only about 5 per cent of British beef sales. Robert Robinson who spoke for the cattle industry at the time said 'It sets an impossibly high precedent for food safety – we're talking about a one in a billion chance.' And the Worshipful Company of Butchers invited 100 diners to wear black armbands at a six-course beef dinner where they could 'say goodbye to the roast beef of Olde England'. Of course consumer responses varied quite considerably, while for some the removal of beef-on-the bone further exacerbated their fears over safety, others felt that the patriarchal approach of the British government had gone too far. CNN reported one consumer as saying 'People should be able to choose for themselves, buy what they want, eat what they want' (www.cnn.com/WORLD/9712/15britain.beef/).

The following three letters were published by *Time* magazine on 19 January 1998.

No one knows for sure if certain beef products are dangerous or not (Dec. 15), but it is better to ban them now rather than find out too late. The problem is that the people in charge are not liable for the decisions they make, so they often take the easy route of not upsetting commercial interests. How could the expert committee conclude in 1988 that it was 'most unlikely' that bovine spongiform encephalopathy would have any implications for human health when it knew almost nothing about the disease? Agriculture Minister Jack Cunningham's courage in banning beef on the bone deserves our respect. It won't bring him votes, but it might save the health of the British people.
Kai Stricker
Bergheim, Germany

As a beef farmer, I found your report a refreshing and well-balanced contrast to some of the antifarmer and antimeat articles I've seen elsewhere. There is a need for balance in the coverage of the crisis. The Sunday roast is a cornerstone of our

culture, but people are more likely to die from the alcohol consumed with the meal than from the beef. Should we ban beer and wine also? We should outlaw cigarettes and crossing the road long before we ban beef on the bone. If consumers and farmers combine in a campaign against this ludicrous law, maybe the government will do a U-turn.
Howard Franks
Biggar, Scotland

The panic over mad-cow disease results mainly from people's unrealistic desire to lead a completely risk-free life and their inability to assess the amount of risk. After Britain's latest beef ban, I wonder how many farmers will commit suicide because they have lost their livelihood. Compare that with the number of consumers who would have died from eating possibly infected meat.
Stephen Turner
Cambridge, England

The combined contraceptive pill

In 1960, the first oral contraceptive was marketed in the USA. The 'Pill' as it became known, has often been referred to as a revolution in birth control. It was considered to be a method of contraception both safe and effective and the result of course was that the adoption of this innovation was both rapid and widespread. The Pill became available to British women in 1961. Within two years of its introduction, it was being used by well over a million women rising to ten million a decade later. At the beginning of the twenty-first century, the Pill remains a popular form of birth control, used by some 100 million women worldwide. The Pill was more than just a form of contraception as it gave women the ability to control their fertility for themselves in a manner that had not been available to them before. Despite its early popularity, the possibility of health-related risk involved in taking the Pill surfaced within the first couple of years of its use. Studies indicated that it did carry the increased threat of blood clots, strokes and heart attacks because of the levels of the hormone oestrogen contained in the Pill. In 1962 there was evidence of at least 11 Pill-related deaths. Women activists in the USA brought these dangers to public attention. In the early 1970s a 'mini-Pill' with reduced oestrogen was finally introduced although some companies continued to produce high-dose Pills until the late 1980s. Research continued in the development of the Pill and then in 1995 the government warned that seven brands, containing the newest formulations, including forms of the hormone progestogen known as gestodene or desogestrel, increased the risk of thrombosis. The announcement was the result of information from a World Health Organization study which had found that women taking these pills faced double the risk of thrombosis in the legs as those taking other brands. The Department of Health said that 26 women taking pills containing desogestrel had died from blood clots in Britain in the past 14 years and 12 women who had been taking gestodene pills had died in the past nine years. The chairman of the government's committee on the safety of medicines wrote to doctors telling them to advise women on any of the seven brands to switch to another, and advised women not to panic or to suddenly stop taking the Pill but to continue until the cycle was finished and then consult their doctors. To put the figures into perspective, the *Daily Telegraph* reported that at the time about five in every 100,000 women not on the Pill experienced a thrombosis each year, rising to 15 for those on pills considered safe and 30 for the seven brands. Doctors worried about shortage of supplies of 'safe' pills and were not always sure what to advise their patients. One doctor was reported as saying that she had just spent 20 minutes with a lady on the Pill who wanted to know what to do and had more information than the doctor had. The doctor then voiced the fears of many doctors and pregnancy advisory clinics saying that it was likely that women would stop taking their Pill and become pregnant. Unfortunately this is what appeared to happen. There was a dramatic reduction in women taking the Pill and an extra 10,000 abortions were recorded in the following year. Scientific debate about the health risks of oral contraceptives continues, but what appears to have happened in 1995 is that some women were unable or unwilling to assess the risks and live with them or at the very least wait until they could switch to an alternative pill. Pregnancy holds many risks (including higher levels of deep vein thrombosis) as does abortion, but one of the problems in this case was probably the way the risk was portrayed to the women. Almost every news account at the time described the risk in relative terms, saying that women taking the new pills doubled the risk. The issue though was that the level of increased risk was still relatively small and this was not adequately described in the early reports.

Risk Perception

So what do these two case studies really mean in terms of risk perception, relationships and consumer orientation? Perceived risk is probably an under-rated phenomenon in relation to what we buy, how we buy and particularly in relation to the adoption of new ideas and things. In some areas, some of us can tolerate high levels of risk, others cannot. For most of us, the actual calculation of risk is really very difficult, just as imagining the odds on winning the lottery are. More important is how close a relationship we have with the product, service, idea and the role it has in our lives. Perhaps the risks in taking the Pill were perceived as greater because women were faced with potential risk every day as they took their daily dose; it was medicine, prescribed by doctors and as such unfamiliar territory for many. While not denying that many people and communities even as highlighted by the letter from the German correspondent felt similarly at risk from beef-on-the-bone, it is possible that the relationship between the meat we eat and ourselves is perceived in quite a different manner by many consumers. We are in a position to make choices, where to buy from, butcher or supermarket, what cut to buy, whether it is organic or not, we still have at least some control in the relationship and so our perceptions of risk can somehow be contained within this relationship. There may not necessarily be a rationale or logic that can easily be explained, especially in any numeric sense. Calculating personal risk from information related to numbers of women who have suffered from deep vein thrombosis or predicted sufferers of CJD is unlikely to follow a well-defined route. Consider the notion of risk compensation when people appear to take more risks after improvements to safety have been made. For example, it was assumed that childproof packs for medicines would increase safety but there is evidence that child-resistant bottle caps are associated with an increase in fatal poisoning of children possibly because parents left the medicines accessible as they thought they were safe. Similarly research in both the USA and the UK showed that after compulsory seat belt wearing and improvements in car safety had been introduced, the decreases in serious injury did not materialize probably because people were just driving faster, thinking that they were safer. As individuals we will make some kind of decision based on a range of issues, many of them incalculable – the result may often appear to be surprising but this in essence is what is at the root of the problem for most suppliers, that in Gabriel and Lang's terms, the consumer really is 'umanageable' (1998).

Conclusion

In this chapter we have explored the rise of relationship marketing and some of the consequences of the ubiquity of the relationship metaphor. A case has been made that there was a strategic failure to analyse the nature of relationships within a social context and hence to embrace the consumer as an active participant. In practice, this meant a failure to understand the value of relationships to the consumer. We have looked at a number of theoretical perspectives which illustrate the need to understand the social complexity of relationship marketing. Value to the consumer was explored in terms of efficiency, affective and risk management dimensions.

We then turned to the practical implications to gain an understanding of consumer frustrations and the unintended consequences of the marketing effort. The examples used drew out a number of contradictions in the application of relationship marketing. These have significant implications for practical marketing issues such as the choice between customization and personalization. The failure to embrace the social context and anticipate active interaction by consumers points the way to acknowledging the need to deal with a spectrum of possible relationships which go well beyond the deficiencies of a simple loyalty principle. The product, brand and nature of the consumer interaction are critical to the type of relationship likely to be effective.

Finally, we employed the perspective of relationship as a means of risk management for both producer and consumer with respect to some examples of major economic and social impact. These illustrated that the failure of relationship marketing has reinforced a lack of consumer confidence in both business and government which has changed social attitudes to risk. This poses a major challenge which marketing theory and practice must engage. We will approach this by investigating some critical aspects of the marketplace and the consumer.

Chapter 2

New Products and their Meanings

Many studies of consumer facilities and habits bear uncanny resemblance to detective novels: in the stories told of the birth and ascendancy of consumer society, the plots tend to grind relentlessly towards the unmasking of the scheming culprit(s). There is hardly a piece without some singly or severally acting villains – be it a conspiracy of merchandisers, the sly intrigues of their advertising henchman or brainwashing orchestrated by media moguls, explicitly or implicitly, the shoppers. Consumers emerge from the story as victims of collective brain-damage: gullible and duped victims of crowd hypnosis. (Bauman, 2001: 18)

Introduction

So far, the argument of this book has been that the notion of relationships between supplier and consumer as promoted by marketing is in reality to do with the balance of power between these two parties and the impact of other outside interests which may affect that balance. In trying to deconstruct what that power really means and who has it, it could be suggested that the consumer's ability to innovate and be creative has often been underestimated by companies. At this point it seems important to position oneself in relation to consumption. Miller tells us that consumption has through history been seen as intrinsically evil; in particular, consumption seems to have become terminally associated with materialism, the capitalist system and is incompatible with environmentalism (Miller, 2001). Miller goes on to say that much of the study of consumption is far removed from the actual experiences of most consumers based as it is on Veblen's (1899) notion of the conspicuous consumer who was characterized by a small sector of the nouveau riche. It would be like suggesting today that we could take the conspicuous consumption as evidenced by the celebrities featured in Hello!

magazine or *Vogue* as indicative of the majority of consumers in Britain today. Miller implies that there is no reason to present the idea of consumption as intrinsically good or bad. Consumption just is. Therefore, when Miller says he wants to give credit to the way consumers consume, he also proposes that this does not detract from critiquing the way goods and services may be sold by companies, or how workers may be exploited by them. It is important that we do break down the mystery of relationships and open the door to a deeper understanding of consumers' views on consumption. From the individual consumer's point of view one question to be considered is, what kind of connections will be required, needed or desired with the different products, brands and companies interacted with? There is already a host of literature which analyses such connections, often within a cultural turn. The simplistic supplier-oriented view of companies offering relationships through loyalty cards, special offers and other promotional mechanisms is countered by sociologists and anthropologists who have long studied and speculated on what people's associations with the things around them were. Increasingly those things have a commercial origin. It is worth looking in more detail at some of this conceptual thinking and how it may help develop an understanding of consumers' roles in consumption. To pursue this further it is necessary to consider both the individual consumer and the object of their consumption. This chapter will focus on the object of consumption, the product and brand. The next chapter will focus on the consumer as classified by marketing. Then in Chapter 4 we will begin to outline consumer responses to their marketplace in the form of their innovation, adoption, and resistant behaviour.

Product Life Cycle or Cultural Biography

It has long been realized that goods provide us with more than just utility in the economic sense of the word. They may, for example, constitute meaning, hold value, or be used in communication (Lury, 1996). Part of the usefulness of goods, therefore, is what they do for us beyond their purely functional value. According to Lury, this is a reciprocal arrangement as 'It is in acquiring, using and exchanging things that individuals come to have social lives' (ibid.: 12), but similarly it is through this process that we give 'life' to things. Appadurai (1986) also has examined the social lives of things, how they acquire and lose value and change meaning over time. Things have meaning and act as communicating mechanisms about ourselves but over time these can change. This 'social history' of objects is of particular interest to anyone concerned with the introduction, development and consumption of 'new' objects, ideas and services. Appadurai is also concerned with the life history of an object as it moves through different contexts and uses and forms a 'cultural bio-graphy'. Take the life story of the BMW in Britain, for example. It began as a symbol of German engineering and excellence; it was a luxury car, expensive enough only to bought by the relatively few. Edwards (2000) uses the BMW as an example of Teutonic class superiority, 'Upmarket German vehicles are routinely associated with German engineering typified in the Audi 'Vorsprung durch Technik' (progress through tech-nology) campaigns, incorporating a kind of Germanic gobbledegook; while BMWs as the "ultimate driving experience" have almost become the Aryan race of vehicles' (ibid.: 74). Gradually, however, the BMW has become more widely available, partly because the company, recognizing its potential status, developed more and relatively cheaper models. As company cars became more common, so executives and middle managers were able to communicate their 'value' through the BMW badge. The exclusivity of the car, however, declined as in the 1980s it became associated with a type of brash, mostly young men who needed to flaunt their ambition. So much so that Audi, a direct competitor, was able to run a TV advertisement which virtually said that choosing not to drive a BMW said more about your individuality (and driving an Audi said even more). Now despite BMWs still being at the top end, in price terms of the car market, if you travel on virtually any British motorway, you will be able to literally feel their ubiquitous quality. A BMW is in effect 'worn' by its driver and clothes are probably the most obvious way that people in the West identify to others who they are and communicate meaning. For the BMW has also become appropriated by others and communicates differ-ent messages in different places, as Schor remarks with reference to the BMW's position in the USA, 'It is unlikely that the Bavarian Motor Works intended to have its cars known as Black Man's Wheels' (1998: 41). Sahlins (1976) has demonstrated how clothing can communicate distinct social identities, show membership of and discrimination from different societal groups. The wearing of objects has, however, become increasingly subtle. As Baudrillard ([1970] 1998) points out, a rich man who decides to drive a 2CV super-differentiates himself, by his manner of consuming. The BMW may have become too common, so discreet (which as Baud-rillard defines, it might also be called super-conspicuous) is his choice. Thus while different makes and types of car may have product life cycles it is also possible that the very idea of what 'wearing' the car says also has a life cycle, say, from functional vehicle to symbol of wealth, to increased differentiation through discretion. There may be differences, however, in the role that objects actually play; so while Sahlins would suggest that people use objects to differentiate themselves from other people, for Baudrillard the relationship is turned on its head and people act as expressions of differences between objects (Lury, 1996). Such a difference would be important not only in terms of examining the relationship between the consumer and the object but also in assessing the role of the consumer in consumption. Is the consumer using the object or the object using the consumer?

Appadurai's notion of the 'life history' of a thing is in many ways a direct reflection of the marketing notion of the product life cycle. The concept of the life cycle was not developed to study the social or cultural life of things but rather to trace the sales and profit of goods over time with a view to developing appropriate marketing actions for different stages of the product's or brand's life. The idea here is quantitative in nature and largely to do with the rise and decline and possible re-emergence of the product and how this is likely to be linked to the company's profits rather than what might be happening to it in terms of how it is used and its role in people's lives. By identifying what might be happening to our goods at certain stages of their lives we can decide what are the most appropriate and cost-effective actions to be taken. Yet, some writers in marketing have glimpsed the social life revealed in something as apparently simple as the product life cycle (Wasson, 1971; O'Shaughnessy, 1995). The standard product life cycle as suggested by the s-shaped curve is only one of many potential routes that a product may follow, willingly or not. For example, a truncated cycle has no introductory stage because the product has little learning requirement but does have lasting appeal, so there is no decline to chart; a good example of this is the television. The 'Skyrocket cycle' applies to fads as once the novelty has worn off, then sales will decline very rapidly, as is the case with some children's toys which enjoy a brief craze period until the next one comes along. Finally, fashion cycles show oscillations of movement as fashions such as flared trousers come and go and come again. Some products or brands inevitably do die, Rinso, Oxydol, the Cortina and the Corsair, Strand cigarettes, Aztec, Spangles, and Radion are just a few no longer with us while Kit Kat and Persil seem assured longevity. Whether these brands always die because of natural causes, or receive a push, does rather imply that their social life is dependent on a number of participants. There is another relationship going on here and this is not just between the brand and the customer, it is also between the brand and the company. If the brand is not performing in the way the company wants or had envisioned, the company will have little compunction in killing it off. Again, the balance of power is crucial here. Novo is an interesting example that illustrates the triangular relationship between a brand, its potential customers and the company that developed it. Rowntree developed Novo in the 1980s as a healthy eating product which attempted to combine wholesome cereal bars with chocolate. The concept was a little mixed in that it implied healthy eating with a degree of indulgence. Rowntree's marketing director at the time saw the paradox: 'We believe that there was too great a difference between the product itself and the position it was trying to establish as a confectionery product. The product doesn't deliver what the positioning suggests' (Hoggan, 1990). What the market research found was a dilemma in consumer's minds; while people did want to feel less guilty when eating chocolate, they still wanted a taste similar to the chocolate bars they were used to. So what did Rowntree do? They dropped the brand because it did not 'deliver' to their pre-agreed objective, and as the marketing director matter-of-factly put it, when this happens 'we pull the plug' – no resuscitation available for brands that don't deliver.

Reconstructing the Lives of Goods

Some products or brands do rise from the grave. A good example of such resurrection is Action Man. While Barbie's long-lived history is well documented (Rogers, 1999) and while she has experienced a number of metamorphoses and plastic surgery, she has matured over time with only limited dents to her popularity. Action Man, however, has received a somewhat rockier ride. This soldier toy was released in the UK in 1966, based on a US toy called GI Joe, developed by Hasbro, and launched in the USA a couple of years earlier. Palitoy saw a major opportunity and bought the licence from Hasbro. Interestingly at the same time Pedigree was developing a similar 'boy's' doll named 'Tommy Gunn'. The two dolls appeared on the UK market at about the same time but Tommy soon lost out to Action Man. Between 1968 and 1980 Action Man developed his range of outfits and military styles, appearing in the uniform of the Grenadier Guards, the 17th/21st Lancers and the Household Cavalry (www.galeed.co.uk). This was no small feat when one considers that introducing a doll to boys in the 1960s was a risky undertaking. To begin with, Action Men had painted heads with hair that felt like flocked wallpaper. The company developed many versions of Action Man, and he had a number of accessories built around the army theme. Interestingly, the manufacturers responded well to problems that children had in playing with the toy and spent money to develop it and make it a better plaything. For example, originally Action Man's hands were moulded into a shape that was supposed to hold weapons but they would not grip unless you tied the hand to the object with cotton or an elastic band. In the early 1970s the company developed soft hands which gripped. Actions Man's evolution included growing hair and developing eyes that moved from side to side and then in the 1980s he was finally able to sit down properly after his thighs had been redesigned. So here was an object that really did have a life and one that changed and developed over an almost 20 year period. In the early 1980s his fate, however, seemed to be sealed with the birth of *Star Wars* and then followed a period when other TV and film-based toys such as Ninja Turtles, developed their own lives. The introduction of computer games was another potential nail in the Action Man coffin. But Action Man returned in 1993 with a new body and a whole range of job profiles: Duke, in Desert Storm Gear, a Ninja Commando, Cobra Commander and a Marine paratrooper. The range continued to develop and included a snow board rider with working ice saw and a swimmer who could do the crawl and had his own set of goggles. He appealed to a new generation of children, that found him just as appealing as their fathers and uncles had done in the 1960s.

The life cycle of products is also closely linked to the life of the consumer. How our needs change, depending on economic circumstances and changes in lifestyle, impacts directly on the types of products we want and will accept. This is not just an issue as to whether there is more choice in terms of brands and products but it is also to do with the time we have available to do things other than work. The increase in labour-saving domestic equipment may lead to more free time or it may change patterns of domestic labour. Game and Pringle (1984) point out that while washing machines revolutionized the chore of laundry, the nature of the job shifted such that women can now find themselves washing clothes on a daily rather than weekly basis. Similarly, in food preparation, processed foods might mean simpler cooking processes but might also lead to more time spent on preparing different menus for household members. Increasingly our leisure time is transforming into consumption time. If we watch TV cooks such as Delia Smith or Jamie Oliver preparing meals on the television, we can almost immediately purchase the book that will send us back into the kitchen to spend more time as work or leisure, depending on one's point of view. Martha Stewart would have American consumers decorate their homes and take care of dinner table etiquette and in doing so, send them down to the store for the goods to differentiate their house and their table from that of their neighbours. We are effectively consuming on numerous levels, from the TV programme through the book and products we then buy at the supermarket as a result. Our holidays too may become shopping trips. Take Las Vegas as an example of a holiday shopping destination. In the 1990s gambling was its number one attraction for visitors but now the city's convention and visitors' authority says that this takes second place to entertainment which includes dining out, floorshows and shopping. Las Vegas caters for all markets from Versace to Banana Republic. Shopping is not necessarily just a by-product of taking a holiday either; the Travel Industry Association of America reported that shopping was the first or second reason given for actually taking a trip (La Ferla, 2001).

However the changes, such as those described above, have impacted on consumers and their behaviour, one thing is certain, that the progression of time and the development and introduction of new things into the market place have brought significant changes in consumption. This may of course be seen just as a reflection of a post-Fordist world of ensuring continued consumption through specialized and flexible production. It is also about the changes which have occurred as production and consumption have progressed throughout the centuries through continued innovation and development; in other words, a reflection of the history of production and the history of consumption. Just as the spread of ideas and eventually, literacy, followed the invention of the printing press in the fifteenth century, so did the invention of the washing machine revolutionize the time women had available for other activities. Notwithstanding Game and Pringle's points regarding domestic labour noted above, the introduction of the washing machine did mean that there no longer had to be a whole day devoted to washing the family's clothes. Once the automatic washing machine followed the twin tub, which followed the tub and mangle, women could incorporate the weekly washing into their routine, no longer having to be directly involved with the process. So innovations bring with them time and labour-saving productivities. Perhaps more of an issue is how consumers deal with this innovation in terms of actually improving their consumption lives. Gabriel and Lang accept that compared with the Middle Ages there is an increase in the choice of, say, transport, but question whether having the opportunity to choose between 50 different detergents actually constitutes real choice. They have a point, while lives may be improved by the discovery of life-saving drugs, labour-saving inventions and international transportation, does the proliferation of brands, flavours and formulations that are the lifeblood of fast-moving consumer goods manufacturers and their agencies make any real difference to us when we do our weekly shopping? If anything, they can make life more difficult. The more choices we face, the more information we potentially have to base our choices upon. But how many of us have the time or indeed the inclination to pick up every pack, examine and compare the contents to determine what will provide us with best value. Even if we did, would we know what would be the best value? Different ingredients may be difficult to compare. Fletcher describes what the experience of supermarket shopping can be like:

On a recent trip to my local supermarket I found – excluding different pack sizes – 293 varieties of cat and dog food, and 46 varieties of loo rolls. There were 107 different breakfast cereals, 11 different mueslis and another 14 different oats. There were 158 different beers and lagers and 31 – yes, 31 – different sorts of water. In every case, the numbers were bigger than when I carried out a similar bit of research a couple of years ago. I could have continued counting the varieties of this and that all day. Yet from this cornucopia, the average shopper will select just 35 items in about 25 minutes. To some this process is fun. To many, it is purgatory. (2000: 36)

Fletcher goes on to describe how little of the information there is now available to consumers can actually be comprehended, simply because there would not be enough time for us to read the labels, note and understand the contents. He even questions whether this information would make any difference to us:

You don't know the chemical specification of the fibres in your clothes, you haven't a clue how your TV works, you feed your beloved pets minced goo which could be reprocessed dung. US studies have shown that only 65 per cent of women and 25 per cent of men try on jeans before buying them, and that 14 per cent of women and 28 per cent of men do not look at the price tags when shopping for clothes. So much for price as the economic arbiter of choice. (Fletcher, 2000: 40)

But really, should any of this be a surprise? The theory of 'satisficing' behaviour is useful in answering this. In the 1950s Simon investigated decision-making in a work situation and found that executives tended to accept the first option which they found as being 'good enough' to solve the problem. Now in a workplace situation, this of course could mean that better solutions might be missed but in the supermarket such an approach might be considered the most sensible way to optimize both our time and the amount of attention we are prepared to spend on choosing relatively mundane products and brands. Information overload is not just related to everyday grocery products either, consumer technology products increasingly provide more functions than are required and this can make them difficult to use. This growth of unnecessary functions has been called 'feature creep' (Ford, 2001: 16) and may reflect an inability to engage realistically with real-life consumers. It goes back to the early problems cited in relationship marketing, too much concern with the supplying of new and different things and too little understanding of how people actually consume. As there appear to be fewer problems to solve for consumers, it seems that features replace meaning. While some new features can be fun or interesting, fewer and fewer of them appear to be actually adding value or helping consumers' lives. There are of course exceptions, for example, the head of a London design group, Ideo, saw the Palm V as an important product because it revitalized what might have been considered a 'dead category' into something that people really wanted. Closer inspection of why this should be, however, revolves around two things in particular, one that it has been made small enough to actually fit into your pocket, and because it now looks less like a gadget and more like an everyday accessory. This is less one might argue to do with the technology and more to do with making the product more consumer friendly.

The Meaningful New Product

Occasionally there are still examples of real innovations which are really solving a problem for the consumer, or really making a noticeable improvement in how something is done. These meaningful innovations make genuinely functional differences to consumers' lives. The Anywayup Cup was developed by Mandy Haberman, a graphic designer by training. Mandy had been interested in the problems of feeding babies since her daughter was born with Stickler's Syndrome, a congenital condition which affects the child's ability to suck. This resulted in the Haberman Feeder which was sold throughout the world to specialist units, hospitals and clinics. Mandy's meaningful invention, however, came about after visiting a friend whose children were spilling juice over the carpet from their training beakers. Anyone who has watched toddlers with these beakers will recognize the problem; the child wants to be on the move, carry their drink with them but seems to have no concept of which way up their beaker should be until it comes time to take another sip. The parent is left with the problem of either trailing around after the child reminding them that they have a beaker or constantly clearing up dribbles around the house. Mandy Haberman developed a beaker which used a slit valve to control the flow of liquid through the spout of the trainer cup. Although it took some time for the cup to go into production, largely because it raised little initial interest with potential producers, once it did, the consumer response was phenomenal. In 1996, they reported selling at a rate of 60,000 a week. Rapidly the Anywayup Cup became stocked by major supermarkets and chemists around the world and by 1999 world sales were at seven million per year and rising. In 2000 the Anywayup Cup was awarded a Gold Medal at the Salon International des Inventions in Geneva and best 'Product – Consumer' at the Design Effectiveness Awards. While one would not want to underestimate the design and innovative thinking that clearly went into the development of the Anywayup Cup, a key aspect to its success must be in consumer acceptability. This was a readily understandable concept that solved an immediate and everyday problem felt by parents of small children – an innovation in response to a consumer need (www.mandyhaberman.com/the_story/).

Unlike the Anywayup cup, the invention of Post-It notes does not seem to have developed out of a gap in the market or in response to a particular need but once used, becomes almost indispensable, as much at home as in the office. The adhesive used was developed in the late 1960s; it was made of minute spheres which created only a light contact with surfaces but was not developed by 3M until the inventor Art Fry used it to deal with a particular problem he had of wanting to mark a page in his hymnal without damaging the paper. Post-It notes are sold in 200 countries and include variations such as narrow strips to accommodate Chinese and Japanese writing style. A key to the success of the Post-It again seems to be how easy it is to use and understand by consumers everywhere as Fry explains, 'The Post-It isn't machinery. It's simple, fast, portable; we use a lot of electronics without much understanding. But the Post-It is understandable. People can find their own creativity with them' (Sims, *The Business FT Weekend* magazine, 2000: 20). In other words, the Post-It succeeds because it can be understood and used easily by anybody, it does not require training or technology or re-learning and is useful; so much so that it is particularly adaptable for a myriad of applications. Although designed for the office, it is equally useful in homes to leave messages and reminders. Students use them for note taking and reminders in books and, as *The Financial Times* article indicates, these are just the tip of their potential, 'In Dick Francis's novel *Longshot*, for example, the lead character carries Post-Its as a survival tool, using them to mark trails, label maps and start fires. Less desperate office workers will have noted how well a pad of Post-Its doubles as an emergency coffee-cup coaster' (Sims, *The Business FT Weekend* magazine, 2000: 20). While quite different in terms of their inception and development, these two examples have a fundamental similarity in terms of consumer acceptance and ease of use. Regardless of what difficulties they may have encountered in development, they are both easy to understand, use and incorporate into existing ways of doing things, they are fundamentally non-technological from a consumer perspective but actually very useful. This is not to argue against technology or consumers' abilities to use and adapt to new technologies, as there are clearly plenty of examples of useful and usable technology, it

is rather to pinpoint the difference between innovations that are meaningful to consumers and those which only add to information overload.

Conclusion

While relationship marketing may not be satisfactory, this does not mean that
consumers do not have connections with the products and brands they
encounter. The act of consumption by people is very different to the picture
sometimes produced from studies of consumption. To investigate the
connections and identify what marketing should derive from them it is
necessary to examine the key roles of product and consumer. Therefore this
chapter has focused on the connection between consumers and the
products and brands they employ in their lives. For this purpose it has
primarily focused on the nature of the product and its path through time.
Marketing has positioned goods, products and brands, as traversing through
some life cycle from birth to death but this is no template for today's
complexity of product and response from consumers. Why some brands
continue to live a charmed life and others do not cannot be simply explained
by a predictive diagram. Sometimes the consumer does play a major role;
children, for example, may respond positively from one generation to the next
to the same playthings and reject others after a few months' interest.
Sometimes, as was the case with Novo, the company very clearly gets it
wrong and retrenches, but some other brands are removed for more complex
tactical and strategic reasons which the consumer will never know about.
Finally, some brands follow a cultural biography, changing and shifting their
meaning and value to consumers over time, here the connection is more
subtle and the supplier needs to respond and change both the brand and the
way it is communicated to keep up with its shifting nature, and they may not
always be able to control the consumer's response in so doing. Finally, we
considered some meaningful new products which made a ready and easy
connection with consumers such that they were adopted and understood
rapidly. The examples were essentially new products of a functional nature
but, as we shall see in future chapters, consumers are just as able to respond
to symbolic new products and to alter and shift the nature of the product for
their own means.

Chapter 3

Paradoxes of Meaning

Market segmentation is inherently a technology of domination. Segmentation is about 'classifying, organizing, and labelling consumers.' (Horkheimer and Adorno, [1944] 1996: 123)

Introduction

We have seen that the central problem for both marketing theory and practice lies in the terms of the relationships that are feasible with active consumers in fluid settings and we have examined some aspects of the product within such settings. This chapter explores how consumers use goods and the meanings that are assigned to those goods. It describes how the assigning of meaning has come about through the increase in choice and the increase in the consumers' economic ability to make those choices. Consumers today, as never before, define their self-identity and indeed their social or group identities through their possessions, the meanings attached to them and their messaging roles. However, setting up and maintaining relationships with people displaying such varied motivations are difficult. It is basic to the implementation of relationship marketing that suppliers can effectively define market segments. This becomes much more problematic in the face of complexity and fluidity and, indeed, some analysts of postmodern consumer behaviour seem to deny the very possibility of breaking consumers into groups, despite the clear commercial imperatives. How can marketing even be sure whether a relationship is feasible when goods are constantly changing in meaning for consumers? The chapter further explores this fragmentation and looks at marketing's response in the form of approaches to segmentation and typologies of consumers such as psychographics which depend on an understanding of the contexts which determine consumer attitudes. While arguing that categorization is the fallback position of marketers and consumers alike, it concludes that this is not the answer to a better understanding of consumers. On the contrary, a rich understanding of consumers is critical to effective categorization and the development of meaningful relationships which acknowledge the needs of consumers. Finally, the chapter explores some of the implications of how consumers today engage with consumption and possessions to define their identity which has profound consequences for how marketing can embrace meaning, particularly in relation to innovation.

What Do Goods Mean to Us?

The consumer acquiring and using goods for purposes of identity and communication is a major theme in texts on consumption and consumer behaviour (Gabriel and Lang, 1998). Interestingly this process of identity and communication has both a paradoxical history and present life. Consumers can, while seeking to identify with particular others or groups, also wish to differentiate themselves and present their own unique identity to the world. Indeed, this paradox is central to Gabriel and Lang's version of the consumer. Aptly entitled *The Unmanageable Consumer*, the authors take us through a catalogue of approaches to consumers and consumption. Among their versions of consumers are the Consumer as Rebel and the Consumer as Victim, the Consumer as Citizen and the Consumer as Chooser. This is in fact less a version of alternative styles of consumers but rather a description of different theoretical positions with regard to consumption. To some extent the authors present the perhaps inevitable historical shifts in people as consumers and their approaches to consumption. One of the most significant consumption shifts is in the increase in real or perceived choice, as choice brings with it other inevitable shifts in consumption and production. Of particular importance is the relationship to one of the central issues discussed later in this book, that is the changed nature of innovation in postmodern society. Choice may be seen as the precursor of innovation as much as innovation is more usually perceived as the precursor of choice. Once the link between choice and innovation is established, an understanding of the relevance of innovation in postmodern society becomes critical to understanding consumers. Innovation may drive production for many companies aiming to provide more choice, but such innovation and choice may be received and perceived quite differently by consumers as they are inundated with choices, decisions and newness. What the response is depends at least to some extent on the type of people and indeed consumers we are.

Part of the argument made by Gabriel and Lang is that within all of us is potentially every type of consumer. We can, they say, be 'irrational, incoherent and inconsistent just as we can be rational, planned and organized. We can be individualistic or we may be driven by social norms and expectations. We can seek risk and excitement or may aim for comfort and security' (1998: 4). Organizations and their marketing departments do not have a good record at realizing this aspect of the consumer. Certainly if it has been recognized, then it has rarely been obvious in terms of the outputs by marketers and advertising agencies. Advertisements whether on billboards or television are simple, they usually appeal to a limited range of emotions and motivations, to be 'better' than others, to be up to date, to find love, and to embrace our families, all inevitably through the purchase of a range of consumer goods. Much of consumers' apparent irrationality can be explained by the phenomenon of choice. All consumer behaviour is choice behaviour (Tuck, 1977) and as citizens in twenty-first-century Western society the one thing it would be difficult to deny is that we have choice. Not only do we have choice but we have more choice than ever before; whereas a hundred years ago a family might have owned a couple of hundred possessions in their homes, now possessions are numbered in the thousands (Cova, 1999). The problem for the marketing organization can be summed up in terms of the nature of the relationships it can feasibly have with its consumers. A supplier organization may seek to segment its market but it will have to produce enough of one type of good to make its efforts cost-effective – firms cannot truly aim to understand the differences of each of their consumers; they have to be aggregated, just to make business viable. On the other hand, each consumer is unique, and so while thousands of people may buy the same brand on the same day, their reasons for doing so may be quite different, just as the way they use the brand is different, what other brands and products they use, what they buy next time, and what TV programmes they watch. They are just too different to actually be manageable. Cova points to the 'instability of the preferences of the consumer' (1999: 71), indicating, he says, the unpredictability of the free choice of the postmodern individual in every part of their life such that they may in the same day purchase food from a discount store and from Marks and Spencer, dress in the morning like a housekeeper and in the afternoon like a model, making the postmodern consumer leitmotif 'it is as I wish and when I wish' (ibid.: 71), as the mood takes him or her.

However probable Cova's picture of a postmodern consumer really is, the meanings consumers derive from goods is clearly diverse and complex, serving alternative purposes at different times and in different circumstances. Similarly, the meaning of the goods themselves is in transit between the various parties involved with them and so it becomes important to address the relevance of such meaning as it affects the consumer. McCracken (1986) suggested that cultural meaning is located in the culturally constituted world, the consumer good and the individual, and this cultural meaning travels the world to the good and from the good

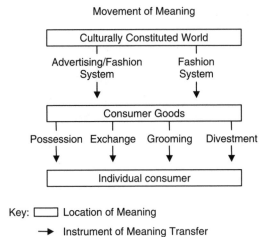

Figure 3.1   Movement of Meaning
Source: McCracken (1986: 72)

to the individual. In his conceptualization he introduced the aspect of the mobile quality in terms of the meaning carried by goods, with this meaning constantly in transit. Similarly, Appadurai (1986) looked at the paths and trajectories of things as their meanings transform and Hebdige (1979) followed objects' 'cultural significance' by mapping the paths through which an object passes along its life history and the meanings it acquires and loses as it moves on its course. A key theme in all these examples is the idea of the object and its meaning moving through time, mutable and changing in that time. Lury (1996), in commenting on Appadurai, remarked that the importance of this approach is that rather than focusing on just one moment in the life of the object, a product or idea is not defined at any one instant in time, but rather it is dynamic, changing, and will have different meanings from one time to the next. Lury also highlighted the temptation to make one moment the 'determining instance' (1996: 19) which then dictates the meaning of the object in other contexts, identifying production, mediation or reception as being likely points for such a 'determining instance' to take place. McCracken (1986: 72), however, does make an attempt to identify if not a 'determining instance', at least a determining process as he analyses the movement of cultural meaning through what he calls 'Movement of Meaning' (see Figure 3.1). In this conceptualization McCracken suggests that meaning resides in three locations, the culturally constituted world, the consumer goods and the individual where meaning is made and transferred through advertising, the fashion system and consumer rituals. There is, however, an apparently one-way flow here, where the culturally constituted world gives meaning to consumer goods via advertising and the fashion system which in turn moves the meaning from the consumer good to the consumer. In comparison to this formal conceptualization, Lury talks of the 'delicately balanced sequence of relationships' (1996: 20) and while, on first reading, this may appear without the form of McCracken's conceptualization, it may, however, help to develop McCracken's somewhat tight conceptualization. If the meaning of objects flows and changes over time, it is difficult for meaning to reside in any location but rather it is in continual flow and flux between the various participants, whoever they may be. As consumers and people we play different roles all the time, depending on our situation, the time, stage in our life, responsibilities we have and many other factors. We are in different situations with other people; our roles at home, and at work are not the same, just as we may alter what we say and how we say it with the people we come into contact with. This in turn implies potentially distinct meanings for objects at any time. The meaning of a good is interpreted by the user and non-user alike and this gives it its multi-layered complexity. It is also important, as Edwards has made clear, that we consider what the limits of influence on consumers are:

> However, what is also very clear, although often missing in many analyses, are the limits of advertising in impacting on personality or identity. Although affluent and style-conscious young men looking to extend their egos may enjoy driving their glamorous vehicles, others perhaps couldn't care less, can't afford it or refute it outright. (2000: 75)

The reasons for being a consumer of glamorous vehicles, and for not, are likely to be many and are not all influenced by the firm and its advertising agency. If you consider a collection of what are essentially everyday products, say, cigarettes, mobile phones, computers, make-up and convenience food and think about the likely differences in attitude and preferences between non-users and users, you can begin to see how such complexity might be constituted even among ostensibly similar users. One working mother may feel convenience food is an essential part of her weekly store cupboard, another may feel convenience food to be a sign of failure and resist buying it. What could be called the 'relationship of meaning' is outlined in Figure 3.2. It is fluid across participants and time but is likely to always include certain participants, whom we can describe as producer, consumer and mediator. The flow between and among the participants is the consumption meaning. The terms producer, consumer

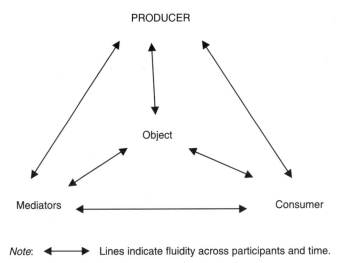

Note: ◄──────► Lines indicate fluidity across participants and time.

Figure 3.2   The relationship of meaning

and mediator are used relatively loosely here and it is likely that a typical relationship would include, say, the producer of a particular good or brand, the mediator as an advertising agency or other form of inter-mediaries such as television, magazine or perhaps an opinion former such as a celebrity wearing a particular fashion item in a certain way, and the consumer as a person, buying, using, and divesting of the object. The actual component players, however, could be highly varied in any one configuration or at any one time, so that it can only ever be a snapshot in time of one scenario. In particular it is important to remember that a consumer's responses from one such scenario to another might well differ so as to defy prediction of meaning. The nature of the relationship between the object and the consumer has to be dependent upon what the consumer is looking for or expecting. This view of the relationship accepts Cova's (1999) point that it will not be the producer who decides the nature of the relationship but rather those who use the product or service. It does not, however, mean, as he has also suggested, that only those goods and services which have linking value, i.e. allow and facilitate social interaction of a communal type, will be valued. Meanings may be func-tional, symbolic, hedonic or indeed anything else the consumer brings to the product in a given situation. If the meanings of objects as Cova suggests are no longer fixed in their function, then while they obtain a relative function rather than a universal function, the nature of that function is no longer open to any kind of prescription in terms of the utility and meaning the consumer takes from it. Instead we always have to look afresh at the meaning of the relationship to the consumer.

What Do Goods Mean?

If the relationship between goods, producers and mediators is fluid and changing, such that things do have different meanings and relative value, should a question such as 'What do goods mean?' even be posed? It can and should because in the paradigm shift from the modern to the postmodern there has been a movement in the understanding or the meaning of what goods are consumed for. So Elliott can say, 'Central to postmodern theory is the proposition that consumers no longer consume products for their material utilities but consume the symbolic meaning of those products as portrayed in their images: products in fact become commodity signs (Baudrillard, 1981)' (Elliott, 1999: 112). Elliott presents the symbolic meaning of goods as constructing the social world, with social symbolism on one hand, and on the other constructing our self-identity, which he terms self-symbolism. Thus one role is a social process where goods are grounded in their social context, and another is to develop an identity. Goods are no longer objects of economic exchange but help us identify ourselves and enable us to construct and maintain social relationships. So goods in Baudrillard's terms have evolved into signs. Goods have no absolute life, rather, they are used by the consumer to create and maintain their identity through their display and the identity they bestow upon the user. The goods are used to create the person from the consumption. As such, the good loses its material meaning but rather it is the *idea* associated with the good which is being consumed. We will see later that this conceptualization of what products are used for has major implications for understanding the nature of innovation. If the thing itself is less important than the meanings it conveys, how can this be incorporated in the development of new things? New products effectively have to create or develop new, better or more appropriate meanings for people, the symbolic innovation may be much more important than mere functional novelty.

Interestingly Baudrillard also suggested that this central role of signing in postmodern society drives the need for innovation when he said that 'The consumer society needs its objects in order to be' ([1970] 1998: 47). He went on to describe this need in terms of destruction and loss rather than gain and benefit. It is as if through the inevitable cycle of use and loss, whether we interpret the use as functional or symbolic, that consumer society benefits and this requires ever more new things to be available. But in turn these new things are no more than gadgets to be used as signifiers of social practices. When a thing is new, Baudrillard suggests, it may experience a sublime period almost equal to the emotion of love but he is careful to position this experience as the opposite to consumption, saying that in this moment fashion and reference to others have no part, but there is an intensity similar to that which a child experiences with his objects or toys, 'the exaltedness of the new' (ibid.: 113). The new, however, quickly becomes a gadget which, according to Baudrillard, is not utilitarian or symbolic in character but rather 'ludic', that is, used in a playful way. The notion of playing helps define the relationship between objects and consumers, whether it is playing as in the fascination with the technical apparatus of computers and mobile phones or the playing with colours and mechanisms. If we relate this back to Lury and McCracken, we can consider that what is being defined here again is the relationships between things and consumers. Thus the meaning of the relationship revolves around play, the relationship is non-functional although what play implies may still be somewhat vague in this analysis, 'there is nothing here of the relation of rider to horse, worker to tools or art-lover to work of art. The relation of man to object is strictly magical, which is to say that it is bewitched and manipulatory' (Baudrillard, [1970] 1998: 114). Nevertheless, there is something interesting in the idea that play is a way of working things out, a sort of rehearsal for the serious and so we could imbue it with some functional value. For Baudrillard the meaning of something new seems always formed within the idea of a gadget, whether a new form of typewriter or dictation machine, something that has novelty value but little else. Rather than asking where and when something is useful, Baudrillard turns this notion on its head and asks where objective uselessness begins? This is not to say that goods have no meaning but, rather, goods become marked by how they are used rather than what their use is, because functional usefulness is subsumed by utility in other terms such as social prestige and fashion. Children go to school with backpacks which have been functionally designed to be worn with two shoulder straps but they wear them slung as low as possible, hanging off one shoulder, functionality subsumed by fashion. Trainers originally designed for athletes or recreational sport are worn on the street with no laces and some of the latest designs feature no backs to the trainers at all, certainly eliminating their functionality for running. Once again we can shift attention to the consumer in terms of how things, be they gadgets, innovations or simply objects of playful gratification, are used, consumed and understood.

What Do We Mean to Goods?

The relationship between goods and the consumer brings us once again to consider typologies of consumers. Cova (1999) explores the impossibility of the quest to classify consumers and suggests giving it up, and instead take an interest in consumption. His message is one of abandoning the simplification of segmentation and instead turning attention to the situations, surroundings, rituals and trends in consumption. However, like it or not, classification is still a fundamental part of how society and business works, with demographics and consumption presented in stark figures. While segmentation may be a fact of marketing life (Wensley, 1998) ostensibly enabling companies to make choices and decisions, it does mask the 'how' of consumption. Cova says that the days have gone where we would have expectations of what car a secretary would drive, and it would cause a scandal if she drove to work in a car associated with another class. Maybe today it would not actually cause a scandal but it would definitely be remarked upon and talked about – such classifications continue to exist in all walks of life. Similarly, Cova suggests a government minister could as easily drive a 2CV as an unemployed person a BMW. This is an appealing idea perhaps but still the exception rather than the rule. For each example, a linkage would be made by others of what the car implied or what the driver was trying to say – we do not live in such a declassified society and most government ministers drive or are driven in prestige cars just as most unemployed people do not. There is another way to look at the nature of classification, which is to suggest that the differences are not as extreme or as distinctly noticeable as they would have been at the beginning of, say, the twentieth century or even in the 1950s or 1960s but an awareness of social differences is still fundamental to much of society. It is the kind of view as expressed by Marcuse:

> If the worker and his boss enjoy the same television program and visit the same resort places, if the typist is as attractively made up as the daughter of her employer, if the Negro owns a Cadillac, if they all read the same newspaper, then this assimilation indicates not the disappearance of classes, but the extent to which the needs and satisfactions that serve the preservation of the establishment are shared by the underlying population. (1986: 8)

While Marcuse is making a political point about the acceptance of the norm, one might also summarize by saying appearance is not everything. The problem is that marketing is interested in numbers and generalizations, not individuals and not exceptions. If there are enough people to incorporate into broad classifications, then the segmentation game will continue. The critical question is whether the segmentation methods used retain their value?

However fragmented and different people may be, as consumers they have been and are always likely to be targets for segmentation. Identifying groups with similar patterns, whether they are behavioural, socio-economic, age- or sex-related helps in the process of identifying markets for products and particularly those markets most likely to adopt a new product or brand. Brands are repositioned to be more attractive to certain clusters, and gaps in the market of consumers who are not adequately served by what is available on the market are identified. Such a need has inevitably led to the categorizing of consumers into groups. It might be argued that this was an easier task earlier in the twentieth century when distinctions between classes were clearly pronounced, where there was relatively little disposable income for most and equally little choice on which to spend it (Bocock, 1993; McKibbin, 1998). 'Fordism' (Gramsci, 1971) is associated with an undifferentiated mass market of consumers where for the first time many people could own a car as long as they accepted they had no choice of colour (Bocock, 1993). But this very lack of choice held within it the inevitable kernel of future choice; if in the 1920s the only colour Ford to buy was black, then it was to be expected that before long this choice would become wider – in other words, rather than seeing this as a signifier of mass undifferentiated consumption, it should be seen as the beginning of increasing differentiated consumption. Bocock has identified the increasing choice available once a pattern of 'mass consumption' developed among the working classes which would not have existed in the 1920s and 1930s where products were designed and targeted only at the middle class. Once the working class had enough money to cover their basic needs, they would become aware of new things and services, televisions, cars, foreign holidays. The result is the emergence of choices being made by them:

> New groups of consumer emerged in this period of 'Fordist' mass production and mass consumption, who began to exercise choice in what they bought. Brand images were established by advertisements for everything from infamous soap powders to cars, drinks, cigarettes, clothing and kitchen equipment. It was young men and women, who still lived with their parents, but had reasonably well-paid jobs, who formed the first group of specifically targeted and differentiated consumers, followed by women who took on paid work in order to be able to buy extras – the new consumer durables as well as new types of foodstuffs, including such 'novelties' as frozen fish fingers and take-away curries. (Bocock, 1993: 22)

Consumers emerge ready and increasingly able to spend their money on new things, they are eager buyers and users of novelty. It was also to be expected that increased choice would be followed by increased classification. Classification gives companies a sense of control once behaviour becomes more complex and varied. To begin with, classification was principally occupation rather than consumption led, as occupation was considered to play a major role in consumption. The occupation classified was that of the male head of the household, and it was assumed that his income would dictate the consumption patterns of the other members of his household. This method dates back to 1946 but is still in use today dividing the UK population into the following categories:

Grade A – Upper Middle Class. The head of the household is likely to be a successful business or professional man, senior civil servant or has considerable private means.

Grade B – Middle Class. In general the heads of B grade households will be quite senior people but not at the very top of their profession or business.

Grade C1 – Lower Middle Class. In general the C1 grade is made up of the families of small trades people and non-manual workers who carry out less important administrative, supervisory and clerical jobs, i.e. what are sometimes called 'white-collar' workers.

Grade C2 – The Skilled Working Class. Grade C2 consists in the main of skilled manual workers and their families.

Grade D – The Semi-Skilled or Unskilled Working Class. Grade D consists mainly of manual workers, generally semi-skilled or unskilled.

Grade E – Those at the lowest levels of subsistence. Grade E consists of old age pensioners who do not have an occupational pension, casual workers and those who, through sickness or unemployment, are dependent on social security schemes or very small private means.

In the late 1980s O'Brien and Ford undertook an extensive study to identify whether social class was still relevant in an increasingly egalitarian society. They were particularly concerned that it did not act as an accurate gauge of disposable income:

A C2 or D may not intellectually be performing the same role in the job market as a B or C1, but may well have more available cash with which to acquire the trappings of our society. The financial chains of private education are likely to constrain the AB as much as the black economy and overtime can enhance the apparently lower wage of the C2D. (O'Brien and Ford, 1998: 290)

O'Brien and Ford were suggesting that classifying people by some supposed relatively constant factor such as the head of the household's occupation did not give us any indication of how much disposable income they have and in turn, it did not readily tell us what they will spend it on anyway. This again is questioning whether we can, through classification systems, be sure of what we may be predicting simply because we really do not know anything about the complexities of each person's life. What we are doing is trying to avoid this complexity by identifying a simple proxy for which there is data that we believe captures enough of the determinants of consumer attitudes and behaviour to allow prediction. However, both the relationship of the proxy to behaviour and the stability of the proxy itself may be highly questionable. Indeed, the constancy of social class was in itself put into question. O'Brien and Ford said that in March 1987 the Broadcasters Audience Research Board (BARB) reported that 32 per cent of their TV audience panel had changed social class over a 12-month period. While this was later considered to be somewhat smaller due to misclassification of some respondents and problems with the level of detail obtained from interviews, it highlights the problems of consistency in classifications of this type. Indeed, when O'Brien and Ford themselves looked at the consistency of social class measures, they found that it was difficult to replicate successfully from one period to the next.

Spending patterns differ markedly over a consumer's lifetime so another approach to classifying consumers that has proved popular is to organize them by life stage, assuming that people will have different constraints and aspirations at different points in their life. One example of this was known as SAGACITY which included four main stages: the dependent stage when individuals are still living at home, or studying full-time if not at home; the pre-family stage where a household has been established but a couple have not yet had children; the family stage when there are dependent children at home; and the late stage when the children have left. These stages were combined with income and occupation to create 12 groups altogether. O'Brien and Ford's life stage groups included six categories, again principally defined by age, marital and working status and the presence of children. They also identified the percentage of people belonging to each group but ending up with a miscellaneous assortment of 18 per cent who did not fit into any of the categories outlined below.

Granny Power: People aged 55–70, living in households where neither the head of household nor the housewife works full-time. They have no children and no young dependent adults, i.e. no non-working 16–24s live with them (14 per cent of adults).

Grey Power: People aged 45–60, living in households where either the head of household or the housewife is working full-time. They have no children and no young dependent adults (12 per cent of adults).

Old Silver Power: Married people with older children (5–15 years) but *no* under-fives (18 per cent of adults).

Young Silver Power: People who are married, with children aged 0–4 years (16 per cent of adults).

Platinum Power: Married people aged 40 or under, but with no children (7 per cent of adults).

Golden power: Single people, with no children, aged 40 or under (15 per cent of adults).

(O'Brien and Ford, 1998: 293–4)

However, again, we need to confront the lack of stability in the behaviour of the identified segments. What is interesting about this life stage classification is that it has largely been superseded by the growth in the older consumer and the incredible variations in their lifestyle and life stage which cannot be simply reflected by age. During the twentieth century there was a shift in the stereotyping of the older person which went together with a change in expectations and consumption. Middle age, for example, was revamped from a time to be staying at home and gardening to a time to be enjoying the 'best years of your life'. This process, however, required women, in particular, to age 'well', to exercise, think positively, eat carefully and use appropriate cosmetics (Benson, 1997). Recent research has begun to focus on those people now in their forties and fifties that belong to the so-called baby boomer generation (Barak, 1998; Moschis et al., 2000). Increasingly, the life styles and consumption choices of those now in their forties and fifties (variously categorized as prime-lifers or baby boomers) have become of interest to marketers. It has been argued that this generation of middle-aged has the greatest power both in political and economic terms (Barak, 1998). Household income has grown together with discretionary income (Lee, 1997) and products and services have proliferated for a generation of people often both willing and able to spend their money. Improvements in medicine and education have meant that they are also better able than ever before to enjoy their good fortune and look forward to many more years of activity and good health than their parents or grandparents. At the same time that many older people may be enjoying a different kind of life to their grandparents and even their parents, women are often putting off starting a family until they are in their thirties or forties. All these factors are helping to disrupt some of the accepted norms of previous generations and marketing assumptions. The problem for marketers is exacerbated by the fact that while such de-chronologization may free some people from the constraints of age and time, it brings other problems with it. These changes have led to a much wider variety of ages at different stages in the family cycle, such that age norms are invariably questioned. The typical age structured roles are changing but the social institutions have not kept pace with this, producing what has been referred to as 'social lag' (Riley and Riley, 1994). Such social change has altered the nature of human lives. One aspect of this that has impacted upon middle-aged women in particular is that they are often part of what has been termed the 'sandwich generation' (Moschis et al., 2000). They may find themselves still fit and relatively youthful yet required to be responsible for both their parents and their grandchildren.

In light of the ongoing disruption of previously held norms of behaviour identified by or associated with age, sex, status, social class or income, it was only to be expected that styles of life would become the often preferred form of categorization. As Featherstone remarked over ten years ago, 'we are moving towards a society without fixed status groups in which the adoption of styles of life (manifest in choice of clothes, leisure activities, consumer goods, bodily disposition) which are fixed to specific groups have been surpassed' (1991: 83). But why the concern with categorizing people in any kind of way? From a marketing perspective it may be seen simply as a matter of developing cost-effective strategies in terms of identifying groupings, establishing appropriate products and forms of distribution and communication. An implication of different sets of consumption dependent on groupings is that it is a way of establishing and maintaining difference between these groups. This is not only pertinent to what goods people buy, what television programmes they watch and what new things may appeal to them but also to a broader concept of education and taste which become components in consumption and identification (Bourdieu, 1984). Here the social and educational structures which maintain taste take on a greater significance in classification than income. This still does not imply, however, that structures are bounded in such a way that there are consistent, long-standing social or consumption patterns. Indeed, a distinctive feature of the postmodern world is the proposed increased fluidity between group boundaries such that people do not necessarily feel aligned to the same group into which they were born but increasingly move from one to another in their consumption choices (Bocock, 1993; Hall, 1992). It should be noted, though, that the nature of consumption choice and relationships between person and product, in a postmodern model, may well be an important aspect of analysing this fluidity and as such have as much to do with the character and availability of these choices as it does with changes in the people consuming them. For example, Bocock uses a number of examples to exemplify fluidity which are fundamentally product led. First, he suggests that the BBC's radio stations 1, 2, 3, 4 were categories in which audiences were seen as fixed rather than moving from one station to another whereas now we would expect much more fluidity between people's music choices, but this may have as much to do with the recognition by radio producers that they can gain a larger share of the overall listening audience if they spread their taste boundaries wider and provide greater choice and variety in music. In a similar vein, Bocock suggests other signs of fluidity and the breakdown of social boundaries:

> Rock music goes into churches; the best champagne is drunk by footballers; pop stars are more likely to be purchasers of a Rolls-Royce car than a member of the English landed aristocracy. The former sense of a clear social status group hierarchy disintegrates in postmodern conditions, not only in Europe, with its feudal past, but especially in the 'new worlds' of the Americas. (1993: 81)

But do these examples even rely upon the same causes for their existence? Rock music, it might be argued, has been taken up by churches due to a perceived need to modernize and try to bring younger people into a church fighting against a secularization that has as much to do with Darwin as it does with the consumer society. Footballers and rock stars are paid a great deal of money, partly no doubt because of their talent and also because they are celebrities. There is nothing new in celebrity, it existed with Nell Gwynne and Madame de Pompadour, and with Mary

Pickford and Douglas Fairbanks reigning supreme in their mansion PickFair and presented to the public in magazines such as *The Picture Goer* just as today's footballers and rock stars appear in *Hello!* magazine. There is little doubt, however, that the cult of celebrity has grown in proportion to mass communication and our consumption of it is accordingly greater. One has to consider whether it is the fluidity of the consumer that is the problem or that the appearance of fluidity is more a symptom of changes in the choices available. This is not to say that there have not been major breakdowns in social class over the last century but it is not quite as revolutionary as Baudrillard's secretary arriving to work in an upmarket car while the government minister drives his 2CV.

To a certain extent the more modern typologies of consumption may be seen as trying to reflect the increased complexity of consumption. Take psychographics, for example, from whence much of today's lifestyle categorizations derive. The history of the term may date back as far as the First World War when it was used to describe people by their physical appearance. In the 1920s the term was used to classify people by attitudes but no attempt was made to form segments from this information. Others suggest that the term first actually appeared in Grey Advertising's publication *Grey Matter* in 1965 (Piirto Heath, 1995). While methodologies vary, the aim of researchers employing psychographics was to find a quantitative segmentation tool which went beyond demographics (Demby, 1994). Demby gave a broad remit for psychographics giving as a definition:

> The use of psychological, sociological, and anthropological factors, such as benefits desired (from the behavior being studied), self-concept, and lifestyle (or serving style) to determine how the market is segmented by the propensity of groups within the market – and their reasons – to make a particular decision about a product, person, ideology, or otherwise hold an attitude or use a medium. Demographics and socio-economics also are used as a constant check to see if psychographic market segmentation improves on other forms of segmentation, including user/nonuser groupings. (Demby, 1994: 26)

The psychologist Ernest Dichter had worked extensively in the area of consumer motivations (1964) and had done much work putting psychological, sociological and anthropological concepts into projective tests and, in part, developed from his work, researchers designed computer clustering programs in the late 1960s which allowed qualitative data to be standardized into a quantitative form with the object of predicting the likelihood of sales to particular segments. One of the key drivers of developing techniques such as psychographics, which potentially allowed the studies of sizeable populations, was the development of the computer itself as it became possible to deal with much larger amounts of complex information about people. Important to the conceptual development of psychographics was an acceptance and indeed a desire to examine the fluidity of individuals in consumption situations. Demby outlined that his thinking had developed out of a view that it was more useful to know whether a person who currently earned $25,000 a year was someone who had previously earned $50,000 but whose circumstances had changed or whether it was someone who had just had a raise to $25,000 or indeed had been earning that amount for some time. From such information he believed it was possible to build meaningful segments as a person's reactions to products and media might be significantly different depending on which situation applied. Later he developed the variables to include the activities, interests and opinions (AIO) originally developed by Tigert in the 1970s, including holiday and travel habits, food preparation and dining, beverage consumption, product benefits sought, self-concept, media habits, and so on. It is important to note, however, that the consumer's measurable demographic characteristics were often included as well. Increasingly psychographic studies included product-specific questions about purchases that had been made as well as future intentions. The psychographics industry burgeoned to encompass different approaches and applications. Wells' critical review of psychographics (1975), still considered one of the most important works on the uses and limitations of the technique, identified five types of psychographic studies. There were psychographic profiles based on general lifestyle dimensions, whereby Wells said that the 'psychographic information can put flesh on demographic bones' (1975: 198). Using large questionnaires, which included questions on demographics, product and media use and lifestyle, the main aim of such approaches was to identify differences between users and non-users of certain types of product. Product-specific psychographic profiles focused on a limited set of product dimensions of relevance to a particular brand, so a company might identify the orientation of users, potential users and non-users. Such information could be particularly useful for positioning or repositioning a brand. A third type of study took personality traits as descriptors whereby a dependent variable, Wells used ecological concern, was analysed against other independent variables which would include personality traits such as tolerance and risk-taking. These would be evaluated to identify which had most impact on ecological concern. Next, general lifestyle segmentation studies used large, nationally representative samples with questions numbering as many as 300, including items on lifestyle, product use, and exposure to media. Respondents were classified into relatively homogenous groups to form typologies, some of which are described below. This kind of study, unlike the previous three, did not assume members of any target group might be similar. Rather, it accepted the possibility that users of a product could fall into several different segments. An early British example of such a study was Leo Burnett's British Men and Women which subdivided the population into six types for men and seven for women. Below is a description of the seven female types.

Gloria: Young, swinging, out for a good time. Gloria makes herself look attractive. She doesn't want to be tied to the house and kids. She works, but only for the money. Age 28, average in social grade. 12 per cent of population.

Helen: Well educated and a realist. You need rational arguments to persuade her. Helen is well-off, well-groomed, confident and responsible. Age 35, highest in social grade. 11 per cent.

Iris: The smart, smiling Mum in most TV commercials. Iris is completely happy with her nice home and lovely family. She's friendly with everyone in her street. Age 39, down-grade. 15 per cent.

Joan: Uncommitted and depressed. Joan is a grey woman without many interests or enthusiasms. She is liable to head-aches. Age. 46, average in social grade. 21 per cent.

Kathleen: A prim, rather cold but contented middle-aged lady. Kathleen dresses sensibly and tolerates no nonsense. 'Plain living and high thinking' is her motto. Age 51, up-grade. 14 per cent.

Laura: A busybody who is active in the Women's Institute. Laura tells other people how they should behave. Tough, optimistic and independent. She is a high Tory. Age 54, up-grade. 13 per cent.

Maggie: an old working class woman, old fashioned, poor and worried. But Maggie is very courageous and cheery. She's anxious to please and make friends. Age 56, very down-grade. 14 per cent.

The problem for such general psychographics is that while trying to bridge the divide between basic demographics and lifestyle, it over-simplifies the complexities of very real differences between people both as individuals and as consumers. While such snapshots may have been useful for advertising folk unable to imagine what a 'real' person would think or do, they are a prime example of marketing's lack of reflexivity. Today, as Lury has made clear, it is perhaps the consumer who is best able to reflect on their own advertising persona.

> since the audience is increasingly made up of a media-literate generation, its members, rather than seeking the truth, in turn self-consciously mimic the media – they adopt the persona of fictional characters as a way of expressing themselves, they discuss their personal lives via analogies with the story-lines of soap-operas, and talk in the catchphrases of celebrities and the slogans of advertising campaigns. They are reflexively aware that advertising is trying to persuade them to buy particular products. They know when they've been tango-ed! (1996: 70)

Wells' final category, product-specified segmentation, was similar to lifestyle segmentation in its approach but focused on product-specific rather than general psychographic items. Piirto Heath (1995) sites the example of research into stomach ailments where 80 product-related items such as attitudes to treatment and symptom frequency were asked. From the responses the 80 items were reduced to 13 highest discrimina-tors by factor analysis and finally just four groups were identified: Severe Sufferers, Active Medicators, Hypochondrias and Practicalists. Piirto Heath thought that the benefit of such segmentation was its ability to dis-criminate between brands which in turn could be used in developing appropriate communications better fitting to the different groups. In the 1980s the advertising agency DMB&B used a similar technique to find groupings in terms of healthy eating. This study conducted by the British Market Research Bureau had a sample size of 11,000 respondents with questions mainly on diet and health. It identified seven typologies which were labelled 'Superfits', 'Younger Concerned', 'Older Concerned', 'Selec-tivists', 'Traditional Healthers', 'Dismissers' and 'The Untouched'. For each there was a small sketch of the type of person identified in the group. So for example the Selectivists were described in the following way:

'Middle England',
not so ideologically convinced of 'nouveau regime' but

mild neurosis/guilt = pragmatic selective experimentation,
two motives:
- care for family
- self-presentation: the body beautiful

key engine of change: food suppliers' actions
experiments often transitory:
- lean cuisine acquires chips
- family put on trial

Additives a natural target: feeling of doing something, and
no family comeback.

The usefulness of this kind of study may well lie in its attempt to understand the differences between people and their relationships with a
particular type of product, more than the segments it proposes. Consider
in this light a quotation Wells used which described the difficulty that an
advertising copywriter had in identifying how to communicate with his
intended audience: 'A writer writes out his personal collection of life
experiences and his knowledge of people, and he imagines and projects
them and he tries to translate them into his viewer's or his reader's terms.
But he's feeding off himself. He's just one person' (quoted in Wells, 1975:
197). What is being described is the problem of getting closer to your
audience when they may be quite different to you, so by giving thumbnail
descriptions (often with pictures) of the type of person to target, the
copywriter might actually feel closer to the consumer. Additionally, in the
DMB&B study, there is a detailed commentary which makes tentative
predictions about how different groups' attitudes are likely to develop, as
well as quite detailed implications for food suppliers. For example, one
implication they state is that the 'purity' of food will become a major
factor influencing food purchase. Clearly, history shows that this has been
the case, partly no doubt fuelled by problems with BSE, but nevertheless
the organic movement and the anti-GM lobby group can also be seen as
having their origins in an increased requirement for so-called 'purity'.

Despite the tangential benefits, the primary objective of psychographics is still the desire by marketing to categorize people as consumers.
But one might argue, marketing *is* about segmenting potential customers,
targeting with the right product and positioning your brand in the
marketplace such that it appeals, and to do this one effectively needs to
categorize people into substantive groupings. Understanding consumers
effectively corresponds to what they mean to goods, such that one can ask
questions of the consumer as related to the good – is this the type of
person who would be interested in a new low-calorie snack food? Categorizing, although it sounds somewhat crude when put like this, is above
all a normal human activity which helps us deal with one another. As

such, it is perhaps more about understanding people than consumers although it may well be couched in consumer terms. Teenagers categorize one another as a matter of course and often through the brands they buy, Shazzas wear Kappa, and Gazzas wear Nike, while Skaters wear Quiksilver. But all of these categories, whether produced by market research companies or young people on the street, can only be caricatures of people as they are at best rough approximations of what they might be, do, and indeed buy. They may be useful for marketing firms in their continuation of segmentation into groups but it would be a mistake to think they give a greater or deeper understanding of consumers. Segmentation remains a tool of mass marketing and consumers know this. The more mature, fragmented, sophisticated or changeable different markets become, the more difficult it will be to maintain the illusion of getting closer to the customer through this tool. Categorization and segmentation are not in themselves bad or doomed to fail. It is just that we should now be developing the techniques after getting close and understanding consumers, not in reverse as a tool to do so. Otherwise as fast as we create, measure and attempt to use categories, they will fall apart in our hands.

Conclusion

Much of this chapter has dealt with the fundamental relationship between the person and the things they possess which identifies a key aspect of consumer culture in the twentieth century (Lury, 1996). Individualism and the mass consumer society have led people to define themselves and others in terms of the things they possess. If we identify ourselves through possessions, then we as consumers enter into a relationship with those organizations which supply us with these possessions. This inevitably leads, on the supplier side of the relationship, to identifying consumers by what we purchase and possess. Segmentation through classification is an obvious route for marketers to take. On a human level, by identifying ourselves with our belongings, we build at least part of our self-identity out of these possessions and what we think they say about us. The essence of this approach to consumption might be summarized by the concept of 'to have is to be' (Dittmar, 1992). From a consumer behaviour viewpoint, self-identity is much more than a cultural resource or possession primarily because consumer behaviour is always about choice. Whether to choose to buy a product or service or not, to buy one brand over another, whether to buy the same brand as last time or the one that has the special promotion. All of these choices impact on us as consumers everyday. Additionally, consumers have an uncanny ability to associate with some of their possessions and not others, to regard some in a purely functional way and others as more symbolic or indicative of their identity. Thus the meanings that different products have for us in themselves help to create the kind of relations we have with them. Rather than surmising product and brand choices from lifestyle alternatives, we may wish to seek a better understanding of the meanings of things to people and hence their relationships with them. To do this would require in-depth discussions and interpretation of motives and may not be an easy to follow route for those wanting quick fixes. It would, however, allow consumers to set parameters which suppliers have not even envisaged and this in turn could be a fruitful and worthwhile avenue to pursue in finding *why* and *how* people consume rather than just *what*.

Chapter 4

Whose Marketplace is it Anyway?

To be in the company of like-minded, life-styled consumers is to share the experience, as mass marketing ecstasy operates under the guise of individualism. You can have it your way, tailored to who you are. Be free. Be what you want to be, as long as you buy something – anything. Or, until the realization one day, that the longevity of belonging is compounded daily, revolving, slowly, enslaving the collective summation of one's life's work and hopes. This is good health in the United States of Free Trade Uber Alles. (Hand-Boniakowski, 2001)

Introduction

This chapter begins by again questioning why consumers would want or need to develop long-term relationships with companies. Examining a number of situations where the supplier side appears to have manipulated its power relative to its customers, the suggestion is made that consumers increasingly require equity in their commercial relationships and will make choices according to whether they perceive they have been treated justly. While suppliers continue to believe that it is they who set the game plan and manage it, they will be open to anything from customers leaving them to outright hostility. The balance of power is shifting. The shift may be slow but it is real. One of the most important catalysts in this movement has been the Internet and its ability to bring consumers together to readily and easily exchange information and experiences. Suppliers appear to have a problem with the Internet. It is not just a medium for more advertising or indeed selling, it truly is a two-way communication and consumers can use it to talk to one another, set up their own websites, complain and agitate. Consumers are beginning to take over the marketplace in small but significant steps. Not only are they talking to one another and trying to talk to the suppliers, but they are also developing ways and means of developing their own responses to marketing. This can be identified through the concept of use-initiation whereby the consumer develops new uses or ways of doing things with or to products, different to that intended by the supplier. While this could theoretically be useful to marketers, watching how consumers respond to products in use, more often the response is defensive, especially if this process appears to threaten the producer's position. Marketing now has the choice as to whether to confront the issue of 'real' relationships and respond to a range of consumer concerns, some to do with the nature of products and firms and some more to do with disjunctures between the promise of the brand and the activity of the corporation (Holt, 2002). Whatever the source and meaning of the consumer response, importantly what is needed for marketing is to ensure that unhappy consumers do not change into consumer 'terrorists' of whatever kind, as this is not only bad for marketing in practice but also an indication of its failure as a discipline.

The End to Inertia

While the 'risk' for the consumer of lots of associations might lead one to believe that Sheth and Parvatiyar were right and people will choose long-term relationships to aid cognitive ease, it seems just as likely that many of these relationships will prove unsatisfactory (Fournier et al., 1998) and the consumer will return to the marketplace to transact and innovate. Consumer inertia will increasingly be a thing of the past and, while too much choice will still produce cognitive upheaval and discomfort, many consumers will nevertheless increasingly look for and get equity and value through tackling companies head-on.

In this movement banks, insurance companies and other such 'tied-in relationships' will be particularly threatened by the value-seeking consumer. While your salary may continue to be paid in to one bank, this does not preclude relationships with other financial providers, indeed, in the UK, in the light of demutualization, relationships with a number of banks, building societies and insurance companies seems to have proved a positive financial boon for consumers. Financial service companies have a poor record at fair relationships. The newspapers are full of stories of people charged outrageous sums for minor misdemeanours. Much of this comes about through the automation involved in banking, where ludicrous slips get through because no individual checked the process. Too often banks are seen to be squabbling over a few pounds of their customers' money while making huge profits themselves. Now that some consumers are shopping around for bank services and indeed changing their banks when they feel they are not getting value from their existing provider, one sees the inevitable backlash from these so-called relationships.

The problem for many people wishing to change banks is getting all their services such as standing orders or direct debits moved from one supplier to another quickly and efficiently. Some banks were found to be dragging their heels and not responding to customers' requests to move their business to their new provider, such that the regulators had to step in. Indeed, at the time of writing, regulators in the UK are putting the finishing touches to plans to enable consumers to move current accounts to a new bank within five days or be able to claim compensation from their existing account holder. Commentators estimated that this could lead to a trebling in the number of people moving their current accounts (Winnett and Toyne, 2001). Essentially what the banks have been doing is creating barriers to exit which are either financial or time and trouble, but, from the consumer point of view, just knowing that you are locked in is not good for the relationship. It may be too cynical to suggest that the banks will find another way of making their customers' lives more difficult, but in customer relationship terms they certainly have a chequered record. In the post-loyalty card world of the twenty-first century, supermarkets too are faced with a different environment. Prices are again seen as a field ripe for bewildering the customer. While price wars are not new in supermarket history, the issue is how the war is fought and against whom. Too often it would seem the customer is ultimately defeated. So, for example, in September 2001 when Tesco was said to have 'slashed' the price of 3,500 goods, it was reported that many were only reduced by a penny (Fletcher and Mills, 2001). More interesting still was the assertion that often before a price cut, prices were increased, thus making the price cut de facto unreal.

> All of the leading supermarkets employ large departments with responsibility for pricing and collecting prices from rivals to ensure they remain competitive. But they also 'manage' prices in the run up to a price-cutting campaign, claims one former supermarket chief executive. 'The classic is turkey prices in the weeks up to Christmas. The prices progressively go up before coming down with a great splash. Big price reductions in particular are managed. If you are about to offer something half price, you push the price up a bit beforehand.' (ibid.: 8)

Once you have incurred the initial search costs of finding the 'best' supermarket, these costs are sunk and act as a barrier to exit. The supermarkets action as described above may be to tax those captured to cross-subsidize potential new consumers. In a time-poor economy it is just too expensive to shop around.

Consumers Taking Over the Marketplace

While newspapers may report on the inequity of the supplier–buyer relationship, the question remains as to whether this really matters to the customer. Do many of us notice how and when prices change in the supermarkets we frequent? If we did notice, would it matter to us and would we do anything about it? As usual, with the consumer, the answers are unlikely to be a straight yes or no. 'Barclaycard drops its annual fee' read the headline of *The Sunday Telegraph* Money Section (Simon, 2001) and under this the sub-heading read 'Bank cuts credit card rate but levies swingeing extra charges in small print'. The article goes on to describe how Britain's biggest credit card provider was abolishing its £10 annual fee and cutting some of its interest rates but, as it gave with one hand, it took away with the other, and the bulk of the article described how a raft of additional charges such as an automatic £15 each time a credit limit was exceeded would be payable. The article also reminded the reader that Barclaycard still charged a £10 service fee to customers spending less than £200 on their card in a year and not incurring interest charges. Such an example illustrates another key problem with relationship marketing. From the supplier's side of things, some relationships are worth more than others. If a customer is not profitable, the supplier has to consider whether it is worthwhile engaging with them in a relationship, and we know that for large and small companies alike throughout the world, relatively few customer segments prove profitable (Sheth, 2001). So maybe it is more realistic of Barclaycard to charge non-interest-incurring, small spending accounts. On the other hand, however, it does raise the question of whether only certain types of people will be worth having a relationship with and the accompanying issues of exclusion this raises. Barclays Bank also hit the news when soon after a major advertising campaign featuring actors Anthony Hopkins, Robbie Coltrane and others extolling the virtues and benefits of banking with a 'big' bank, it then went on to cut 171 branches while quadrupling the chairman's salary to £1.76 million (Worthington, 2001). Against such odds what can consumers do and indeed what are they prepared to do for a 'fair' relationship? If this is a relationship at all, it is one of unequal partners; the big boys have a mighty punch but every now and again there are acts of resistance which appear to show that some consumers are quite capable of reclaiming, at least some of the marketplace for themselves.

Let us continue with credit cards as an example of such small acts of resistance. It is important to remember that the nature of these cards is that they can act as an aid to money management as well as a payment method. Increasingly in the 1990s consumers were using their cards as a means of payment and taking advantage of the interest-free period. As early as 1988 it was noted that Access were worried that their card was being used 'as a method of payment rather than simply as a means of credit' (Worthington, 1988). At the time both Access and Barclaycard had about 40 per cent of their customers regularly settling their account each month thus using the free credit period to defer the time when they had to part with the money from their bank account. While a small point in itself, the clashes between banks and consumers which have continued since the 1990s highlight an important implication for the supplier–consumer relationship which was well developed by Burton (1994). She presented two implications of consumers paying off their credit cards monthly and using them as a convenient method of payment and interest-free credit. First, she noted that financial institutions did not always identify and conceptualize consumer behaviour accurately; they had expected credit cards to be used for obtaining credit in exchange for interest income and not all credit card users wanted to do this. Second, as consumers have become better informed, they are more able and aware of 'how to play the system' to their advantage. (1994: 72). While Burton's conclusions reflect behaviour in the consumer financial services sector, the two key points still act as messages for the promulgators of relationship marketing. First, companies who set the rules of the relationship need to think carefully what these rules really mean for both sides and, second, they need to consider how their consumer partners might want to play their hand. Having set the rules of the relationship, to change the rules is to breach the trust that is basic to a customer-oriented marketing concept.

An interesting, if unusual, example of a consumer getting the better of the rules of the game occurred when Phil Calcott, a physicist, bought 3,000 bananas from his Tesco in Worcester and made a profit of £25. Spotting an offer of 3lb of bananas and 25 Clubcard points for £1.17 he quickly calculated that 25 Clubcard points would buy him goods worth £1.25; Tesco were effectively paying their customers 8p to purchase 3lb of bananas. Mr. Calcott bought bananas worth over £350 and then started to give them away by standing in Worcester High Street and shouting 'free bananas'. It wasn't long of course before the publicity reached Tesco and the offer was withdrawn. A point, however, had been made. Companies spend time and energy developing relationships that suit them and consumers know it, but chinks in the armour can and will appear. Just such a chink was found by an 89-year-old pensioner of Barclays, Mrs Jessie

Bonner-Thomas, who stood up at the AGM at Barclays Bank and brought 'fat cat salaries' and branch closures back in the public domain. National newspapers, radio and television picked up on how Mrs Bonner-Thomas had taken the board of Barclays by surprise with her comment that, 'I received a letter stating that circumstances beyond your control only allowed you to increase my widow's pension by £1 a week. Circumstances within your control allowed you to give the new chief executive Matthew Barrett a £1.3 million hello' (www.socialistworker.co.uk). And the anger of Mrs Bonner-Thomas was shared by many others at the AGM who had read in the Barclays annual report of promises to increase the convenience and access to services weeks after they had closed over 150 branches.

Shifts, Fault Lines and More Resistance

The balance of power between customers and suppliers is changing. While globalization brought with it the inevitable shift of production to cheap labour sources, thus reducing the cost base of many supplier companies such as Nike and Gap, so did the Internet release and reduce the cost of information and product and brand switching for the consumer. Just as the law has made it easier for couples to divorce if they find they are mutually incompatible, so the Internet has made it easier for consumers to find out if they really do want a relationship with a company and, if so, what kind of relationship that should be. Why should I stay with a company if I can find something cheaper or better elsewhere? These decisions will be defined by other forms of value and equity too, not only those related to the functional attributes of consumption choices, price and availability. Increasingly our choices of relationship will be defined by production as well as consumption issues as consumers express a wider range of values. This has been hinted at by some writers such as Miller (2001) when he argues that consumption is often the scapegoat for an ideological concern that wishes to castigate Western society for the poverty that continues to exist in the world: 'the desire to give credit to the way consumers consume and the authenticity of some of their desire for goods need not detract from the academic critique of the way companies attempt to sell goods and services, or exploit workers in doing so' (Miller, 2001: 241). He continues to say that his view does not contradict the critique launched by Klein in her best-selling book *NoLogo* (2000). The increasing importance of the role of production directly for consumers, how it affects their choices and relationships will be discussed further in Chapter 9, but a potentially critical prediction for marketing is that the attributes which will concern consumers in their choices in the future will be more complex and sophisticated. Consumers will be less easily convinced and more critical in their choices and will want to see their needs and concerns answered.

Creativity in Relationships

On the way to understanding the nature of how their goods were produced and what this might mean for them, some consumers began to get more involved with the consumption of goods. Miller (2001) describes people's relationships with things and other people as a 'constant struggle'. In reality, customers have been quietly fighting back for years, trying to ensure just, equitable transactions between themselves and suppliers even if they have been less interested in the relationship proffered. One of the most interesting areas of creativity is where consumers use products or services in ways that were not intended by the supplying organization. Sometimes this can aid the organization by doing some 'in the field' product development but it can also lead to using products in ways not conceptualized by the supplier and which they do not necessarily approve of.

Such creative behaviour has been identified in the theoretical literature. In 1980 Hirschman suggested the term 'use-innovativeness' might be used to refer to the deployment of an already adopted product to solve new consumption problems. Foxall (1994) evolved the term into 'use-initiation' suggesting the behavioural context in which the consumer initiates novel functions for existing items. This makes the important distinction between the behavioural action of doing something different with an existing form of product and a personality type which may have an innovative tendency. As consumers, if we have ever used a product or service in a novel, different or unintended way, then we have effectively partaken in use-initiator behaviour. For example, Foxall suggests that the use of household bleach as a germicide might constitute such use-initiation. Other academics have explored this area of using products in different ways. Price and Ridgway (1983) referred to variety seeking in product use, suggesting that previous products might be used in a single novel way or an existing product might be used in a number of different ways. Their examples included recycling a tin can that had been used for soup as a container for nails and a home computer which had been bought for game playing to do word processing. All the previous examples seem fairly simple, functional and unlikely to have much effect on the marketplace but they are just the tip of the iceberg. Once we accept the concept of use-initiation, its implications become enormous and together with this, the potential impact upon the marketplace. Extending the mortgage on your home is a well-known route to equity release, whereby the freed money may be used for all kinds of alternative purchases by the consumer. Other creative, although doubtless somewhat dubious, use-initiation schemes have been developed by consumers over the years. In the past, students and others in need of cash would exchange goods which had been paid for by cheque at Marks and Spencer to aid their liquidity problems. Here we see the relationships of a different kind, where the customer identifies ways that they can achieve their goals or meet their needs.

Use-initiation has some affinity with the concept of bricolage, an idea developed by Piaget and Lévi-Strauss which was used to describe how objects can acquire new meanings from recontextualization. Lury refers to the 'mods' of the 1960s as bricoleurs as they transformed the meaning of commodities such as the scooter from their traditional meaning to something else which expressed their own style. There are many examples in the history of fashion where items of clothing have been re-invented often in the same form but producing a very different meaning. The desert boot, for example, was developed in the 1950s by Nathan Clark. He had developed a simple functional boot based on crepe-soled boots worn by British army officers that they had discovered in the bazaars of Cairo. Desert boots were designed in soft but sturdy suede in dark neutral colours. This functional boot was adopted by jazz aficionados in the 1960s and later the 'mods' were also to be found wearing them, protecting their ankles when riding their scooters. As a fashion item the desert boot lost favour in the 1970s and 1980s only to be re-born in the 1990s when a new generation of trend-setters such as the Gallagher brothers from Oasis re-adopted the functional shoe for their own expressive needs. Similarly, the duffle coat developed in the 1890s specifically for use in the British Navy and used extensively by the armed services in the Second World War, also found a new life in the 1960s when it became part of the fashion uniform of folk followers. Now it has somewhat returned to its previous functional role, being a stalwart of school clothing shops for outdoor wear. More dramatic in use-initiation manner was the appropriation of everyday objects such as safety pins and razors to be used as jewellery by punks in the 1970s and 1980s, followed by seizure (often literally) of car marques to be used in a similar manner. Another interesting interpretation of brico-lage has been in relation to computer use (Turckle, 1991; Shih, 1998). Turckle makes special references to the 'second nature' of the computer which she says is as 'an evocative object and expressive medium that people use for self-expression and self-reflection' (Turckle, 1991: 8). Turckle goes on to say that this expression largely comes about through the type of interaction between the user and the computer, whereby the computer might be analogous to a tool such as a hammer or to a creative instrument which is 'played' such as a harpsichord; thus the computer supports a variety of styles of interaction or use with potentially different outcomes. Turckle uses the example of Anne below to show different ways something may be used.

> Anne, a fourth-grade student in a class using the Logo computer language, has a style of work typical of the bricoleur. Her favorite hobby is painting, and she has become expert at writing programs that produce striking visual effects. In one, a flock of birds (each of them built from a computational object known as a 'sprite') flies through the sky, disappears over the horizon, and reappears at some other place and time. A classical method for achieving this end calls for an algebraic style of thinking: one would make the program store each bird's original color as the value of a variable, change all colors to invisible, and then recall the appropriate variable when the bird is to reappear. Anne knows how to use this algorithmic method but prefers a different approach, one that enables her to turn programming into the concrete manipulation of familiar objects. As Anne programs, she uses analogies with traditional art materials. When painters want to hide something on a canvas, they paint it out, covering it with a color that serves as the 'background.' Anne uses this technique to solve her programming problem. She lets each bird keep its color, but she makes her program 'hide' the birds by placing a screen over them. Anne designs a sprite that will screen a bird when she does not want it seen, a sky-colored screen that makes the bird disappear. Anne is programming a computer, but she is thinking like a painter.

Shih has taken the idea of bricolage and applied it to consumer behaviour on the Internet. He notes that the nature of the medium allows bricolage in ways that traditional media would not, but this still requires motivation and creativity on the part of the consumer to use it in a different way. Shih highlights that the consumer having the ability to control the flow of information on the Internet can create the order of information and thus embark on a conversation with the text but on his or her terms. The embedding of hot words and icons means that linearity of presentation need not be followed but rather information can be manipulated to meet the consumers' needs at that moment. While the data available is still in terms of what has been produced by the site, the important point is that each consumer will deal with the various links differently or have a different strategy in assessing the links and absorbing information from the page. Thus each person's interpretation and understanding of the information presented may be quite different.

There is also a potentially subversive aspect to use-initiation and bricolage, although it is important to stress that whether such actions would be considered subversive is largely dependent on one's point of view. Appadurai says that society outlines the cultural and legally approved 'paths' for the circulation of objects. Appropriate forms and types of exchange, under different conditions, allow goods to be exchanged through formal economic and legal rules, as forms of credit, as loans, regulate the quality of products, and the appropriateness of selling second-hand goods or using them as gifts. But there are tendencies for interested parties to engineer 'diversions' to step off prescribed paths, so passages are dynamic and contexted. In fact, the paths and circulation of goods are equally susceptible to innovative dynamics and change as they are to political, economic, technological and social drivers. An important dynamic is between what is expected or allowed and what is taken over and manipulated by the consumer in a way unanticipated or unexpected by others with a vested interest. A case in point is that described by Lewis (2001) in his book *The Future Just Happened* when he presents the case of 15-year-old Jonathan Lebed who outwitted the US Securities and Exchange Commission, the regulatory authority of the US stock market. Jonathan had been charged with stock market fraud for using the Internet to promote stocks from which he had made money. Lewis's argument is that Jonathan Lebed was being prosecuted for something that, if he had been an adult working on Wall Street, would have been acceptable. Lebed had 'made a mockery of the financial order' (Lewis, 2001: 48) not for any malevolent reason but simply because he had cleverly found a way of making money on the stock exchange, this was unacceptable to the idea that 'high finance' was only for the elite and not something that ordinary people should or could dabble in. Lewis recounts his meeting with Richard Walker, the Stock Exchange Commissions Director of Enforcement who here attacks Lebed use-initiation:

'This kid was making predictions about the prices of stocks.' Before I can tell him that that sounds a lot like what happens every day on Wall Street, he says, 'and don't tell me that's standard practice on Wall Street,' so I didn't. But it was, and still is. It is okay for the analysts to lowball their estimates of corporate earning so that they remain in the good graces of those companies. It was okay for analysts to plug companies with one hand and collect fees from them with the other. The SEC might protest that the analysts don't actually own the stocks they plug, but that is a distinction without a moral difference: they profit mightily from that stock's rise. It was okay that Mary Meeker of Morgan Stanley and Henry Blodget of Merrill Lynch had plugged a portfolio of Internet company shares that, inside of six months, lost more than three quarters of their value at the same time that they were paid millions of dollars, largely as a result of the fees their firms raked in from the very same Internet companies. But it was, for some reason I do not fully grasp, not okay for Jonathan Lebed to say that FTEC would go from 8 to 20. (Lewis, 2001: 55)

Another potentially 'subversive' form of use-initiation is that of young Mozambique boys keen on playing football. Millions of free condoms are handed out every year in Mozambique and children have discovered a really important use for them. They make them into footballs. The condom serves as a bladder used in the soccer balls that existed in days of yore. They blow it up and thin wrap a case of paper round it, using this to shape it roughly round. Then they wind string round it until it is thickly covered and becomes perfectly round. The result is a small but effective football about the size of a melon. The creativity of active consumers through use-initiation, whether deliberate or in the form of bricolage, fundamentally challenges the unspoken premises of relationship marketing and requires more thought about the nature of interaction with consumers. Just as mass media are a one-way communication system while the actual process of communication is not, rather depending on some kind of interaction between sender and receiver in the interpretation of the message (Castells, 2000), so too is the relationship in marketing. Whatever the supplier intends in the relationship, it is in some way decoded, interpreted and acted upon by consumers in different ways. Use-initiation such as that practised by Lebed or the bricolage of the mods are different forms of response. Such an analysis was developed by Castells (2000) from Eco's conclusions on the non-existence of Mass Culture when he said that 'the sender organized the televisual image on the basis of his own codes, which coincided with those of the dominant ideology, while the addressees filled it with "aberrant" meanings according to their particular cultural codes' (Eco, 1977: 90). Castells uses Eco's essay to suggest that one of the ironies of intellectual history is that it is often those who advocate social change who are also those who view people as passive receptacles. If people have some level of autonomy in organizing and deciding their own behaviour, then messages sent through the media should interact with their receivers (Castells, 2000). In turn, we might suggest that the same is true of broader interaction between customer and supplier. Mass marketing has been replaced by mass marketing. The trendy marketing speak of today's 'segment of one', 'one-to-one' (Peppers and Rogers, 1993) and customer-centric marketing (Sheth et al., 2000) will be no better than the mass marketing of the past, if the nature of the interaction and of the consumers' response is not acted upon in any meaningful way. Henry Ford's saying that customers can have any colour of car as long as it is black is retold in marketing classes as a joke but there is a fundamental aspect of this anecdote that still beleaguers companies and stems from an approach that places internal constraints and stock-holder interest before customers' wishes.

Eco's point, as presented by Castells, has another lesson for consumer research, which lies in the nature of how we organize our worlds. As people and as consumers we organize. We organize differently at different times and for different reasons and depending on a host of factors such as our personalities, our ideology, age and gender. In perceptual research the notion of organization is important as it helps to understand how people select and attend to the many stimuli that they are assailed with every day. It also goes part of the way to understanding how and why we interact differently. One reason is that we bring our own history, our existing beliefs, attitudes and preferences to what we see and experience. A famous example of how people respond differently to what is ostensibly the same experience was a study conducted in the 1950s by Hastorf and Cantril (1954). An American football game between two university teams, the Princeton Tigers and the Dartmouth Indians was particularly rough and unruly with quite serious injuries on both sides. Princeton won the game and a week later the researchers asked the undergraduate spectators for their reactions to the game. The responses showed significant differences in what was 'seen' by either side, for example 69 per cent of Princeton students described the game as 'rough and dirty' while only 24 per cent of the Dartmouth supporters thought this. Shown a film of the game, the Princeton students 'saw' Dartmouth make twice as many rule violations as did the Dartmouth students. This experiment led Hastorf and Cantril to conclude: 'The data here indicate that there is no such "thing" as a "game" existing "out there" in its own right which people merely "observe" (1954: 133). The game 'exists' for a person and is experienced by him only insofar as certain happenings have significance in terms of his purpose. The same information will always be interpreted differently, both in terms of qualitative and quantitative assessment. Some people will take notice of messages or new products that another would ignore. Some would read into the message something completely different to another.

The response to the Benetton advertisements of the late twentieth century is a case in point. While for the some the sight of a newborn baby or a man dying from AIDs were liberating images, for others they were completely unacceptable vehicles for advertising clothes. More recently pictures of Sophie Dahl advertising Opium perfume were variously described as 'porn chic' and 'a sort of pre-raphaelite muse seen hanging in the world's finest art galleries' (*The Sun*, 2000: 17). Finally, the Advertising Standards Association (ASA) ordered the removal of the posters for Opium perfume, saying that it had led to more than 730 complaints, with more coming in each day, so making it the most complained about advertisement since 1995. Most of the complainants argued that the poster was offensive, degrading to women and unsuitable in a public place. The ASA's ruling Council considered that the advertisement, on a poster, was sexually suggestive and likely to cause 'serious or widespread offence', thereby breaking the British Codes of Advertising and Sales Promotion (ASA press release, Monday, 18 December 2000).

While such differences in responses to advertisements are not unusual and we expect consumers to react in different ways to different stimuli, after all, different generations have different values and norms, what is less usual for companies is when the consumer bats the ball back to the supplier but with their own spin on it. It is one thing to interact with communications and send letters of complaint to the ASA, it is even acceptable to use-initiate if we do it in our own homes and don't cause too much of a stir. When active consumers become a problem is when they start interacting and use-initiating in a way which challenges the status quo, then business may react by calling in the authorities to suppress the development, as Jonathan Lebed found out.

The Consumer Fights Back with a Bit of Creativity

Some of the biggest problems are going to face companies when consumers really take over the Internet and start interacting and use-initiating all over the place. Already the Internet is being used in all kinds of different ways by consumers. The companies who thought the Internet would be a ready-made goldmine are finding, like the credit card companies did before them, that it is not easy to conceptualize what consumers will do and that a little knowledge is a dangerous thing when consumers have worked out what to do with that knowledge. The importance of the Internet and the power it brings to customers have been well documented (Seybold et al., 2001). Consumers have used the Internet to change the power relationship with companies. Often this has been purely deliberate, to improve their competence in the marketplace.

They have checked out prices and compared offers, bought from one company, then another and then gone strolling down the high street, or flicked through a catalogue to buy something else. The biggest advantage the Internet has to those consumers who can be bothered to do the searching is as a source of information. Where it is not worth the time and trouble to go into two or three different shops to compare prices on a vacuum cleaner, say, the Internet can make it worthwhile. Consumers have used the Internet to find out about, and to access, services such as importing cheaper cars from abroad (www.broadspeed.), to reduce their gas and electricity bills (http://www buy.co.uk), to download music, to trade stocks and shares, to manage their bank accounts and much more. The most liberating aspect of the Internet for consumers has been essentially in two areas: access of information and the ability to communicate easily with one another. Information on the Internet empowers consumers, not only in terms of being able to access and compare prices but providing them with tools that they otherwise would not have had or would have had trouble getting hold of. They can gain information about health issues such as new drugs and treatments, government statistics and details about companies which are not generally available. The consumer becomes empowered as long as they have access to a computer. Possibly the most important aspect of this empowerment is the scale on which it allows conversation. One message can be easily transmitted to numerous people and in turn these can become the catalyst for many more conversations. It develops exponentially and is therefore potentially perilous to anyone trying to maintain a false or inappropriate position. We know how the Internet has been used by those wishing to disrupt petrol distribution in the UK in 2000 (www.fuelprotest.com) and by the Consumer Resistance brigade of Seattle and Genoa, but what happens when it is used to explore issues about companies and how they treat their customers? An isolated consumer can easily be told they have an unusual problem or issue possibly with an inference of some failing on the consumer side. However, once consumers as a group can connect to discern a pattern, there is a fundamental change in the power distribution in the relationship.

In *The Cluetrain Manifesto* Rick Levine writes up a conversation from a newsgroup which started with a consumer's query as to how much a service for a Saturn car should cost. 'It's just ordinary people, talking about their cars' (Levine, 2000: 55). The conversation starts with Ross asking why, when his car manual said that at 9,000 miles and 15,000 miles all his car would need would be an oil change, his dealer had apparently done much more and charged him for it. Ranger replies that the charges seem high and suggests Ross shop around for a better price. Someone else gives Ross a URL of a retailer and information on what the retailer recommends in addition to the owner's handbook. Another gives details of a similar situation, one saying he is boycotting a particular distributor and so the conversation continues, passing on valuable snippets of information. As Levine points out, at this point there were no messages being posted from the dealership about which the original complaint was made, and he suggests that this could be a sign that indeed something not quite right is going on. Additionally, there was no intervention from Saturn directly, which could also be a bad sign. Then a Saturn employee comes on line and explains how as Levine puts it 'this game is played' (2000: 58). The end result is that the Ross is able to use the material he has collected with his conversations on the Internet to get a better deal from his Saturn dealer including a free 18,000 mile service. Levine suggests that this conversation is about people wanting to help each other in a consumption situation; they contribute to the well-being of others and in so doing, they may also fulfil motivations ranging from revenge to finding out who to trust. All of which is probably the case but, in addition to this, the consumers are using creativity to identify issues and situations which previously would have remained opaque because companies found it easier for themselves to leave the customer in the dark. Here again the company has not actually taken part in the discussion, only a Saturn employee who, as Levine explains, may not have been officially sanctioned to say anything, but the nature of the Internet is such that individual dealings with the company are no longer isolated. The most important relationship is that which is going on between and among all those consumers and not between the consumer and the company. You need never feel alone in your complaints to a company, if you have the time and inclination to share your feelings with potentially millions of others.

Consumer Creativity or Terrorism?

Sheth suggested that a dissatisfied customer with no choice might well become a 'terrorist' (2001). The comparison between a dissatisfied customer and a 'terrorist' may seem somewhat extreme but it may also contain within it the seeds of what happens when companies and indeed governments do not listen to the people who are all inevitably consumers. A dissatisfied customer can become a 'terrorist' in business terms, if they feel they have not been dealt with fairly, they can bombard companies with complaints, letters, telephone calls and tell others about their experiences. But what happens when this 'terrorism' becomes formalized in some way? Indeed, the question needs to be asked, what is happening with the relationship between consumer and producer for 'terrorism' to become formalized? One reason is because individuals have asked questions which either have not been answered by companies or have been answered unsatisfactorily; this may not matter with one or two customers but when more and more feel this way, it becomes a problem. Also consumers may feel they have less and less choice in terms of what businesses they can actually deal with. Klein illustrates this feeling well when she describes a phenomenon that is quite familiar to many of us:

> Everyone has, in one form or another, witnessed the odd double vision of vast consumer choice coupled with Orwellian new restrictions on cultural production and public space. We see it when a small community watches its lively downtown hollow out, as big-box discount stores with 70,000 items on their shelves set up on their periphery, exerting their gravitational pull to what James Howard Kunstler describes as 'the geography of nowhere.' It is there on the trendy downtown main street as yet another favorite café, hardware store, independent bookstore or art video house is cleared away and replaced by one of the Pac-Man chains: Starbucks, Home Depot, the Gap, Chapters, Borders, Blockbuster. (2000: 130)

High streets in Britain look alike just as malls do in the USA. Klein suggests that three industry trends brought about this ubiquity of similarity. First, price wars by the big players systematically underselling their competitors out of business. Second, 'blitzing' out competition by setting up what Klein calls chain store clusters. As an example, Klein sites Starbucks' strategy of saturating an area with stores until the coffee competition is so fierce that even individual Starbucks stores can find their sales dropping. But while cannabilization may mean a slow-down in sales in individual stores, the overall combined effect for Starbucks is positive. Clustering can only benefit large chains which can afford to let some individual stores suffer if the effect is positive for the company as a whole. Finally, there is the growth of the huge flagship stores, built in prime locations, acting, as Klein says, as a 'three-dimensional ad for the brand'.

Strategies such as those described above when combined with the swarms of ads bombarding us from every space, on buses, tickets, taxis, bus stops, the Internet and even in schools, may make some consumers desire some blank space or at least some uncommercially sponsored space. As Klein again notes, most consumers cannot buy the advertising space in order to respond, so for some the activity of culture jamming as a rejection of a one-way information flow is the only response. Culture jamming parodies advertising usually by transforming billboards by altering the message of the advertisers and creating what Klein refers to as 'semiotic Robin Hoodism' (2000: 280) with a view to improving and augmenting the message and as a result unmasking some aspect of the branded message. Culture jamming might be considered an extreme form of use-initiation, where an advertising message designed for one use is put to another use by those who have to consume the advertising. Klein traces the history of culture jamming back to Paris of the 1960s where the Situationists first expressed the idea of *détournement*, where an image or a message or a thing might be taken out of its original context and new meaning ascribed to it. Again technology has been adopted and adapted by culture jammers for their own means. Downloading digital versions of advertisements from websites has allowed changes and parodies to be made easily while the tools of desktop publishing allow new versions of ads to be made from scratch through easily reproducing and copying images and colours. The Internet's distribution advantages are not lost on the culture jammers either; it may be easier to get a message across to more people through an Internet site than by clever graffiti on a few billboards.

Now culture jamming has become an almost mainstream activity through the Canadian Adbusters magazine and website which produces its own goods such as calendars and 'uncommercials' to attack subjects like the beauty and car industries. There are of course many groups around the world trying to make themselves heard and get a message across to a wider audience and much of this is done over the Internet. In the UK WyeCycle, a group of people committed to recycling waste, have a website which lists ten ways to create a better world (www.wye.org/business/directory/wyecyclebetterworld.htm). Each of the ten ways begins 'Don't shop at supermarkets . . .' and goes on to attack the big supermarkets for pollution, control over the food chain, industrializing farming, putting high street stores out of business and dismantling local communities, to name just a few of their grievances. Perhaps this is pretty low-level 'terrorism' but, as companies and politicians have been discovering, the range of activities that individuals, consumer groups and anti-consumerism groups can devise is vast and can have repercussions for their businesses and their activities more broadly. Consumers do not need to actively participate to have sympathy or empathy with an activity against a business which in turn can affect that business.

While we are most concerned with how this situation affects consumers, it is also highly relevant to broader, political issues. Take the G8 summit in July 2001 in Genoa. The groups protesting covered a huge range of political and social dimensions from the Genoa Social Forum to Ya Basta, and Globalize Resistance, most of them have a global network of supporters which are able to communicate with one another. They did not all share the same interests, Globalize Resistance, for example, is an umbrella group linking environmentalists, peace activists and political campaigners. What they did have in common was a desire and a need to express their concerns to world-wide governments who they doubtless felt were not listening to these concerns. Ironically they are mirroring organizations like the G8 and the World Trade Organization by uniting together with the view of getting their point across. Of course, there have been many different views on what happened in Genoa and who was to blame but one thing was sure, the 'terrorists' were heard. An interesting note on this particular piece of creativity or 'terrorism' was sounded by Tony Blair in an article in *The Sunday Times* defending the summit when he said, 'Since Seattle, the minority know one thing. Have a cause and put it reasonably and coverage is limited. Have a cause and commit an outrage and you will lead the news' (Blair, 2001: 2). Unfortunately for the leaders of the G8 countries, it is not only the minority who have learnt this particular lesson. One of the biggest mistakes that governments and businesses alike make is to forget that consumers are, if they wish to be, better informed than ever before. If consumers choose to take an interest in something, then they know what they are talking about because the information is more readily available than ever before. It is misreading or indeed ignoring the knowledge and activism of the consumer in the street, that can be most damaging for business and governments alike. In the same article quoted above, Tony Blair also presents the decisions made at Genoa thus, 'Africa, not anarchy, was our focus in Genoa. We took decisions on Third World aid, climate change, world trade and global financial systems.' The tone continues in the 'we know best' attitude of many Western global nations of the twenty-first century, and the trouble is that people have heard this before, but still too often do not get answers to their questions of how money is spent and decisions are made.

Whatever the long-term effects of demonstrations in Seattle and Genoa actually are in terms of how businesses and governments respond to and debate with both consumers and activist groups, some campaigners are already taking a more pragmatic route and finding other means to achieve their aims without head-on confrontation. For example, Friends of the Earth used £30,000 of its money to ensure that as a shareholder of Balfour Beatty it could propose a resolution at the company's annual general meeting. Friends of the Earth were concerned about the environmental impact of the Ilisu Dam project on the Tigris in Turkey. The building of the dam could make 30,000 people homeless, drowning dozens of towns and villages. Friends of the Earth proposed that Balfour Beatty should adopt tight guidelines in dam building contracts. Although the resolution did not succeed, Friends of the Earth regarded the whole process as successful as they gained awareness and press coverage as well as finding that a large block of largely institutional-held shares abstained from the vote, suggesting sympathy with the resolution (Reece, 2001). At the time of writing Balfour Beatty had pulled out of the dam project, which Friends of the Earth accredited in part to their public campaigning (Friends of the Earth, 2001). Another peaceful and successful, at least in terms of the publicity gained, activity has been 'Buy Nothing Day'. 'Buy Nothing Day' which started eight years ago was focused originally upon the North American public, falling as it does one day after the US Thanksgiving, which is traditionally their busiest shopping day of the year. Now consumers in more than 30 countries choose not to consume for 24 hours and to celebrate their non-consumption through activities and events designed to gain a broader publicity for the act of non-consumption.

Conclusion

This chapter has examined some of the changes taking place in the marketplace, especially in terms of how consumers are reviewing their relationships with companies. While suppliers often continue to do what seems appropriate to them and then respond defensively to consumer complaints and concerns, consumers are looking for and finding opportunities to take over the marketplace. There can be little doubt that one particular innovation, namely the Internet, has proved particularly helpful in this. Information can be exchanged and developed, knowledge is increased and the consumers are empowered. Others, who have become increasingly savvy in a complex marketplace, find ways to reroute and contest the less consumer-oriented companies. The failure of companies in the marketplace to innovate and respond directly to the consumer has led the consumer to take over and begin an interesting and continuing process of use-initiation. The response from suppliers has unfortunately tended to be defensive, perhaps a reflection of a view that assumes it is companies who innovate, not consumers. But in an endeavour to search and gain meaning and function from the marketplace, use-initiation will continue and it will be less and less easy for suppliers to stamp it out. Far more creative would be to respond to it and help consumers develop something even better. If consumers want to complain, then be sure to answer the complaints. If they want a credit card that they can use as a charge card, let them, plenty others will want the credit. Above all, treat the customers as if they really are partners in the marketplace rather than as adversaries. If this change in thinking does not come about, it may lead to a more aggressive reaction from consumers as some at least move into 'terrorist' mode. And yet, consumers should be a resource of ideas, collaborators, co-developers in the production of new and better ways of doing things. Companies need to be aware that consumers are not the goose that lays the golden egg, to be used and manipulated on a whim. Within every problem the consumer has, there is potentially a solution, a better, more efficient, effective way of doing things and they should see this as a missed opportunity and not potentially a threat.

Chapter 5

Innovation and the Creative Consumer

The period of newness is, in a sense, the sublime period of the object and may, in certain cases, attain the intensity, if not the quality, of the emotion of love. (Baudrillard, 1998: 113)

Introduction

Innovation and how producers and suppliers engage with consumers in the process of innovation are central to the challenge to marketing theory and practice in postmodern societies. The following chapters will argue that there has been a fundamental shift in the meaning of innovation as consumers are no longer only focused on the functional attributes of new products but on other aspects of value as already discussed. Innovation is a relationship issue. To be successful, innovating suppliers need to forge relationships with appropriate consumers. For consumers the choice whether to accept and use the innovations is more to do with what they want from the products, services and relationships on offer than some notion of whether they are innovative or not.

In the initial examination of relationship marketing as the dominant paradigm it was argued that it had failed in its understanding of the consumer. Lip service has been paid to a consumer-centric approach. Consumers continue to be treated as passive and attempts to make relationships reciprocal have been flawed. We saw that our concept of relationships needed to be broadened to embrace the complexity of the active consumers in fluid settings. In no aspect of the challenge to current marketing is this more apparent than in the problem of successful innovation and in particular understanding consumers' response to innovation.

This chapter will review the nature of innovations and their relations to the consumer and to marketing. It will begin by discussing briefly what drives people to want new things. It will examine some of the history of innovation research in this area and how it has been and can be applied in the marketing context. In particular, it will review and consider the usefulness of classifications of innovations and innovation adoption and will do so within the context of both the functional, where the technical feature of products are uppermost, and symbolic, where the role and implications of sign value are more important.

The Importance of Innovation to Marketing

One piece of received wisdom in marketing is that it is vital for consumers to be willing to accept new products and brands. Research and development departments in companies and indeed universities exist because they will ultimately bring into being new products, services or technology which can eventually be developed into a form which consumers will purchase. It is the need for profit, Lury (1996) argues, that has led to the production of an ever-expanding range of products, which in turn need to be marketed and which may imply the control over and manipulation of the consumer. This, Lury suggests, might imply a passivity in the consumer which does not recognize consumers' active role in the consumption process. The marketplace requires consumers to be willing and indeed want to accept innovation in order for it to remain dynamic. This is equally the case both for entirely new technologies or ways of doing things, such as when the television, the telephone or the microwave were introduced, and for new forms of existing products, such as digital cameras, minidiscs or electronic organizers, and importantly for the symbolically new, the latest Beckham hairstyle, Prada handbag or café latte.

Hirschman (1980) said that if people did not adopt new ideas when they came to the market, consumer behaviour would be no more than a series of routinized buying responses to a static state of products, a stationary marketplace. While Hirschman's remarks were most likely made in relation to what might be termed 'purposeful' innovations, i.e. where there is something intrinsically different and implied better, such that they would improve some functional aspect of consumption, in a postmodern world the remark is equally applicable to innovation in sign value (Baudrillard, [1970] 1998). Today use value has been replaced by exchange value and sign value, such that the manipulation of sign value and meaning becomes part of this innovative process whereby it is essential for its maintenance for it to be accepted by consumers. The significance of the latest bag from Gucci or Hermes or watch from Tag Heuer or Cartier is lost if it is not accepted and maintained by consumers. Consumers may be manipulated by advertising and PR, but it is their acceptance and ultimately purchasing that are needed for the continued innovation in terms of use value or sign value to persist. As a recent BBC programme made clear, as long as there have been people, there have been things and people love things (*Shopology*, BBC 2, 10 September 2001). But if it was just the things themselves that mattered we might reach a saturation point and lean back and just marvel at all we had collected. The story, of course, doesn't follow such a simple plot. Bauman (2001: 24) cites Pascal's observation that 'it is the hunting, not the hare, that people call happiness. Admittedly, temporary identities can only be conjured up through differentiation from the past: "today" derives its meaning by cutting itself off from a "yesterday"'. One might define this as being the transience of novelty which ensures the durability of novelty. The uselessness of an innovation may follow or it may not. As Baudrillard ([1970] 1998) implies, all new things can be seen as gadgets, their objective usefulness subsumed by their social role. But for marketing it is perhaps more important to understand the social role of new things as the functional role is more easily copied, less likely to maintain its uniqueness in the fluid, changeable path of the postmodern world.

New Things and More of Them

How new products come to be accepted in the marketplace such that they make 'yesterday's luxuries turn into today's necessities' (Douglas and Isherwood, 1996: 70), has fascinated economists, anthropologists and consumer researchers alike. Marketers are endlessly exploring why some products succeed and others fail, why some become household items long before others do or indeed never do, while some others become relegated to some kind of time-warp limbo as described by Douglas and Isherwood, 'consider the solid silver cigarette cases of forty to fifty years ago, which no longer carried, have not yet joined the display of Georgian snuffboxes in the curiosity cabinet, but lie instead stacked in attics, awaiting a decision as to their value-antiques or just their weight in silver' (ibid.: 70). Similarly, we can compare the seemingly timeless success of Barbie, launched in 1959 to the short fashion cycles of Pokemon, Pogs and Furbies. Why do Teletubbies appear to have become a classic while Ninja Turtles are consigned to near oblivion? Such success and failure scenarios are not limited to the perhaps fickle children's markets; food, confectionery, soap powders, soft drinks and many more product categories boast astounding successes and often difficult-to-explain failures. Again classification has helped marketers and in particular the identification of two supposedly key players in the diffusion of innovations into the marketplace. The 'early adopter' and the 'opinion former' may, depending on the commodity in question, be one and the same person. The consumer who adopts early may also tell people about his or her success and have their opinions listened to. Alternatively, the opinion former may have adopted later but be more efficient or more credible as a source of reassurance, thus acting as a medium for further mass adoption. The classic S-shaped curve, generally linked to the diffusion of innovations into the marketplace, shows a slow demand which quickens and then becomes steeper before gradually flattening off. It implies that a few people initially adopt the new item, after this the word is spread, whether through word-of-mouth, advertising or some other vehicle, whereby after some period of time it becomes a basic part of everyday life.

While it is quite possible to present a supposedly scientific response to how innovations come to be adopted and used, there will always be a more personal, possibly idiosyncratic aspect to whether or not we accept certain new things and how we integrate novelty and newness into our lives. The story of Diderot's dressing gown not only produces an empathy of understanding of how something new can come to permeate your whole life but also it produces a feeling of poignancy and, paradoxically, loss that is brought with it. The Diderot story has been used by economists, consumer researchers, anthropologists and theologians as a parable for modern consumption. In his essay, 'Regrets on parting with my old dressing gown', Diderot wrote about a gift he had received of a beautiful scarlet robe. Soon after receiving this gift and discarding his old ragged dressing gown he quickly found that other possessions around him no longer gave him pleasure. In the light of the splendour of his new dressing gown everything else in his study appeared shabby and so unsettled, he replaced his desk, chairs, engravings, and threadbare tapestry and bookshelves until everything was new. But once Diderot had replaced all his worn old things, he found himself seated amidst these new acquisitions, unhappy. Now he regretted the 'imperious scarlet robe' which had driven him out of his crowded but comfortable study. McCracken (1988) uses the Diderot example to reflect that objects do not communicate in isolation but together with other things, thus producing what he refers to as the 'Diderot Unity'; once one part of the picture is replaced, total harmony is lost and we are driven to make further changes. The drive for harmony and consistency underlies much of the consumption of new things. Our old world is reflected in the new thing and found wanting, a new home needs new furniture and a new dress can make old shoes look shabby. The desire for unity and harmony in our lives need not, one might think require the continual purchase of new items. It may be less about unity and more about a continual upgrading, what Schor compares to an escalator moving ever upward. As we continue to acquire, we acquire more and so on up the consumption escalator as acquisition has an unremitting upward propensity. Resisting the new and returning to a

Diderot-like shabby simplicity may for some be a choice in itself and one which requires a quite different kind of relationship with the world of consumption.

With such a consumer escalator as backdrop, the scene is set for the continued introduction of new things. Creatively consumers deal with such a phenomenon in a number of ways, for some, consumption may bring a meaning in itself, for others, the desire to resist or even stop the escalator is the route to more successful consumption. The important thing to recognize is the awareness of consumption that most consumers have. We can reflect on what we are doing or what is happening to us, just as Diderot, perhaps belatedly regretted his scarlet robe. Accepting that such knowledge and fluidity are attributes of modern consumers is critical to developing a more subtle synthesis of how they respond to new ideas, things, and symbols in their lives. In particular it is increasingly important to accept that newness in itself is unlikely to be the goal for all consumers. This suggests a more complex understanding of the relationship between innovation and the consumer which questions much of the theory related to the adoption. In particular, if marketing assumes that the objective is to find those people who will adopt new things, it is anyway potentially undermining its own relationships by encouraging new and different transactions. A more reflexive mode might be to re-examine the nature of existing relationships and improve and develop these along lines which appeal to their consumers. Before developing this further, however, we should examine the existing modes of thinking in relation to innovation in marketing terms.

Innovation: Theory and Practice

In the marketing literature, the perhaps unwritten rule has been that in trying to understand more about how consumers react to innovations, what we are interested in is how to develop more effective marketing for our new products. Relatively little research has been done into how consumers feel about adopting or not adopting new commodities and it is only recently that a literature has developed which focuses on resisting consumption. Resisting consumption is, however, again something different to the consumer's non-adoption of new items. Resistance may imply a positive response to the world of things and more things, and often has a political dimension to it, such that business may suggest that such people are unlikely to be mainstream consumers and their actions are therefore extreme. Non-adoption of new items is worrying for business, because it implies that there is something wrong with the product, the way it has been packaged and distributed or the way it has been communicated to consumers. While businesses may be willing to spend millions developing and improving such non-adopted items, they are much less likely to spend the same amount trying to convince the resistors that they should buy.

Rogers (1995) has been a key driver in developing innovation theory as applied to consumer behaviour and marketing. His work emphasized the importance of the relationship between the nature of the innovation and those who adopt it. He suggested that, while the research literature indicated that much effort had been spent in studying what he called the people differences (determining the characteristics of different adopter categories), relatively little had been devoted to analysing innovation differences. One might add that an examination of the relationships between different people or adopter categories and the innovation differences might in turn lead to a deeper understanding of reactions and responses in the marketplace. Take, for example, the use made by older people of the Internet. It is perceived by many as a younger person's medium, while older people are often profiled as being technologically challenged (Corlett, 1999). Market research by Computer Industry Almanac reported that in Europe one out of five Europeans were using the Internet in 2000, the average age was 32 and over 60 per cent of the users were male (commerce.net, 2001). But the nature of the innovation is such that many of these people have to use computers and the Internet at work and so in effect have had to adopt it, while many older people have not been given the opportunity to learn and become familiar with this technology on an everyday basis. Interestingly when older people are given the opportunity to use computers, they generally adapt to them quickly and easily and have rapidly developed successful methods to use them effectively for their purposes. In Australia the Melbourne PC user group reported the biggest increase in growth in the 55-plus group in Internet use (Australian Bureau of Statistics, March 2000, http://www.abs.gov.au). Sites such as AARP.org in the USA, fifty-plus.net in Canada, onlineseniors.net in Australia and www.idf50.co.uk in the UK are full of information on health, travel, and bargains that older people can take advantage of, together with intellectual and political debate. This shows the dangers of a preconception which can colour how we view the evidence.

.To better understand consumers' relationships with innovations and also the relationships between business and innovation, there are a number of factors worth further examination within the history of innovation research as it applies specifically to marketing and consumption. The principal components of innovation research broadly reflect how the work has developed in this field and the particular interests of different researchers. The classification made by Mittelstaedt et al. in 1976 highlights these key areas. Four themes were identified: the innovation itself;

the channels through which it is communicated; the time over which it is diffused; and the members of the social system into which it is marketed. Of these four themes, much of the academic research has focused on how innovations diffuse across a community over time (Midgley, 1977; Rogers, 1995) and what constitutes an innovation in terms of the nature of the innovation (Robertson, 1967, 1971; Hirschman, 1981; Rogers, 1983). As noted earlier, researchers have also been fascinated by the idea that they might be able to identify something significant in those people who adopt early which might be useful in marketing terms. This research has focused on the possibility of linking their buying behaviour to specific identifiable personality traits (Midgley, 1977; Horton, 1979; Rogers, 1983; Foxall, 1989; Goldsmith, 1987; Mudd, 1990). Another interesting avenue of research has been to try to ascertain whether there is something which might be described as inherently innovative in certain people (Midgley, 1977; Midgley and Dowling, 1978; Hirschman, 1980). In other words, a predisposition as a person to be innovative which may reveal itself in terms of the type of consumer one is and which might present a propensity to try new things generally.

While much attention has been given to exploring the nature of innovative behaviour, much less attention has been applied to the question of why people do *not* adopt new things (Sheth, 1981; Ram, 1987; Ram and Sheth, 1989). In terms of understanding the consumer, this last point is particularly important and reveals the continued production orientation of much of this research. It is of course little wonder that businesses are perhaps more interested in the positive side of consumption, but understanding why people do not consume is potentially more important for some increasingly overcrowded markets.

The Nature of Innovations

Much has been written about innovations but often without in-depth consideration as to what constitutes an innovative product, idea or service. When in 1991 Gatignon and Robertson made a content analysis of marketing and consumer behaviour journals between 1984 and 1988, they found that articles tended to assume that what was being studied was an innovation. However, as they point out, there are different approaches to defining what is an innovation. Citing Rogers' definition that an innovation is, 'an idea, practice, or object that is perceived as new by an individual or other unit of adoption' and therefore 'If the idea seems new to the individual, it is an innovation' (Rogers, 1983: 11), they proposed that the definition would then rest on each individual's perception. The subjectivity of this view is important as it accepts the differences in people's perceptions of what is innovative as well as their situation. What might not be considered innovative in one situation might be revolutionary in another. Consider the case of the plastic container. In the West we are used to receiving many of our grocery goods, drinks, etc. in plastic containers, we probably think little of them, the plastic container is essentially packaging and little else. In Africa the plastic container not only revolutionized life for thousands, perhaps millions of people but is also acting as a purposeful innovation in a number of different ways. First, one has to remember that the consumer of the plastic container in Africa is likely to be a child, as half the population of Africa is under 15 years of age.

While everyone else is still asleep, little boys are rising in the darkness and running to springs, ponds, rivers – for water. Modern technology has proven to be their great ally: it gave them a gift – the cheap, light, plastic container. A dozen years ago, this container revolutionized life in Africa. Water is the sine qua non of survival in the tropics. Because there is generally no plumbing here and water is scarce, one must carry it over long distances, sometimes ten or more kilometres. For centuries heavy clay or stone vessels were used for this purpose. Traditional African cultures did not know wheeled transport, so human beings carried everything themselves, most often on their heads. The division of domestic labor was such that carrying water was women's work. A child could never manage such a large and heavy receptacle, and in this bare-bones world each house usually had only one.

Then, the plastic container appeared. A miracle! A revolution! First of all, it is relatively inexpensive (although in certain houses it is the only thing of any value): it costs around two dollars. Most important, however, it is light. And it comes in various sizes, so even a small child can fetch several liters of water.

All the children carry water. You see entire flocks of youngsters, playing and teasing one another as they walk to a distant spring. What a relief this is for the exhausted African woman! What a transformation in her life! How much more time she now has for herself, for her household!

The plastic container possesses countless advantages. Among the most important is that it holds your place in line. Often you have to stand for days in a line for water (in those places,

> that is, where it is delivered by truck). Standing in the tropical sun is torture. It used to be that you couldn't just set down the clay pot and go sit in the shade: it was too valuable to risk its being stolen. Now, however, you place your plastic container in the line then go find yourself some shade, or go to the market, or visit friends. Driving through Africa, one sees these kilometre-long, colourful rows awaiting the arrival of water. (Kapuściński, 2001)

Kapuściński's story reveals the complexity of defining what an innovation is. Something as simple as the plastic container which, in the West, has virtually no contemporary significance, can revolutionize the lives of an entire continent of people. Not only has the lightweight plastic container allowed women to be released from a laborious and time-consuming job, but it has also allowed the inclusion of children into the maintenance of the household as it is light enough for them to carry. Having little intrinsic value it is unlikely to be stolen as was the case with clay pots and so people can leave the plastic containers in line waiting the arrival of the water lorry while they go and use their time elsewhere. Thus the plastic container becomes a purposeful innovation within the context of the combination of situation and circumstance facing these people in Africa. It also means that the relationship with the product is entirely different to that in the West where plastic containers, while useful in some contexts, may be a problem in others, for example, as visual pollution of the environment.

Such a subjective approach to innovation places the user as central to understanding the nature and role of the innovation. There have also been a number of attempts to classify innovations, and thus attempt to develop a universal basis of criteria external to the potential adopter. Robertson (1967, 1971) suggested three types of innovations: the continuous, the dynamically continuous and the discontinuous, which we will consider in terms of how they might help make links between the object and the user. The continuous innovation is in a sense the least inventive of these three types. It creates little change in behaviour patterns of consumers as it generally involves no more than the introduction of a modified rather than 'new' product. Most new products introduced to the market in the past few years are of this kind. A new model of car or type of television or a differently flavoured or packaged toothpaste would be considered a continuous innovation; nothing fundamental has changed in the nature of the good, it is more a question of size, styling, aesthetics or fashion that brings novelty to the new item. The consumer does not have to learn anything new in order to use the commodity. Mars introduced 'New Snickers Crunchier', this is a classic case of the continuous innovation. Now with crisped rice, as well as crunchy peanuts, caramel and milk chocolate, the name, shape and size remain the same. The risk involved in trying the new Snickers is negligible, it is almost ensured trial by even the least variety-seeking chocolate bar consumer. Such 'new' products appear almost daily and give rise to the notion of increased product variety but, as Gabriel and Lang ask: 'Are the 10 different variants of a car model or the 50 detergents on a shelf different products?' (1998: 30). The answer is probably no, what such continuous innovations really seek to do is to provide some novelty in the status quo. This is a relatively low-risk manoeuvre to introduce more variety and more choices into the market, it may help maintain an existing relationship with Mars Snickers and it may induce non-users to consider trying it, as such it appears to be primarily a tactical move.

A dynamically continuous innovation, however, does create some change in behavioural patterns although these are unlikely to be great. In product terms it usually involves the creation of a new product or the modification of an existing one. Examples could include the introduction of compact discs or the bag-less vacuum cleaner developed by James Dyson. Both were new products, quite different to the previous products but which a consumer would quickly be able to read and understand within the context of listening to music and vacuuming carpets. Similarly, the digital camera, which requires the learning of new ways of developing and printing pictures and uses a different type of technology, is fundamentally, from the consumer's perspective of taking a picture, little different to another modern instant camera. Continuous innovation may also be related to the size or form of the product developed. Miniaturization, for example, may transform the nature of a product and the way in which it may be used. Consider, for example, the process of miniaturization for music, from gramophones, through tape decks and hi-fis to portable cassette players, mini-disc players and mp3 players. The increased portability of each item may mean more space for other items whether in the home or on the move. A new car will feature CD, tape cassette and radio as standard, a home can have TVs, music systems and radios in every room and a handbag can hold a mobile phone, a camera and an Mp3 player easily. Lee (1993) refers to such size differences as changes in commodity-form, the reduced size leading to the creation of 'new' space within the home environment which allows for the addition of more, new commodities. Another form of innovation is the compound commodity (Lee, 1993) which combines objects to produce a new commodity form. Examples include the combination of shampoos and conditioner, washing powder and conditioner and gin and tonic in a can.

Robertson's third category, discontinuous innovation, brings about the greatest change for users and change which does require the establishment of new behavioural patterns. The microwave oven, while now placed firmly within the context of home food preparation, required a major rethinking and understanding of cooking and so may be classed as a discontinuous innovation. Other discontinuous innovations from the past would include the television, the video recorder and the telephone. Discontinuous innovation may be extended into the social realm, Hirschman (1987: 57) suggested that for a couple their first baby is a discontinuous innovation, while one might also consider a similar case being made for a child's first day at school. Retirement, redundancy and going into hospital for the first time might be similarly classified. Throughout our personal life cycles we face numerous occasions when we have to adapt to a major discontinuous innovation. Each occasion brings with it the need to learn and adapt to different products and services. When a spouse dies, not only is the remaining partner facing the prospect of learning all about funerals but also possibly how to fill in a tax form, cook and clean, put up shelves or even drive a car, etc., depending on how the division of labour in their household had been distributed.

While Robertson has produced a typology of innovation, it is still ultimately dependent on the consumer's perceptions of the three types of innovation. Differences in acceptance of new technology are relative, and even changes in confectionery may be perceived by some as more fundamental than by others. While Robertson viewed innovations in technological terms and classified them by levels of technological difference, a significant shift occurred with Hirschman's (1981) classification. The simple but key distinction which she made was in differentiating the innovation into the technological and the symbolic, thus introducing a more subtle and perceptual angle to the division. Here technological innovations are similar to the discontinuous in a functional sense, while the symbolic innovation conveys new social meaning. In marketing, classic examples of symbolic innovations have been designer mineral water or margarine repositioned as low fat spreads as they take an existing product category and give it new meaning. Water, the essential commodity of the Africans, can be positioned in the Western marketplace either as the purifying body cleanser of the Evian ads, or as the quirky, fashionable alternative to alcohol as with Perrier.

Hirschman's division emphasizes the importance of the sign of the new thing and implies repositioning in tune with what might be current or fluid in the consumer's mind or approach to things. The key to symbolic innovation is redefining an existing product or brand in a new way that has meaning for the consumer. Lewis and Bridger (2000) take this a step further, implying that a product can be made 'original'. One of the examples of an 'original' product which they use is *The Simpsons* television cartoon which they say stood out from the sameness of much TV cartoon shows at the time with its 'gaudy mix of yellow characters in multicolored setting' (2000: 42). *The Simpsons*, they suggest, have become regarded as an authentic work of art because of the way they grabbed the viewers' attention. They cite alongside *The Simpsons*, so-called functional products, the watch, and the vacuum cleaner. In fact, all three of these products have undergone a high degree of symbolic innovation, which is reflected in different brands with different degrees of success. *The Simpsons*, while watched by millions of children, is not a cartoon of the 'Tom and Jerry' or 'TopCat' kind; it is not received as children's entertainment so much as a satirical burlesque on American society and mores which has a universal appeal across age ranges. It is less a different kind of cartoon and more an entertainment which happens to be in the cartoon form. Some see its role as even more profound:

> *The Simpsons* remains at the vanguard of a revolution in animated comedy that is now so firmly established that only one of Sky One's regular Sunday evening shows (the nightmarish Dream Team) contains real actors. And what gives *Futurama, King of the Hill* et al their edge is what *Simpsons'* creator Matt Groening describes as animation's 'rubber-band reality' – allowing the realistic and the surreal to co-exist convincingly. (Pettie, 2001: 10)

The Swatch Company SMH successfully reinvented a relatively cheap watch into a fashion accessory and through judicious marketing and limited production runs, it also transformed into a collectable item, and one which collectors were prepared to pay thousands of dollars for. An interesting aspect of the Swatch's symbolic innovation has been how it has come to have different meanings for different groups of consumers around the world, thus reinforcing the fluidity of the sign and the object. While in the USA it was associated with 'teeny-bopper' fashion and was largely sold through department stores, in other European countries it had a higher profile fashion image and was distributed in jewellery shops (Pinson, 1987). Symbolic innovation brings to the discussion a concept which takes us beyond the technical functional metaphor of innovation. While the producer can aim to develop or reposition a product or brand such that it will be perceived in the marketplace as new and dynamic, symbolic innovation also hands the metaphor back to the customer, such that they can consume and use things in ways that may be different or unintended by the producer, thus bringing their own symbolic use-initiation into play.

Another important categorization of innovations with both theoretical and practical implications was that developed by Rogers. His models were developed out of research work for the American agriculture business sector. The original model (1962) was primarily concerned with how innovations in areas including seeds, equipment and agricultural practices such as planting systems were diffused among individual farmers in their communities. Since the original model developed in the 1960s Roger's concept of the diffusion of innovations has gone through a number of iterations. From a consumer point of view, there are some interesting and relevant aspects to the model and in particular to the understanding that Rogers shows with regard to the differences between individuals and their perceptions of situations. In the original model, regard is given to how farmers would vary individually along six theorized dimensions which were anxiety, individualism, mental and conceptual skills, status, cosmopolitan orientation and opinion leadership. The model assumed that the early adopters of innovations were likely to have a higher status, be more cosmopolitan, intelligent and socially secure. Another important aspect of the model is the classification of innovations. The basic principle behind the classification was the relationship between the characteristics of the innovation and its likely commercial success. The attributes identified by Rogers as affecting this relationship were relative advantage, compatibility, observability, complexity, and trial-ability. Generally these feature have been seen in terms of the functional attributes of innovations but there is merit in examining each of them also in the light of understanding how consumers come to accept or reject new things for their symbolic or sign value as well as their functional value.

The relative advantage of a new product refers to how it was likely to be perceived by consumers in terms of its superiority over those products already available to them. Many new products or services are functionally presented as doing something better, faster or cleaner than their competitors. The claims of many fast-moving consumer goods come into this realm with their so-called abilities to 'last longer' be 'new, improved', 'faster acting', etc. A critical aspect of relative advantage is that it is dependent on how consumers perceive its advantage rather than how it may objectively perform. The Automatic Teller Machine helps banks by removing the customer from the bank branch and allowing wider distribution for the bank's services, at supermarkets, shopping malls, airports and stations. As an innovation it may provide relative advantage for consumers who do not want to travel to their bank branch and can pick up cash while out doing other things. ATMs are not necessarily as easy to use for all types of customer, especially the elderly, or those with impaired vision. Similarly the introduction of self-service supermarkets meant that the customer was doing increasingly more work for herself. As Bowlby has shown, this required people to get some kind of enjoyment out of what was additional work:

> there is also the novelty of people 'content to wait on themselves'. That they should be doing it at all is one thing; that they should be content to be doing it is something else again. The word implies that they are already at ease with the transformation, not just putting up with it but positively enjoying it. (2000: 136)

Again self-service stores were a positive advantage for the owners of the business as consumers 'left to themselves' meant that the clerk as an interference was removed (ibid.: 136) and thus made them redundant, so reducing costs. What is more surprising perhaps is that the consumer found serving herself an advantage at all, but when Bowlby describes the festive atmosphere of a day out at Big Bear, first introduced in the United States in 1932, it is not difficult to understand the self-service attraction.

> There is a childish element in this. No limits are placed on customers' desires; they can pick up anything they see, and stay for as long as they like. The 'circus-like' scene and the name itself tend to a kind of happy infantilization for everyone. From the start, going to Big Bear was a family outing. It would involve a trip in the 'Model T' Ford, by this time a standard possession for even quite modest households; a free parking lot had been leased across the road to accommodate them. (ibid: 136)

So symbolically the shopping trip had been transformed into a holiday experience. Despite the festive atmosphere, the trip was unlikely to have made economic sense with people effectively doing their own distribution, often driving over 50 miles to reach the supermarket. The functional disutility is effectively outweighed by the relative advantage of symbolic difference for the consumer. Here Bowlby provides what is a good example of relative advantage definitely needing to be in the eye of the consumer. It is the supermarket entrepreneurs who were clever enough to package what was and still is a chore in a way different enough to get people willingly to change their behaviour and work for it too. It is also extremely difficult to identify what relative advantage a consumer will value, the apparently obvious ones are not always those most appreciated. Expectations of credit card use were based on consumers wanting credit and being prepared to pay for it, many of course did, but others saw the prime relative advantage being the ability to charge all expenses on one card and having up to sixty days free credit before then paying the entire bill without incurring any credit. Burton (1994) identified this use of credit cards as a source of interest-free credit as what made Lloyds the first bank to bring in an annual credit card fee. Lloyds introduced a £12 annual fee to its three million card holders in February 1990 in return for lower interest rates on outstanding balances. In other words shifting the relative advantage for customers towards borrowing (and paying for it) rather than paying off their account. Lloyds admitted that 37 per cent of their holders who paid off their bill in full each month would be charged and receive no benefit in exchange. Initially, *The Financial Times* reported that the bank lost around 15 per cent of its credit card customers but Barclays and then Midland Bank soon followed (*Financial Times*, 1990a). Of course it does not all work in the producer's favour. When Piggly Wiggly, often credited with being the first supermarket, opened in 1916, it lost as much as 6 per cent from pilfering. This may, at least in part, have been due to the novelty for customers of having easy access to goods; previously they would have had to pay for everything as they were transacting with the shopkeeper. Piggly Wiggly's owners had to take action in the form of store layout which remains familiar today. Points of entry and exit were separated, turnstiles were introduced at the entry and cashiers had separate spaces with room for only one person to pass through at a time. This resulted in a reduction of such losses down to 0.75 per cent (Bowlby, 2000). Finally, we have a form of relative advantage which may be almost entirely to do with sign value, but is also about the path of the object through time, history and tradition and how values can shift along this path. Lewis and Bridger (2000) describe how the Leica camera is imbued with 'perceived authenticity' so, despite being of similar quality to its nearest rival, it surpasses it through a form of fascination that is partly received from its quality, partly from its history in terms of the photographers such as Henri Cartier-Bresson who have used it and from what is probably some nebulous quality of perceived exclusiveness which gives it above all relative advantage in its sign value. Lewis and Bridger's example, however, shows an interesting side to how functional value can shift imperceptively to sign value largely through maintaining authenticity. When the Leica was introduced, it was truly revolutionary and this is partly why great photographers used it, now that side to its value is of less importance although still significant, while the balance has shifted towards what it symbolizes to those who use a Leica or those who dream of owning one.

In Rogers' taxonomy compatibility refers to the extent to which the new product is consistent with the consumers' existing values and past experience. Things that we are familiar with may be much easier to accept than completely new experiences. Once we had become familiar with supermarket shopping, the move to self-service petrol stations was relatively easy. One also finds that innovative ideas may be rejected in one form only to be accepted at a later date in another form more compatible to the consumers' way of doing things. Home banking is an interesting example of an idea which essentially needed to find a form of distribution compatible to consumers' lifestyle.

Home banking was initially introduced into Britain in 1983. The Nottingham Building (NBS) Society developed a system using Prestel videotex, which retrieved news, and commercial information from a central computer over telephone lines and into subscribers' modified television sets. NBS had hoped to achieve 100,000 subscribers by the end of 1986 but only reached 5,000 (Dover, 1994). Home banking did not begin to be seen as a successful innovation until the service was moved from a screen-based system to a voice-based one as used by Midland Bank's First Direct launched in 1989. While in the twenty-first century the advent of screen-based shopping and Internet banking may seem relatively normal, in the early 1980s they were not. Even if one argues that the telephone was always going to be more compatible at least as a first stage to begin home banking, it is interesting that it was still some years after NBS's attempt that First Direct was able to make a success of home banking. First Direct's formula obviously had a number of advantages over the Nottingham Building Society's, including a well-built system to deal with the volume of traffic. It is interesting to note, however, two key elements to their success that are both linked with one another and with Rogers' concept of compatability. As Larréché et al. say, 'The heart of First Direct was the call centre' (1997: 672). Now after 20 years or more of call centres, we may all be a little more cynical but in 1989, the advantages in First Direct's case outweighed any future disadvantages. Customers were able to call 24 hours a day, from anywhere and only be charged at local rates. So this is the first key reason for its success in compatability terms; the people who used First Direct at its inception tended to be time-scarce business people who wanted the convenience of banking which fitted into their schedule. So a bank that was truly open anytime, anywhere, was highly compatible with their lifestyle. The second key element was that the customer was able to talk to a real person who was backed up by superb database specialists and responsive systems. This not only assisted the operators to cross-sell financial services but also helped them to personalize conversations appropriately with customers. If anything, this was turning the whole self-service revolution back to front. The customer had returned to the old grocery store where the assistant not only knew your name but what you had bought last week. The key difference here was that this time it was dependent on technology. Technology could produce the impersonal ATM machine and it could act as a support to a personalized banking service. But why was this system so compatible? If the customer had not been bothered about losing shop assistants, why should they need banking representatives? The answer is in the nature of the offering; some things we can do more easily on our own and for others we either need or want to interact. The relationship symmetry is completely different from one situation to another. Some people will be happy to get their cash from an ATM but may not know how many dollars they will need on a skiing trip without some extra information. First Direct had put together a highly compatible package. This is an extract from an early First Direct transaction when the customer has called to order foreign currency:

> *Sylvia*: Thank you, Mr. Scott. How many US dollars would you like to order?
> *Mr. Scott*: It depends, I'm going skiing in the States. Can you tell me if there is a cash machine in Vail, Colorado, please?
> *Sylvia*: I'll need to ask you to hold the line for a minute while I find that information for you, sir.
> *Mr. Scott*: Thank you.
> *Sylvia*: Hello, yes, in fact there is a Cirrus ATM machine at the First Interstate Bank at 38 Redbird Drive in Vail.
> *Mr. Scott*: In that case, I'll only take $500 in cash with me and use the cash machine at the resort. (Larréché et al. 1997: 673)

The next attribute we consider is observability, which refers to the degree to which the effect of the innovation is visible to others. Often this is a case of the ease with which a product can be communicated to potential consumers. The more highly visible a product, the more easily it is diffused. Premium priced cars, through association with other people and things, can easily be attached to particular attributes; hence the use of the BMW Z3 in recent Bond films and a similar effect is anticipated with the ubiquitous celebrity endorser of premium priced watches. In the Bond films, the BMW Z3 is observed both as an extension of the man and doing amazing, albeit unlikely, feats such that it is no longer just a prestigious car but something more both in its functional abilities but also through its association with the fearless Bond. We are more aware of different models and makes of car than we are of cookers and vacuum cleaners because we observe lots of different types of cars everyday, whereas domestic appliances, while also part of everyday life, are rarely used in public but confined to the home. They have less obvious social visibility and no evident sign value. Having said this, the home has become increasingly a site of sign value and appliances too are taking on such values. Home decor is big business and the media buttress this through TV programmes and magazines supporting a fashion industry in interior design, while appliances too can become status symbols, the latest Alessi gadget or Aga signal different messages but both built on authenticity and exclusivity. It is notable that the two examples that Rogers (1995) uses, namely cellular telephones and Nintendo video games, have an almost built-in observability; the cellular phone because by its very nature it is used in public places, and Nintendo, through word of mouth in the playground at school. But in his analysis of the Nintendo phenomenon Rogers also points to the very important part that a variety of promotional push can play in the success of the observability factor when he points out that Nintendo had a huge advertising campaign including tie-ins with major companies such as Pepsi Cola, McDonald's, and a Hollywood film, such that its visibility was not left to chance.

Complexity refers to the relative ease or difficulty with which an innovation is understood. While Rogers refers to this attribute in terms of the consumers' perception, he also suggests that any new idea may be classified on the complexity–simplicity continuum, some innovations being clear in their meaning to potential adopters where others are not' (1995: 242). Complexity was also likely to have dogged the NBS in its home banking, with potential adopters having to learn how to use the Prestel system before they could do any banking while First Direct knew that not only did the telephone not suffer from any such complexity problems but that its familiarity gave it positive advantages for trial. The more difficult it is to use a new product, the less acceptable it is likely to be and, as others have suggested, such complexity needs only to be perceived as such to inhibit the diffusion of the innovation (Assael, 1987).

Rogers' final attribute is trialability: the degree to which a product may be tested and assessed before purchase. For lots of new things in the marketplace such trialability has relatively little impact. If you try a new variety of cereal or cosmetic and don't like it, the downside is relatively small, if a product can be purchased in small quantities, then trial again is relatively easy (Shoemaker and Shoaf, 1975). Often new food products are advertised in trial sizes, free samples are sent directly to consumers and sachets of moisturizer and perfume are found in the pages of women's magazines. But buying a high-priced consumer durable and finding it is not suitable is more of a problem and leads to consumers taking longer and considering more carefully whether to purchase an item which has a built-in innovative aspect to it. Marketers have long known that they need to devise methods of letting consumers try or have products demonstrated to them; new cars can be test driven and computers set up ready to let potential customers try them out. Clearly, the ability to test out a new product to some extent helps to reduce the risk for the consumer and probably aids adoption.

Conclusion

Thus far we have considered the importance of understanding the innovation process as it affects consumers and the relationship between goods and consumers. We have considered through reviewing work by Rogers and Robertson in particular how the balance between identifying innovation characteristics and their relevance in terms of consumer acceptance and the type of value particularly related to functional and symbolic aspects is likely to impact upon the nature of adoption and ultimately relationships. While the elements discussed so far do not reflect complete theorizing of the adoption of innovations, an important element which runs through our discussion of understanding consumers is the balance between the production and consumption dialogue; the characteristics of the innovations, on the production side, are balanced by the characteristics of the adopters or non-adopters through some kind of decision process, on the consumption side. That there should be such a neat package of elements as presented in the classifications discussed here is debatable, but that there is some kind of relationship between the nature of the innovation and the nature of the adopter seems at least intuitively likely. This association again reinforces the need to continue to examine the nature of the relationship between production and consumption, the producer and the consumer.

A key move forward in the study of innovations and their relationships with consumers was identified in the work of Hirschman who delved into the possibilities of the nature of innovations and delivered a simple division of technical and symbolic differences. The symbolic innovation has been explored to some extent particularly on the basis of known symbolic innovations. This deserves further analysis as it may help inform the nature of potential relationships and complexities that consumers have or may develop with new symbolic innovations. It may also aid an understanding of how consumers develop the symbols of the new, why one car brand is prestigious and another not and how hobbies, just like clothes, lose their appeal in a desire for new and different experiences.

Chapter 6

Revisiting the Time of Adoption and Resistance

For every learning curve, a plateau phase.
For every dish of the day, a sell-by date.
A backlash to every latest craze.
A riptide to every seventh wave.
For every moment of truth, an afterthought.
For every miracle cure, an antidote.

> From: Armitage (2002), A Tree Full of Monkeys

Introduction

Consumers who adopted an innovation later than the majority, or indeed did not adopt have been termed Laggards (Rogers, 1995). The word implies people behind the times and not in the first wave of the innovative, the fashionable and indeed the marketable. But is it right to generalize in this way? Those who choose not to buy the newest, latest things may have a range of motivations and reasons for not doing so. Marketing needs to understand this to better reflect not only on what choices consumers make but crucially why they buy when they do. There are two important aspects in relation to the timing of adoption. First, we need to examine the role, if any, that time plays in the adoption of new things and, second, we should consider what is implied by non-adoption. Are the non-adopters really Laggards or does non-adoption itself present a positive decision by a consumer knowledgeable in the marketplace? We do not all want the latest washing powder, lipstick or laptop computer and choosing not to buy is a real choice. This might, of course, be countered by the argument that marketing exists to create the market for new goods, but does it really? If there is to be any real meaning in the metaphor of relationship, then it surely needs to have a remit to help guide people in their choices not simply to drive them constantly to buy more things. This is in no way to decry innovation, but the choice not to consume at a certain point in time is not necessarily that of the dull no-hoper. It is a real consumption choice and, as such, marketers should be interested in it. The first part of this chapter begins by reviewing the role that time has played in the construction of the concept of an innovative consumer. The second part then looks at what it means not to be part of this trajectory of continued newness and examines some of the subtleties of non-adoption and even resistance. The chapter concludes by suggesting that we need to examine the nature of relationships with products to better understand how and why some things are not immediately or readily adopted. This approach can also help in understanding the best way to research and present new things to consumers. The reasons and barriers to why people do not adopt are discussed and their implications for marketing are considered.

Why Time Matters

The importance of time in understanding the behaviour of consumers cannot be underestimated. As consumers we organize, use, create, lose and plan our time. The process of ageing reminds us that time has what Adam (1995: 18) has described as an 'irreversible unidirectionality'. As consumers, parents, workers and carers we also know that every day, week and hour contain that same phenomenon. We act in ways that bind the future in irreversible ways. Some are personal decisions over which job we take or what we study at university, other are a small contribution to a bigger decision, such as which political party we will vote for. Research has examined the notion of the time-scarce consumer and what this means both for their approaches to consumption and what implications this may have for marketing and the development of new convenience products and fast food (Gross, 1987). A central proposition forming the core of much of the marketing and consumer behaviour literature suggests that the growth in such convenience products has allowed consumers to trade time spent on, say, the preparation of food and household tasks for goods and services that 'save' time. Thus time becomes open to commodification. It should be said that such commodification may be at least in part due to what tends to be considered the Western approach to viewing time as 'linear-separable' (Graham, 1981: 336), such that it is presented as a straight line from past to future while being separable into discrete units for use or consumption in different ways. Once time has the potential for separation into different portions, we can choose to allocate the units among different activities. Time can effectively be bought in terms of labour-saving devices or equally expended in different ways, wasted, used, spent wisely, etc. (Leclerc and Schmitt, 1999). As an economist might put it, tradeable, predictable time savings can be embodied in the household production function or utility function. Time, as Baudrillard points out, becomes a 'rare and precious commodity' which becomes subject to the laws of exchange-value:

> But, increasingly, free time itself has to be directly or indirectly purchased before it can be 'consumed'. Norman Mailer has analysed the production calculation carried out on orange juice, delivered frozen or liquid (in a carton). The latter is dearer because the price includes the two minutes gained over preparing the frozen product: in this way, the consumer's own free time is in fact time is being sold to him. (Baudrillard, [1970] 1998: 153)

Thus time even has a role in relation to which products a consumer chooses, including new potential labour-saving devices and the relationships that develop with our time-saving, time-extending, or complex devices. But time can also be used to categorize us as consumers. Just as products and objects move through paths of meaning and understanding, so too can consumers move along a life cycle and be categorized by what they buy at different ages or stages of their lives. A new parent is a very different consumer to one whose children have left home, a single woman in her thirties may purchase very different items to a widowed man in his seventies. Once we put the consumer and the product together within a time frame, we potentially have a powerful marketing tool, a way of analysing what kind of person is likely to adopt when. In theory the idea is intriguing and attractive, but the realities of the time of adoption are complex and do not readily respond to neat classification. We can see this by noting the tension above in the arguments that are efficiency based in terms of the time-scarce consumer and those which point to complex sociological drivers. This is illustrated practically in that clearly the income-rich and the time-poor are not the only consumers who buy convenience foods. We will begin by looking at two contrasting approaches to time and adoption, those of Rogers, and Hirschman and discuss some of the criticisms that have been made with regard to the usefulness of time as a construct in innovation research.

Time and Innovation Research

Let us consider briefly the traditional role time has played in much research, at least since the 1960s. A premise of much of this research has been that markets could be segmented on a temporal basis; the earliest adopters could be separated from later adopters by time (Rogers, 1995). Rogers and Shoemaker's definition of innovativeness as 'the degree to which an individual is relatively earlier in adopting an innovation than other members of the system' (1971: 27) made clear the relationship between a person's individual categorization and the time at which they adopt a new commodity. This idea was developed by other researchers taking some measure of time in terms of introduction of an innovation to the marketplace until its adoption as indicative of a person's innovativeness, such that different time lengths of this process were used to segment consumers in terms of degrees of innovativeness.

The classic model of this time-bound innovation consumption was first included in Rogers' model of 1962 (1962, 1983, 1995). Describing the spread of a new idea or product over time and through the social system Rogers showed this diffusion as following a normal distribution curve. Another interesting aspect of this diffusion over time model is that it included characteristics of adopters by time segments, although Rogers suggested these as 'ideal types', with 'conceptualisations based on observations of reality that are designed to make comparisons possible' (1995: 263). Nevertheless such categorization of 'ideal types' is a form of segmentation in that it assumes the ability to make a generalization of some kind about consumers. The standard deviations of the curve identified theoretically the different adopter groups as Innovators being the first 2.5 per cent to adopt, based on the standard deviation from the mean time of adoption. These first adopters were unlikely to engage in an extended decision process, being venturesome to the point of daring and rashness. They were likely to be networked with other innovators although the geographical distances between them may be great. Such venturesome behaviour has its price and the innovators needed considerable financial resources in order to absorb possible setbacks from an unwise choice. Again we see risk playing a role in consumption choice. Another interesting aspect of such Innovators is that they may often be responsible for importing the innovation from outside into their social system and so can play an important gate-keeping role with regard to what they choose to adopt and what not. A keen tennis player told about a new titanium racket by his tennis coach may choose to adopt and pass on information to friends at a tennis club or not, a rock enthusiast who has just been to see an exciting new band may immediately tell his friends or keep his 'find' to himself for a while.

The Early Adopters, the next 13.5 per cent to take up the innovation are, Rogers suggests, the category more than any other which has the greatest degree of opinion leadership, in most systems being respected by their peers and perceived as making judicious innovation decisions. They are likely to be particularly important for functional decisions as they trial the innovations and pass on information, so the later adopters are free-riding on their work. They lack the cosmopolitan nature of the innovator and are much more integrated with a local social system. This Early Majority account for the next 34 per cent followed by the Later Majority the next 34 per cent. The Later Majority, whom Rogers refers to as deliberate, interact readily with their peer group but seldom hold positions of opinion leadership and are likely to take a long period of deliberation before making an adoption decision. They are sceptical and cautious and may find they have to adopt through some economic or social necessity – very reactive rather than pro-active in their behaviour. Finally, the last 16 per cent, described as Laggards, are those who are suspicious of change and whose primary reference point is the past; their limited resources leave them well and truly at the tail end of the curve. Rogers identified the diffusion as a process by which an innovation is communicated by members of a social system through certain channels over a period of time. Time is a critical element here and implies that some people may identify something as an innovation long after it has been introduced to the market. Similarly, one social system may take much longer to adopt an innovation than another. While in the summer of 2001 walking down a high street in almost any city in Europe one would see the ubiquitous mobile phone in the hands of almost every teenager and many adults and children, go to the States and it was clear that this form of communication had nòt yet reached fashion icon stage. Environmental and situational factors clearly have an effect on how long it takes for a new idea to filter through the community. So, while the relentless march of the supermarket in Western Europe has nevertheless taken a good many years to dominate our shopping lives, after 1989, Eastern Europe caught up very quickly in welcoming the supermarket format. When denied of innovations, consumers can move through Rogers' normal distribution curve with no thought to time or willingness to adopt. IKEA opened its first store in Moscow in 2000, and it is now their busiest worldwide; the Muscovite consumers had adopted the concept of IKEA long ago, they just didn't have a store to shop at. Another example of the vagaries of time with regard to adoption is the case of crème fraîche. Crème fraîche has been widely available in supermarkets in Europe for many years. In the USA although actually available in the 1980s, it was treated like a 'gourmet ingredient, lining it up among the esoteric and exotic like something precious, too expensive to use but for that once-a-year tart Tatin', wrote Amanda Hesser, in the *New York Times* dining out section in August of 2001. But at last American dairies are learning how to make crème fraîche and so with recipes and suggestions for its use, the article takes on the role of disseminating the 'innovation' to the readers of the *New York Times*. These are important qualifications to Rogers' approach, as they indicate how there is no one neat path along which innovations and those who adopt them can be charted. The situation is much more dynamic and complex, with the obvious route being circumvented or leap-frogged for a range of reasons.

Hirschman (1987) presented a less linear, more complex, approach to time stemming from her perspective on time as experiential. She 'seeks to understand and measure the contents of the consumption experience from the viewpoint of the consumers' (1987: 75). This experiential perspective has its own temporal basis, accepting as it does that consumers have to engage in planning horizons. Expectations of future activities are experienced as a flow from present to future and continue as the future becomes the present. Important to understanding the choices that consumers make with regard to future consumption is the proposition that the consumer's commitment to future events is a function of personal preference and a sense of social obligation. Such an approach does to some extent decommodify time and moves away from a budgeting of resources viewpoint to a position which accepts that there are conflicting temporal demands and that prioritization of activities will depend on intrinsic personal rewards such as pleasure and satisfaction together with the extrinsic social obligation that a person may feel. Hirschman suggests that such an experiential approach may be useful when investigating consumers' anticipated consumption of events and should provide insight into how they perceive and plan future activities and consumption choices. Thus the consumption of new products and services may become part of the planning process for a consumer and may also be coloured by social factors and relationships. A parent may, for example, plan to buy a new product such as a minidisc player for their child but delay purchase until a suitable occasion such as a birthday or Christmas. The innovation is essentially adopted but the point of purchase is delayed. A similar situation might occur with the purchase of a laptop computer by a parent for a child going to university. There is a sense of social obligation to ensure that the child has the appropriate equipment similar to his or her peers. The purchase is planned for a particular event in the future which makes actual adoption before that event unnecessary and with the rapid changes both in specifications and price in this market, potentially foolish.

Problems with Time and Innovation

While time has a role in consumption, the vagaries of time consumption suggest it is unlikely to really be useful in such a predictive and positive form as suggested by Rogers. Indeed his approach received criticism from many directions (Midgley and Dowling; 1978; Hirschman, 1980; Mudd, 1990; Venkatraman, 1991). Midgley and Dowling (1978) argued that time of adoption, by definition a temporal concept, had no isomorphic relationship with what is fundamentally a hypothetical construct 'innovativeness'. Time definitionally cannot act as a route to measuring innovativeness; one might for example suggest that it is like using feet and inches to measure emotional states. The idea of linking innovativeness to time of adoption led Mudd (1990) to censure it on the basis of 'circularity criticism', i.e. that it will always be the early adopters who adopt early. In turn, others criticized this approach as having little usefulness in actual research. How, for example, could one compare findings across studies when time frames for different products and in different situations would not be directly comparable? (Goldsmith and Hofacker, 1991). This echoes the example of the introduction of Western shops to Eastern Europe; people cannot adopt what is not available, and once it is available, they are so familiar with the concept that a population may adopt all at once. Hirschman's (1987) experiential approach to time also suggests that planning for future events and consumptions is likely to be part of a person's frame of reference. So while the de facto adoption may not be apparent in the marketplace through actual purchase, the innovation has to all intents and purposes been adopted. While Rogers' model is neat and still widely referred to, particularly in conceptualizing how functional innovations diffuse over time, what is needed is a more inclusive view of innovation diffusion such that environmental and cultural implications are incorporated or at least investigated. As already discussed, few of the twenty-first-century's products and brands will be truly innovative or unique but rather they are attempts to alter existing offerings. When a new brand appears, there are generally already existing brands available to consumers broadly similar to this new one, which makes attempting to identify 'real' innovative behaviour by time potentially spurious. Another practical consideration is that innovations are themselves not developed in one moment of time. Rather, a new concept may be improved in the eyes of the consumers over a period and thus expand the market over time. The personal computer is a case in point. In the first few years of the personal computer's life home users became frustrated as to how quickly they were updated and how soon their relatively recent purchase became obsolete, such that programmes would not run. Since that time personal computer consumers have become savvy about how improvements are constantly being made and so may well now delay a new or replacement purchase until some particular innovative, price or quality barrier has been overcome. Just because they have not actually purchased says nothing of how innovative they may be with regard to this product category.

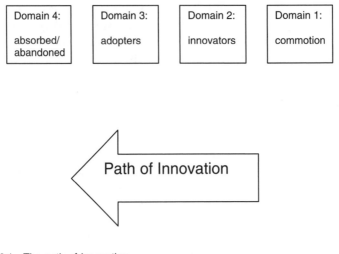

Figure 6.1   The path of innovation
Source: McCraken (www.cultureby.com)

Paths of Innovation

An alternative to the diffusion over time approach is McCracken's 'path of cultural innovation' (www.cultureby.com). In McCracken's conceptualization, as shown in Figure 6.1, we begin to see a more fluid and complex relationship that people have with products and their adoption. Innovations travel along a path made up of four domains. The innovation originates in Domain 1, enters the social world in Domain 2 where it will find its earliest recruits, or as he calls them 'Partisans'. In Domain 3 it begins to win widespread adoption where a fad moves into a fashion item or trend. Finally, in Domain 4 the innovation either slips beneath the surface of consciousness and becomes part of the culture, virtually taken for granted or it is abandoned or returned to the land of the new and becomes re-invented as someone else's fashion or innovation Although McCracken's path is presented as one of cultural innovation, it could equally well apply to other types of consumer innovation including purposeful innovations. The first domain is about commotion. The new thing makes us begin to examine our assumptions and consider the possibilities such that the known world may begin to soften and blur. 'Categories become less precise. Definitions less distinct. It is only when malleable that the world allows reworking' (www.cultureby.com). But at this point McCracken stresses the need for chaos not to take over as whatever the new thing is, it has somehow to be incorporated into the existing construction of our worlds. This first domain is alive with possibility and, just as with marketing notions of different types of innovative products, we have a continuum of novelty from substantial changes not only in what we think and to the way we think, right down to something that is new but not new at all, the classic product line extension or when *South Park* replaces *The Simpsons*, Atomic Kitten the Spice Girls and *The Weakest Link* replaces *Who wants to be a millionaire*?

If it is in Domain 1 that the innovation is produced, developed or thought of, it is in Domain 2 that it begins to create havoc. Here innovators develop the idea, draw on it and create something that may make the previous state-of-the-art look ridiculous.

> Innovators are prepared to embrace new ways of thinking and being. This demands a characteristic set of psychological characteristics, economic opportunities, educational advantages and cultural conditions. Most of all it demands, the inclination, rare in most cultures, to 'step off.' For reasons we understand and some we do not they are prepared to forsake what they know and embrace what they don't. Typically they do not care that other people think the innovation odd or loathsome. ('You've got a safety pin in your nose!') They are happy to embrace what others disdain. They like the 'shock of the new,' or they have a constitution that can endure it. (McCracken: www.cultureby.com)

At this point McCracken's interpretation of diffusions becomes markedly different to that undertaken by Rogers. Rather than smoothing the path for the innovation across society, McCracken now points to an ensuing battle between the innovators in Domain 2 who have appropriated the innovation produced in Domain 1 and the adopters in Domain 3. These adopters cannot stand the full force of the new, they need it watered down, they have weaker palates, and they do not want anything too risky or radical. The key to understanding the nature of the interaction (or conflict) between these domains is contained in the idea that it is the innovators who differentiate and the adopters who imitate which in turn sends the innovators back for more innovation to differentiate themselves from the adopters. Innovation has been appropriated by the consumer as a means to differentiation. McCracken is working within a status signing framework, not one of purposeful or functional innovation. In this sense it is richer in terms of its challenge to postmodern marketing. McCracken's version of diffusion is more complex than that of Rogers, implying all the social consequences of innovation rather than the functional ones. This is less about competing frameworks but rather two quite different ways of casting light on the phenomena of the marketplace. Additionally, McCracken gives history a greater role. The historical setting of McCracken's approach lies in the inevitability of diffusion over time particularly between Domain 1 and Domain 2; it does not matter whether it takes a moment or years but what is inescapable is that what was state-of-the-art will become stale, ridiculous or worse, meaningless, as McCracken says, 'This kind of novelty is a strange beast, both unanticipatable and, then suddenly, inevitable' (www.cultureby.com).

The adopters of Domain 3 interact with Domain 2 but this interaction is largely appropriation which in itself produces a self-perpetuating conflict. Using George Simmel as a reference for this conflict, McCracken suggests that the basis of the conflict is that the motivation for innovators to differentiate comes from the adopters' desire to imitate and the adopters imitate because innovators differentiate: a cycle of innovation, adoption and more innovation.

The final stage in McCracken's diffusion path is Domain 4 where the innovation may face three possible outcomes: (a) it may become a permanent part of the culture; (b) it is dispensed with and falls into disuse and disregard; or (c) finally it remerges redefined by someone else as new or different or as a fashion choice. McCracken points to the Afro-American high 5 as an example of a fashion coming off the street to be transformed into a gesture exchanged between white sports fans and players in all kinds of games from football through to tennis. An interesting example of redefinition is explained in the fall and rise of the preppie look. While McCracken says that by 1987 the button-down shirts, chinos and loafers of brands like Brooks Brothers were 'old', some Baby Boomers, while distancing themselves from the values of the 1980s, were not going to abandon the preppie look, thus ensuring a continued market for brands such as Land's End, Eddie Bauer and Ralph Lauren. McCracken goes on to tell how at the same time this look could endure in one incarnation it was also reincarnated in a very different way:

> Its not entirely clear what happened then. Urban myth has it that the *Saturday Night Live* appearance of Snoop Dog created a small sensation because he appeared wearing a shirt designed by Tommy Hilfiger. Hilfiger helped enormously by reputedly suggesting that his clothes were not intended for Afro-Americans. The reaction from the hiphop world was swift and unsurprising: 'actually, we decide who wears what, not some skinny white guy with bad teeth and big hair.' Sales

picked up and the preppie look rose from the ashes of well earned obscurity to achieve a certain street credibility. So the result was that, while still despised by some, the preppie look simultaneously became part of mainstream culture and had street credibility such that it 'managed to transcend fashion, stay in fashion, and fall from fashion all at once. (www.cultureby.com)

This story once again underlines the problem of time in diffusion research; the unidirectional flow of time becomes less useful when one sees layers of use and acceptance happening in the same time frame but among different groups. What is new or novel when the process is one of continual invention, appropriation, rejection and re-appropriation? The complexity of the marketplace in terms of the number and range of new things is reflected in the complexity of the consumer response. This implies a more intricate relationship with time than is implied in the unidirectionality mode referred to at the beginning of the chapter. Time may be marching on but there are small ebbs and flows within, different from person to person and qualifying the neatness of Rogers' type of continuum. The problem from a marketing perspective is that it undermines again the neat segmentation variables that marketers might want or expect. Tracking the movements and changes within will be more difficult than simply splicing up the marketplace, as the responses will be many, varied and not consistent. The second part of this chapter will look more closely at one form of response which is the rejection of the innovation.

The Range of Resistance

Consumer creativity reveals itself in a wide variety of forms of resistance, some highly pro-active and some possibly unconscious. New ideas and things are not adopted by consumers for many reasons but ultimately they are rejected. Why should consumers go on and on adopting new things? And indeed in purely numerical terms they don't. Midgley and Dowling (1993) summed up the findings of one extensive study by saying that despite the fact that individuals were interested in the particular innovations under study, 'the dominant act of behaviour was to reject adoption' (1993: 624). For some time researchers have been aware and interested in the notion of rejection. Mittelstaedt et al. (1976), for example, presented a model which proposed the concept of symbolic adoption or rejection. Here the process is fundamentally one of understanding and responding to a new thing in the form of conceptually adopting or rejecting it. It is echoed later by Venkatraman (1991) when he distinguishes between product adopters and innovators. One may be conceptually innovative but one needs the means to purchase new products. Mittelstaedt et al. suggested that a new product necessarily involves both an idea and an object with corresponding symbolic and action forms of adoption. An interesting aspect of this model was that it presented a number of routes that could lead to de facto rejection of the innovation. A symbolic acceptance of a new thing is necessary but it is not sufficient in itself to lead to trial, which in turn may or may not lead to adoption. Three possible scenarios are suggested. Individuals may symbolically reject an innovation by deciding on the basis of the available information that it is not for them; for example, a consumer may read a good review of a new film but because it is violent decide not to go and see it. Alternatively, they may symbolically accept the idea of the product but for other reasons be unwilling or unable to move to the trial stage; for example, a student may decide that a store card at his favourite shop would be suitable for him but be unable to obtain one because he does not have a regular income or does not pass the credit screening. Finally, someone may have symbolically accepted the idea but postpone trial until an appropriate time or situation for use; for example, a consumer may like the idea of owning a digital camera but may postpone purchase if their existing camera is still workable or perhaps wait for a specific future occasion to purchase. Gatignon and Robertson (1989) added to the conceptualization of innovation by suggesting that non-adoption of an innovation may be explained by either rejection or postponement with postponers not wishing to adopt at a particular time because they want more information or more time to process the information they have, while rejectors have processed the information they needed to make the decision not to adopt.

Resistance becomes less threatening to marketing if it is conceived, as Ram (1987) suggested, not as the opposite of adoption. He believed that it was better to consider adoption only beginning once initial resistance offered by consumers is overcome. Thus resistance is effectively redesigned as a normal consumer process. He suggested that the most important characteristic for an innovation to be successful is its amenability to modification. The modification to be made is dependent upon what caused the resistance and once the innovation is altered accordingly, it can again be exposed to the consumer and further modifications made if appropriate. Our earlier example of remote banking is a good example of such modification. The initial 'Prestel' form it was developed in was inappropriate and difficult for most customers but once modified into telephone banking, remote banking was rapidly accepted. Ram emphasizes the centrality of the consumer's relationship to the innovation, both in terms of whether a new idea is fundamentally acceptable, and also as pro-actively involved in the development of the innovation. If a company is able to identify what negative aspects of the new thing trouble or displease the consumer, then they should be able to work with them to produce something better.

Involving the consumer may not however, be a straightforward route to success. Martin characterizes the problem by saying that 'Real innovation does not emerge from slavish devotion to consumer feedback' (1995: 121), but contained within this message may be the seeds of a dilemma in developing new things. It is difficult for the potential con-sumer to envisage the new product and what it will mean to them, and so initial resistance may be no more than a reflection of the unknown. Martin tells the story of the Chrysler minivan developed in 1984 when Chrysler was struggling and needed a real success to pull it up. Despite tests which showed consumers were ambivalent towards the minivan, Chrysler went ahead and the minivan did indeed become a major success. Similarly, George Foerstner, President of Amana, believed that microwave ovens could revolutionize cooking at a time when consumers were not only sceptical but also worried about their safety. Both these examples are of ideas which needed to be seen, used and understood over a period of time before they were likely to be accepted but principally because as functional innovations it was difficult for consumers to understand the technical complexity of the delivery of the beneficial attributes. They were probably inevitably going to perform badly in research forums such as focus groups which could only describe the concept and its usefulness but not explore how the innovation might actually improve existing ways of doing things. Interestingly, part of the solution to the dilemma of when do we know whether the consumer really knows best may be supplied by Martin in his example of Urban Outfitters. This chain of clothing stores from Philadelphia competes with retailers such as Gap and Eddie Bauer, though it is considerably smaller. A key to the success of the company, Martin says, is that it never conducts focus groups and has only done a couple of surveys in the whole of its 25-year history. Instead the company uses observational research. It relies on 'customer profiles' produced by videoing people in their stores and around trendy locations such as New York's East Village. Such observation gives the company a direct link into what people are wearing and allows the company to make quick decisions on their merchandise. Martin quotes the founder and president of Urban Outfitters as saying 'We're not after people's statements, we're after their actions' (1995: 124). The germ of importance here is in the way the relationship with the consumer is transacted. The problem with focus group research to develop an innovative product is given away in its name; it is focused, perhaps over-focused. The level of interest a consumer has in a specific product or idea is likely to be limited and an over-emphasis on discussing the nature of such an idea may actually skew the results. By actually looking at what customers do, what they wear, how they like to shop, etc., the company is realigning the centre of attention away from itself and its problems back to the customer and how they like to do things.

Perhaps the best-known 'misuse' of consumer opinion in the development of a new product was revealed in the story of New Coke.[1] In the early 1980s Coca-Cola was seriously worried by the growth in Pepsi's market share while it remained virtually flat. It had also found itself cannabilizing its own flagship brand with alternative diet, citrus and caffeine-free alternatives to Coke. Indeed, Diet Coke, introduced into the US market in 1982, was a particular problem as its increasing popularity diminished the market for sugar colas which, in turn, Pepsi seemed to be winning. Taste appeared to be the nub of the problem. The taste issue was brought to the fore by Pepsi with their 'Pepsi Challenge' advertisements which appeared to show that people preferred the taste of Pepsi. It seemed that Coca-Cola took the results of the taste challenge seriously and its own research apparently found that people did indeed prefer the taste of Pepsi. Coca-Cola developed a new sweeter drink with high fructose corn syrup supposedly closer in taste to Pepsi. In blind tests people apparently liked the taste and so the company made the decision to discontinue Coca-Cola when the New Coke was introduced. This was probably the biggest mistake, something people were used to was being removed and a new product was replacing it, just like that. Much is made of the tradition of Coke, that it had been part of people's lives for over a hundred years and as such had become part of their own identities, and doubtless this was a major factor in the rejection of New Coke. There are other issues too, some with regard to the relationship between the company and its customers when developing and introducing new products and also in terms of the importance of the taste of a soft drink. Coca-Cola's decision to remove the original Coke was determined by market share predictions. It feared that it would make its competitive position worse by introducing a third major player into the cola market. At worst, New and Original Coke might cannabilize one another and let Pepsi in the back door. At best Pepsi was likely to have more market share than one or other of Coke's colas, if not the two combined. This might provide Pepsi with marketing leverage if nothing else. But consider this in the light of our earlier discussion of relationship marketing. From a customer point of view, removing the tried, tested and enjoyed brand, in favour of the new upstart is much more difficult to justify. It smacks of the company knowing best, removing the decision-making process from the customer and this, as we have argued, is critical in terms of the relationship between the consumer and the company. When a company tells us that it is providing us with something new and better, customers still want to make their own minds up. It is the paternalistic, we-know-best approach which particularly rankles. Second, while Coke's market share had been relatively flat, it was still selling plenty of Coke, in other words there was still plenty of people out there happy with the original taste of Coke; such people effectively never had a choice, their drink was taken away from them. Taste may be important, but its importance is relative to everything else, and if a company sees fit to take one taste away and supply another, the customer may decide that they are having none of it, there are plenty of soft drink alternatives about. Donald Keough, the company's President and Chief Operating Officer presented the New Coke saga as an emotional commitment between the people of the USA and Coke, 'The passion for original Coca-Cola – and that is the word for it, passion – was something that caught us by surprise . . . It is a wonderful American mystery, a lovely American enigma, and you cannot measure it any more than you can measure love, pride, or patriotism' (Mikkelson, 1999). A somewhat more cynical interpretation might be that the US consumer was just plain annoyed that a multi-billion dollar company could treat its customers in this way, just playing around with its products, taking away the old and introducing the new and not expecting some kind of backlash. Often it seems companies expect the consumer to take them seriously but are unwilling to reciprocate and give the same kind of respect to the consumer, so some rejection may be a more judgemental response to how they have been treated in the relationship.

The Comfort of the Status Quo

Consumer characteristics doubtless affect the resistance to an innovation. Unless the consumer feels the need for an innovation, he or she may well resist it (Ram, 1987). Again, a consumer may feel comfortable with their existing situation, what Sheth (1981) described as 'habit'. Where the habit strength towards the existing product is high, there is less motivation to change. Ram (1987), working from the Robertson classification of innovation, suggests that the more discontinuous the innovation, the more likely this is to happen. Importantly, both Sheth and Ram identify consumers as having no a priori desire to change. Why should consumers constantly have to change to something new? This is essentially an efficiency type argument, using habit and rules of thumb the consumer economizes on their search and information processing costs with respect to the information about new products. The investment in the search costs to habit formation act as a sunk cost barrier to change, which echoes the more

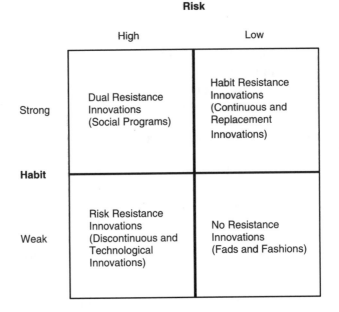

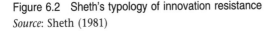

Figure 6.2   Sheth's typology of innovation resistance
Source: Sheth (1981)

positive assertion for maintaining existing relationships by Sheth and Parvatiyar discussed in Chapter 1. The investment in new search costs is costly and risky in terms of pay-off. As Ram explains, change has the potential to disturb a person's equilibrium and therefore resisting such change should really be seen as a normal response of consumers. Sheth also suggests that those who do not wish to change may be both more typical and more rational than the small group of individuals who do seek change. Thus, when Midgley and Dowling (1993) point to their respondents showing interest in the product category but not adopting the product, it may be that their personal characteristics, i.e. not wishing to change, overrode their liking of the product. Additionally, it is clear from attitude research that a favourable attitude towards a product does not necessarily lead to purchase (Tuck, 1977; Ajzen and Fishbein, 1980).

Not only might innovations unnecessarily upset the status quo but they may also be perceived as having an associated risk. Sheth (1981) proposed three types of such perceived risk which might be related to the adoption of the new. The first he described as adverse physical, social or economic consequences; the second, performance uncertainty; and the third, perceived side effects associated with the innovation. These he put together in a typology of innovation resistance (see Figure 6.2). In Sheth's model, dual resistance innovations have the highest prospects of failure and are often found in the area of planned social change. Habit resistance innovations are low risk but require changes in existing habits and practices and generally offer little relative advantage to motivate change. Risk resistance innovations have a high risk perception largely because they generate new habits. These are the most radical and discontinuous innovations and are often technological breakthroughs such as birth control and nuclear energy which may be perceived as risky both in performance uncertainty and potential side effects. Microwave ovens, for example, met high market resistance initially from consumers who thought the radiation might cause physical risk.

Later, Ram and Sheth (1989) suggested a definition of innovation resistance that also included a cultural element, such that resistance could come about because of potential changes from an existing status quo or 'because it conflicts with their belief structure' (ibid.: 6). What that belief structure might be is open to question but an interesting example of such resistance which the authors suggested at the time was resistance by US consumers to goods from developing countries, believing them to be of inferior quality.

Barriers to Consumption of the New

Just as we may adopt or use new things for the different values they offer us, either functional or symbolic, so we may resist adoption in a similar form. In Ram and Sheth's terms (1989), categories of resistance to the adoption of innovations may also be seen as different forms of barriers. These they grouped into functional and psychological barriers. The functional barriers include product usage patterns, product value and risks associated with product usage. The psychological barriers arise from traditions and norms of customers and perceived product image and generally arise through conflict with customers' prior beliefs. The concept of resistance through product usage patterns reflects Rogers' earlier idea of compatibility. Ram and Sheth, for example, suggest that car-pooling met with resistance primarily because it required such a significant change in people's daily routine. They have to synchronize their arrival and departure times and lose the freedom of a flexible schedule. A key attribute of the car is its option value. We value the option of being able to travel exactly when we want. New ideas or products that may appear objectively as beneficial do not always fit in with consumers' existing patterns and ways of doing things and are rejected because they are just not compatible with their existing lifestyle, or put another way, the sum of habits we have invested in. People may also reject because of a barrier in terms of the value the innovation provides. Ram and Sheth present this concept primarily in terms of performance to price value. Using Automatic Teller Machines as examples, they suggest that the value barrier has been avoided here by not charging for usage. The ATM, they say, does not provide value to customers who seek complex banking transactions but may be of more value when placed by situation and time where bank tellers are not available. Such a value barrier also highlights where people may be prepared to pay more for perceived increased value. Some people enjoy the process of supermarket shopping, for them paying for home delivery would have little value, but for the time-poor working mother the value may easily outweigh the service charge.

Risk may also be perceived as a major barrier to adoption. And it may include such things as physical, economic, functional and social risk. Physical risk is commonly associated with new medicines or other products that might have a harmful side effect; currently such risk is focused on the issue of genetically modified food. Economic risk is often particularly located with new capital goods where such products are often perceived as likely to come down in price over time and so people may delay purchase. Functional risk is related to performance, where the customer worries that the innovation may not have been fully tested and thus may not work effectively; new types of consumer durables such as washing machines or vacuum cleaners may be particularly prone to this kind of resistance. Similarly, the idea of shopping over the Internet could for some have both functional and economic risk, where consumers may both worry that they are unable to successfully accomplish a transaction and that even if they are able to, they may have fears about the use of their credit card in this channel. Finally, social risk is the risk that many of us feel when we are unsure that we are buying the 'right' thing, it is clearly particularly related to acceptance and distinction among our reference groups and as such is related to the risk we feel in adopting the 'right' signs. This social risk is much more important in postmodern consumption than previously where risk mainly applied to the functional or purposeful and such a risk is a major driver in consumption and rejection of goods. From the child ostracized at school for the wrong pair of trainers to having the 'right' menu at a dinner party, signing through adoption of right and wrong innovations is powerful and emphasizes the importance of the social and cultural context to innovation adoption and rejection. In terms of the cultural and social context of adoption and rejection, the issue of what is actively not adopted, i.e. a pro-active resistance, is particularly significant within the social and cultural context and in relation to the consumer's own self-identity. Bannister and Hogg (2001) have shown, for example, that people will reject types of clothing on the basis of whom they associate with wearing particular items. Their concepts of the avoidance self and the undesired self highlight the notion that we adopt and reject items in relation to how we see ourselves. While the avoidance self might involve rejection because an item of clothing, while liked, was 'not right for me', the undesired self was linked with active rejection of particular and specific products and brands. A more general image barrier may come about through a perceptual problem which has arisen through a stereotypical view of an organization or country linked to the innovation. For example, consumers might have a huge tradition barrier in terms of accepting a new car from a country like Russia. Signs on the backs of the Skoda, which originated from pre-war Czechoslovakia, saying 'Yes, it is a Skoda' reveal much about the company's understanding of the resistance to their brand. But Skoda have accepted the resistance and the range of reasons for such resistance, both rational and not, and reflexively developed out of their understanding of consumers an effective and humorous response to it. Critics might respond by saying that consumers have been won over by the purely functional fact that Skoda is now owned by Volkswagen. That would surely be a mistake, as we know that such simple logic does not transform the value of an existing brand in a crowded image-conscious market. It owes much to Skoda's improved reliability and better design but Skoda has also carefully positioned its sign values to directly respond to those of the consumer, a brand that doesn't take itself too seriously is one worth taking a second look at.

Conclusion

Time has both a functional and symbolic role in the adoption of new things and in the relations that consumers have with goods. Functionally technical advances and changes that help consumers in some way in their day-to-day lives will be important, especially where increasingly Western consumers are multi-tasking individuals looking to do a number of things at any one time. The symbolic role has become much more important in postmodern society but it is much more difficult to understand and predict consumer behaviour. Being the first to do something, wear something or use something has different levels of sign value to different groups. Writers have considered the commodification of time and how time is experienced but it is how innovations diffuse across populations that have traditionally most interested marketers. Rogers used time as a basis for representing the diffusion of innovation across a typology of adopter types. This classic framework acts as an important entry point to thinking about innovation but its greatest usefulness lies with regard to the purposeful innovation, the technical new of doing something that brings utility to the consumer primarily through the functional attributes that are conveyed, and appreciated in the innovation. While McCracken continues to look at an adoption across time and type, his framework moves away from the principally technological or functional to one which is based on the social process of signing. His domains signify not only an understanding of the shifting relative values of different groups but the importance and juxtaposition of one domain against the other. Thus time is used by consumers so they can judge how they compare and match up to others, they use it in their own relationships and as a sign to others, rejection and disuse are less to do with functional acceptability or suitability and much more to do with signing to others your own innovativeness.

Once we accept the fluidity of diffusion and the continuing shifting relative values that may be associated with different products, we are better able to embrace resistant behaviour as part of the diffusion process rather than opposing it. We have looked at a number of factors that may produce apparent resistance, some of which are to do with the way the product was presented to the consumer and some to do with the problems, risks or barriers the consumer may perceive. Again, rather than a negative response to marketing, this is potentially a useful input to marketing's reflexivity, to better understand consumers' behaviour, both positive and negative.

Note

1   This interpretation of the New Coke case is largely drawn from Barbara and David P. Mikkelson's Urban Legends Reference pages (http://www.snopes2. com/coklore/newcoke.htm).

Chapter 7

When Innovation becomes Creativity

'What's new?' is an interesting and broadening eternal question, but one which, if pursued exclusively, results only in an endless parade of trivia and fashion, the silt of tomorrow. I would like, instead, to be concerned with the question 'What is best?' (Prisig, 1976: 8)

Introduction

Having spent some time studying the nature of innovations and consumer responses to them, their acceptance, diffusion over time and resistance, we will now take a more detailed look at consumers and their part in this process. The individual consumer has been studied in relation to their behaviour and whether or not this behaviour might be described as 'innovative'. This in turn has been considered both in terms of what implications there may be for the marketplace and for a deeper understanding of what is driving consumers' behaviour. This chapter first of all considers some of the characteristics associated with innovative consumers. On the one hand, it examines the issues around associating socio-economic characteristics and innovators, linking to our earlier discussion of segmentation and analysis of risk taking. On the other hand, given the importance we are ascribing to sign values in innovation, it in particular highlights the importance of socio-economic differences and status markers both in terms of aiding identification of innovators and crucially to understanding the role they play in the process of diffusion leading to widespread adoption. It then considers the research that has tried to explore the concept of innate innovativeness and evaluate this in relation to personality differences. It concludes that this concept offers much promise because it embraces the creativity of the consumer in the innovation process and puts the analysis and practice on a firm consumer-centric foundation. Finally, we conclude with the marketing opportunities and challenges for theory and practice.

Socio-economic Characteristics in Historical Perspective

It has been suggested that if companies are able to identify the social, economic and psychological characteristics of early adopters, they should be better able to tailor their product development and create an appropriate marketing mix to meet adopter requirements (Foxall, 1984). It is hardly surprising that companies believe they would benefit from the early identification of consumer innovators, if their adoption and use resulted in the kind of social comparison and adoption suggested by McCracken and Rogers, which leads to diffusion across a wider market, thus helping to make the introduction of new products more effective, and encourage quicker adoption in increasingly competitive markets. Again there could be a potential circular benefit, as successful pursuance of this could ensure deeper understanding and knowledge of these early adopters and their social and consumption habits and preferences. In developing new products and the marketing for these products, marketers could return to them and make certain their views were adequately taken into account (Midgley, 1977).

Over the years much research attention has been given to the discovery of factors which might characterize the early adopter of innovations. Typical of this approach was the work by Robertson et al. (1984), who reviewed research across a range of product categories, identifying a number of characteristics linked to innovators. Not surprisingly perhaps, these included higher income and education, more social mobility and interaction and a relatively favourable attitude to taking risks. Others have suggested that such social characteristics are difficult to apply in a generalized way and may be more appropriate for some product categories than others (Gatignon and Robertson, 1985). Foxall et al. (1998) developed a more comprehensive classification which included social, personal and consumption characteristics of innovators. They presented their five fields as areas where consistency in the general characteristics of innovators had been found. These they described as:

- socio-economic status
- social interaction and communication
- personal traits and characteristics
- product perceptions and appraisal
- purchase and consumption behaviour.

Again, social and comparison factors are significant but others, importantly to do with the consumers' personality and relationship with products, are also included. The role of personal traits, perceptions and purchase patterns will be discussed below but first we will conclude our examination of the impact of socio-economic factors. Foxall et al. identified innovators as having higher incomes and more discretionary income than either later adopters, their peers or the population as a whole. Innovators tended to greater social participation, opinion leadership and were more cosmopolitan than others in the social system. There is both a functional and symbolic dimension to socio-economic factors in innovation. On the functional side, Foxall et al. point to numerous studies that show innovators differ from their social group in terms of social class position, education and privilege, thus affirming quite simply that those with more money have more discretion on what and how to spend it but also that the risk they incur is relatively less than others in their social group. On the symbolic side, the social interaction and communication of innovators appear to be deeper and greater in terms of the media they use and their 'cosmopolitan character'. Importantly, they communicate more and are likely to be opinion leaders, actively communicating their discoveries and new purchases to others. This social dimension to innovation and consumption is embedded in the history of consumption through the nineteenth-century examples of Simmel and Veblen discussed earlier, and makes clear that sign values, while of much greater importance in postmodern society, have always been with us. Literature through the centuries is a very good mirror on status markers and their implications. Jane Austen's novels are full of references to status markers and the battles that ensue over their appropriation, display and rejection. Mrs Elton in *Emma* desperately tries to assert her social credentials through her brother's oft cited barouche-landau, its newness signposted by their first having the carriage 'last summer'. The many references to the barouche-landau are studiously ignored by Emma whose defined social standing does not require her to compete in any way with Mrs Elton. Today authors such as Jay McInerney and Tama Janowitz continue with depictions of status markers in modern American society. Florence Collins, Tama Janowitz's anti-heroine, always wears something a little different to her colleagues at the New York auction house where she works but she is the innovator, the others the adopters.

> She put on a flared striped cotton skirt, in shades of forest green, mustard, dark brown and beige; a pair of dark green patent leather flats, hand-made in a French shop; a brown-and-beige sleeveless floral-print silk shirt with a Peter Pan collar. Around her neck she tied a thin cotton sweater in lime-green. She pulled her long blond hair back in a ponytail and, rummaging for her new sunglasses, put them on top of her

now-sleek hair. She wore hardly any makeup; a little lipstick in a neutral tone, some powder. Though the other women at Qualyle's would be wearing simple black linen shifts, tightly fitted, with jackets they removed once evening came, or suits, Florence's outfit was more expensive than any of theirs. The overall effect was a subtle fifties' parody, a bit different than what anyone else had on but which on her somehow managed to seem like the latest style. Quite often it turned out that what she wore was what the others ended up wearing shortly there-after. (Janowitz, 1999: 120)

History also shows 'higher' social groups have proved useful for producers in the diffusion of ideas and innovations. McCracken retells the story of Josiah Wedgwood giving his plate away to members of the aristocracy with the view that if they adopted it, then it would be seen by others in lower social groups who would want to copy their betters and such imitation would help the awareness and adoption of his product through English society. Even relatively recently, royalty has been imitated, although most of this social status has been taken over by media celebrities. When Princess Diana became engaged to Prince Charles, frilled blouses of the type she favoured at the time were found throughout department stores in England. Fashion designers now offer actresses and models free dresses to wear to prestigious events such as the Oscars with the same intention that Josiah Wedgwood had some years ago, imitation helps awareness and awareness aids adoption.

Personality Differences

While the importance of 'high' status individuals and other conspicuous innovators may be intuitively understandable as a catalyst or precursor to mainstream adoption, the role of personality is more difficult to grasp and define in terms of innovative behaviour. Indeed, it is a difficult question to answer as to whether a person's personality has any role in adoption. This has not stopped researchers specifically trying to pinpoint what it is about a person's make-up that makes one person innovative and another not. Weak though consistent links between innovative behaviour and personality traits such as flexibility in thinking and trying new things, tolerance of ambiguity, self-esteem and sensation-seeking have been identified (Foxall et al., 1998). Such a link between personality and inno-vative behaviour has been cautioned by other studies in this area. For example, Kassarjian and Sheffet (1991) concluded that, despite the many research studies undertaken to produce evidence of a positive correlation between personality traits and early adoption, the correlations produced were in fact so weak as to be either questionable or even meaningless. But Foxall et al. suggest that probably the most important trait to be linked to innovative behaviour is 'venturesomeness', which they define as the capacity to cope with high levels of risk and uncertainty, and to show a self-contained approach and independence of mind in new situations. Foxall et al.'s final two characteristics, product perceptions and appraisals and purchase and consumption behaviour, can also be linked to personality differences because they are about the difference between perceptions and behaviour of those more innovative and those less so. Innovators are thought to perceive the characteristics of new products differently and in particular using Rogers' characteristics described in Chapter 6, they are likely to see more advantage, greater compatibility, less complexity, more conspicuousness and more opportunity for trial than others. With regards to purchase behaviour, an interesting aspect to innovators is that they tend to be more involved with the product category in which they are the earliest adopters. So if you are a heavy coffee drinker, say, you may well be likely to try a new kind of coffee. There may also be similarities in purchase behaviour and involvement across product categories, for example, across different types of domestic appliance. Foxall et al. conclude that this behaviour indicates another attractive aspect of innovators to marketers, i.e. that they not only initiate markets by communicating innovations to others, but that they also consume a disproportionate volume of the products they do adopt.

Attempts to find linkages between people and innovative behaviour continue. Lewis and Bridger identified a group they called the New Consumers, whose wants 'frequently focus on original, innovative and distinctive products and services' (2000: 4). The New Consumers may be any age, sex or ethnic group, independent, individualistic, involved and well informed on consumer matters and their fundamental desire is for what they call 'authenticity'. Such authenticity is difficult to define precisely but Lewis and Bridger refer to a notion of exclusivity framed by quality. They suggest that authenticity is quality that fascinates rather than just quality that is expected. Their understanding of authenticity is most often framed and described in terms of consumption distinctions and decisions.

On the sleeve of a suit by top British designer Paul Smith, for example, you will always find five or six buttons rather than

> the usual four. A BMW M5 is one of the fastest and most sought-after sports cars on the road, yet its only distinguishing feature from a similar car of the same make is a tiny M5 badge on the rear. A mere glance at a shirt collar is sufficient to tell a connoisseur whether it is hand made or mass produced. (Lewis and Bridger, 2000: 150)

This quest for 'authenticity' is, however, probably more to do with the need to distinguish oneself through sign and status markers than anything significantly different about the personality of the consumer. The New Consumer is basically a mainstream version of McCracken's Domain 2 inhabitant but while McCracken describes new Goths and punks, Lewis and Bridger are more concerned with innovation adoption of new brands and modes of transaction such as shopping on the Internet. Much emphasis here is put upon the notion of authenticity as perceived by New Consumers and Lewis and Bridger suggest that 'providing an authentic product or service and then delivering it in an equally authentic manner is not only the way to ensure authentically loyal consumers, but also the fastest route to commercial success in the New Economy' (2000: 199). What may be missing from Lewis and Bridger's analysis here is the difference between those searching for something functionally new and better and those looking for ways to distinguish themselves from others using the signs of the marketplace to do so. Despite Lewis's description of the New Consumers as individualistic, involved, independent and informed, we are no closer to understanding whether their behaviour can be traced back to some aspect of their personality or whether it derives from other drivers.

Is it the Product or is it the Consumer?

As with so much that is concerned with a better understanding of the consumer, we need to keep in sight both the product and the consumer and their relations with one another. In the innovation literature much time has been spent on discussions of whether innovative behaviour might be something inherent in certain types of consumers or whether we show our innovativeness only in certain product categories. In other words, is there a type of person more likely to exhibit innovative behaviour generally, or are we product-led in the sense that we have categories with which we are more involved and hence we are likely to exhibit what appears as innovative behaviour in the sense that we adopt more new things in these categories? Such a distinction was acknowledged by Venkatraman (1991) when he highlighted as a problem that innovators were being identified by their new product adoption behaviour, in other words, in relation to their being relatively earlier than others in purchase terms, and that this alone did not indicate they were innovators.

In response to this criticism and while the correlation of personality traits and overt innovativeness has proved inconclusive, there still have been many attempts to conceptualize a representation of inherent innovativeness (Midgley, 1977; Midgley and Dowling, 1978; Hirschman, 1980). Midgley and Dowling suggested classifying innovativeness into two parts: an observable behaviour which might be referred to as actualized innovativeness and an abstract construct of innate innovativeness. They suggested that at the level of observation, overt innovative behaviour might be accounted for by actualized innovativeness, that is the relative time of adoption of a single innovation along the lines of Rogers (1995). This actualized innovativeness, however, related as it is only to observable behaviour, does not allow for the innate innovativeness that precedes it. Here the diffusion process is seen as essentially a communication process, with innate innovativeness as the degree to which an individual will make decisions independent of the communicated experience of others (Midgley, 1977: 47) and with variables such as interest in the product category, communicated experience and situational variables intervening in the progress of innate to actualized innovativeness. In other words, can we identify to what extent someone adopts new things on the basis of their own judgement as compared to how much and what kind of information they received from the outside world? It seems like an impossible task and one that would not achieve much anyway in terms of our understanding, in as much as it would be difficult to distinguish the differences in any useful way. How well would somebody be able to recall what influences and communications they had received during a possibly complex decision process?

This thinking did, however, lead Midgley and Dowling (1978) to suggest three types of innovativeness identified as specific innovativeness for a single product, for a category of products, and innate innovativeness. They differentiated between actually adopting a product, process or idea and having a tendency towards making innovation decisions independently. This idea of innate innovativeness is probably close to an expression of a person's personality, as previously discussed, and this implication has been recognized by others (Foxall, 1988; Mudd, 1990). Midgley and Dowling did put forward the view that certain clusters of personality and sociological traits may have an impact on the degree of innate innovativeness of an individual, while not completely determining this. While innate innovativeness was not described in detail, it was referred to as 'the degree to which an individual makes independent decisions independent of communicated experience of others' (1978: 236) which led some to consider whether this tendency was intended to be independent of the influence of communication from others. Both Mudd (1990) and Hirschman (1980) concluded that communication was incorporated into this conceptualization of innate innovativeness and if so, such a definition of innovativeness essentially includes two criteria: the degree of receptivity to new ideas and the degree to which the consumer's decision process is influenced by or independent from others in their social system. Exactly what role interpersonal communication plays is not clear and certainly Mudd took issue with the proposition that innate innovators will be seen to be actual innovators more often because their adoption is independent of interpersonal communication. The implication here is that high receptivity to new ideas would be correlated with low dependence on communicated experience.

Another major contribution from the consumer research field came from Hirschman (1980) who suggested that Midgley and Dowling's inherent and actualized innovativeness was closely related to constructs she described as inherent and actualized novelty seeking, which she presented as preceding actual innovative behaviour. There are clear similarities between Hirschman's inherent novelty-seeking, described as a preference for and a desire to seek novel stimuli, and Midgley and Dowling's innate innovativeness, i.e. the inclination and readiness to gain new information through product adoption (Foxall, 1988). Hirschman's actualized novelty-seeking, however, refers to the initiation of behaviour intended to gain new information, and thus is presented as a different phenomenon to actualized innovativeness. Actualized novelty-seeking is an individual's behaviour to acquire novel stimuli and as such mediates to translate the consumer's inherent novelty-seeking into actualized innovativeness. This actualized novelty-seeking can be present in three ways: vicarious innovativeness where new products are learnt about but not yet acquired; adoptive innovativeness where new products are actually purchased; and use innovativeness where existing products are used in novel ways by consumers (see Figure 7.1).

Important to Hirschman's model is the proposition that movement from inherent novelty-seeking to actualized innovativeness is dependent upon the consumer's situational and personal factors. The consumer's creativity in terms of understanding complex products and considering consumption problems is required, which in turn may stimulate overt novelty-seeking and actualized innovative behaviour. Important to the notion of the creativity in the consumption process is that Hirschman presented consumers as needing to be more creative in order to be able to deal with the complexities of modern society. Creative consumers are more

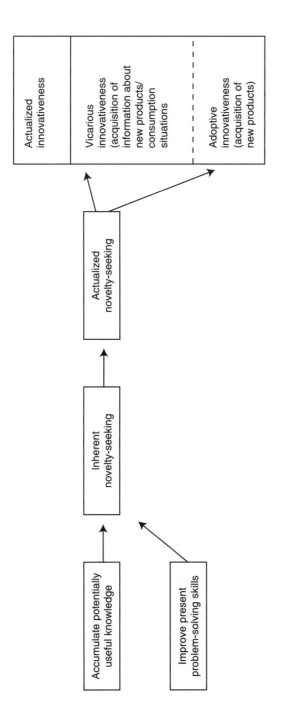

Figure 7.1 Hirschman's model of novelty-seeking and actualized innovativeness
Source: Hitschman (1980)

readily able to identify and evaluate the attributes of innovative products in comparison to existing ones. In consumer research, attributes of course can mean many things and include symbolic and social attributes as well as functional ones. Similarly, this could refer to the ability to read the sign value or capital value of innovative products, indeed, the innovation might itself be in the sense of sign, cultural or social capital significance. But as Slater says: 'most of us, even in the depths of poverty or the heights of conformist affluence, are very far from being mindless consumerist zombies. We can and do reinterpret, transform, rework, recuperate the material and experiential commodities that are offered to us' (1997: 211). Therefore high levels of consumer creativity are not necessarily translated into adoption of new products but perhaps more competent new product evaluation (Hirschman, 1980: 289). This is a significant shift in thinking in relation to innovativeness as it implies an assessment of what is being adopted and its usefulness or appropriateness to the consumer, rather than just a desire for new experiences. It opens the door for different responses being considered as creative responses whether it is adopting a product for use in a particular way or indeed in resisting the product. Exploring the concept of product evaluation also brings the consumer potentially closer to its production and, as we shall in see in Chapter 9, the realignment of production to consumption may bring important consequences for a better understanding of consumers' responses to the marketplace in future years. Higher creativity is also thought to lead to increased use innovativeness, just as we have explored earlier, such creativity may as easily appear on the streets in the form of fashion or over the Internet in the form of mani-pulating existing frameworks for new uses. A novel consumption problem is judged on the basis of whether to adopt a new product or to use a presently adopted product to solve the new consumption problem. This latter is a consumer researcher's analysis but others might also see such creativity as allowing us to deploy devices ironically or to distance our-selves from or to make goods a matter of play which we can transform or resist. This moves innovativeness right away from product adoption and into a completely new mode of creative consumption, whereby consumers really do take centre stage, as it is within their remit how to interpret and use what is on offer, be it functionally, symbolically, playfully or indeed in complete realignment of the intentions of the marketer, such that they initiate a new or different mode of consumption suited to their needs.

Conclusion

Creativity is, after all, perhaps a more useful concept to consider innovation through rather than some notion that is directly related to the adoption of new products. Creativity is essentially a human process while innovation is too closely linked to the nature of new things which in turn is a production rather than a consumer-centric way of thinking. To emphasize this point, consider the development of the mobile phone and in particular the use of text messaging by young people. In Lewis's account of this innovation adoption, one which is almost universally used by young people with mobile phones, he describes the process of development as one of creativity to overcome a particular problem. Lewis discusses how the Finnish company Nokia studied the way children used technology:

> The kids came to each new technology fresh, without preconceptions, and they picked it up more quickly. They dreamed up uses for their phones that, for reasons no one fully understood, never occurred to grown-ups. The instant text message, for instance. The instant message was fast becoming a staple of European corporate communication. To create an instant message, you punched it by hand into your telephone, using the keypad as a typewriter. On the face of it this is not an obvious use of a telephone keypad. The difference between the number of letters in the alphabet and the number of keys on the pad meant you wound up having to type a kind of Morse code. The technique had been invented by Finnish schoolboys who were nervous about asking girls out on dates to their face, and Finnish schoolgirls who wanted to tell each other what had happened on those dates, as soon as it happened. They'd proved that if the need to communicate indirectly is sufficiently urgent, words can be typed into a telephone keypad with amazing speed. Five and a half million Finns had sent each other more than a billion instant messages in the year 2000. (2001: 5–6)

The drive to meet particular needs is essentially human, whether social, functional or symbolic. People look for solutions to problems, for better ways of doing things and making themselves feel better and happier. The drive to produce products is essentially to do with business and while business clearly needs to produce things that consumers will want and use, it is from the consumer's creativity that a product's usefulness is really derived. So young people in Finland use existing technology to overcome their dating problems, UK bank customers may use credit cards so as to delay paying for goods while not incurring interest and young American speculators can use the Internet to make money on share trading. Companies can deny consumers' creativity but not only do they do so at their peril but they also miss out on a huge opportunity. Seeing how people use products and want to use products is potentially a more useful tool both for developing new things and for marketing existing products than segmentation variables developed from lifestyles or existing behavioural characteristics.

Chapter 8

Conspicuous Consumption, Downshifting and Reconsumption

On other occasions you might recoil in dismay when something you had always considered uniquely your own – a remote holiday destination, a favorite restaurant or an obscure piece of music – is suddenly 'discovered' by a great many other consumers. I remember my own dismay when Puccini's aria 'Nessun Dorma' from Turandot, which I had long treasured, was adopted as the 1990 World Cup anthem and stayed at number two in the singles charts for several weeks, its sudden mass popularity somehow robbed it of that special feeling that I had long held for the piece. (Lewis and Bridger, 2000: 81)

Introduction

We have considered the nature of individual responses to innovations and some of the implications for marketing firms engaged in developing new products and long-term relationships with consumers. Consumer relationships with products and brands are much more complex than a simple one- or two-way supplier to buyer interaction. They are made up of a myriad of responses to consuming, some functional, some symbolic, some to do with the utility of the goods and others to do with the sign value of the goods. Bridging the gap between a functional and a sign value orientation in marketing is important, as the framework will then embrace that consumers can be many things. In this chapter we move on to look in more depth at a range of consumer roles and positions in relation to consumption in general before developing in Chapter 9 an argument in favour of reconceptualizing marketing to encapsulate the developing concerns of consumers within a production–consumption continuum. In this chapter we examine the polar opposites of conspicuous consumption and downshifting before moving forward in our thinking to what we have termed reconsumption whereby consumers themselves are moving to a more reflexive position with regards to their own consumption. Consumption can be comparative in nature and the adoption of certain products and brands is often a reflection of the need to distinguish oneself from others. What value consumers gain from such a distinction is open to question.

Consumption as Display

The fact that consumption is not something done in glorious isolation but is contextualized by place, time and social comparisons is fundamental to understanding why conspicuous consumption is even an issue. It is the fact that consumption can be comparative or even competitive in nature which makes spending potentially so conspicuous (Schor, 1998). We are all aware of the brash conspicuous excess of some recent episodes, for instance, the 1980s or even, briefly, for the instant dot.com rich. However, conspicuous consumption is not just a modern-day phenomena. It has a long and complex history incorporating many forms and many types of consumer. As Schor has pointed out, even before Veblen's much cited *Theory of the Leisure Class*, Adam Smith in *The Wealth of Nations* had noted that day labourers would be ashamed to be seen without a linen shirt (Smith, 1976: 869). In terms of presenting ourselves to the world, there are many notable earlier examples of conspicuous consumption, patrons appearing in paintings dressed in the richest garments, regardless of the subject matter. Others, including consumer researchers, have pointed to how different forms of art have reflected and revealed aspects of materialism including the display of consumption activities (Belk, 1986; Berger et al., 1972). Pictures such as Thomas Gainsborough's 'Mr. and Mrs. Andrews' which shows a proprietorial owner overlooking all he owns, and Hans Holbein's 'The Ambassadors' surrounded by the riches they have acquired, reveal how both the picture itself and the contents within can be used as a sign to others of the position and status of the sitter and/or owner. Literature, from Henry James to Scott Fitzgerald, has also contributed to an understanding of consumption, revealing and describing as such authors do the role and importance of conspicuous consumption to people's lives.

Whether display and emulation are in fact central to what we understand as conspicuous consumption should first be addressed, as, at a general level, understanding the consumer is about trying to get to the core of why they shop, purchase and consume the items they do in the ways they do. What Baudrillard might interpret as consumption significant in its sign value might equally be interpreted by another as consumption on some functional or other attribute. Does the executive buy a BMW rather than a Skoda because he really believes it is more reliable or because it is a possession to be proud of and which he knows others will envy? The symptoms of quite different motivation can be the same but failure to identify the different cause is of profound significance to marketing. The question does not have a ready answer. Instead, let us look at some of the contributions to this debate beginning with the contribution of the nineteenth-century economist, Veblen. Included in his interpretation of a conspicuous display of wealth were such prestigious items as clothes, furs, jewels and wives. One aspect of consumption that Veblen did try to clarify was the propensity for emulation 'for invidious comparison' (Veblen, 1899: 109). This propensity, he suggested was a pervading trait of human nature, almost part of the make-up of a human being and stemmed from the need to detach oneself from the mundane (Slater, 1997), such that distance is created. Essential to this was distancing from productive labour, in the sense that not having to work set the leisure classes apart from the rest. This in turn led such people to be able to partake in essentially useless activities in that they did not generate anything productive, leading to further distancing. The concept of waste, of non-functionality, became an attribute in itself. Others have pointed out that Veblen saw both serviceability and waste as potential for the utility of the good from the user's perspective (Ramstad, 1998), so Veblen can first describe the 'functionality' of goods thus:

> Goods are produced and consumed as a means to the fuller unfolding of human life and their utility consists, in the first instance, in their efficiency as a means to this end . . . The marks of superfluous costliness in the goods are therefore marks of worth – of high efficiency for the indirect, invidious end to be served by their consumption. In order to appeal to the cultivated sense of utility, an article must contain a modicum of this indirect utility. (Veblen, [1899] 1970: 154–5)

In terms of what this means now, Ramstad points to pertinent questions of whether today such marks of superfluous costliness are leading consumers to 'free choices' or 'false needs'. The reality of such diametric opposition of these two types of utility, one to do with functionality and the other to do with some indirect sign value or membership of elite or different groups, leads others to question whether this kind of con-sumption is just individuals being manipulated rather than a satisfaction of real needs (Leiss, 1976). This manipulation is exacerbated by the argument that goods do not supply what the advertisers may promise, as Weiss puts it: 'An individual's striving for a permanent place of distinction is like the pursuit of a mirage across the desert. The horizon of social honour recedes as one approaches it' (Leiss et al., 1990).

What is the Nature of Conspicuous Consumption?

In endeavouring to understand the nature of conspicuous consumption and its implications for consumers in the twenty-first century, we shall begin by attempting to unpick its nature. What are the qualities or ingredients of conspicuous consumption? Has it changed over time? And is it static or mobile in quality? Do we buy more expensive clothes, jewels and cars just for their own sake or to make us feel better? Or rather, do they continue to play, just as in Veblen's original suggestion, roles for us in terms of their power for comparison? It seems likely that there is some truth in both assertions but we cannot ignore the reality and importance of the continuance of comparison in social life. Comparison in turn is related to social position, such that as Slater has observed, 'In modern societies it also regulates relations between classes, as well as culture as a whole' (1997: 155). If goods are only relational points of comparison, then Slater adds, no consumption can be final as the need to preserve status has to be 'competitively maintained' (ibid.: 156). 'A holiday in Marbella or a taste for nouvelle cuisine has a certain cachet until ten million other people are consuming it in packaged form. At this point it is devalued because it can no longer discriminate status and its wide availability cancels out the positional gains any individual consumer might have achieved by obtaining it' (ibid.: 156–7). Such a view appears to go against any possibility that while consuming the holiday or the nouvelle cuisine a person may gain pleasure and satisfaction from the thing consumed alone, but it would be wrong to assume this. Certainly preferences, whether based on comparison or not, will change, but the pleasure of functional consumption should not necessarily be dismissed too easily.

It is also worth considering whether built-in obsolescence is consumer or production led. Changes in production have of course affected patterns of consumption. Advances in production, increasingly flexible workforces both in time and geography and the development in the range and extent of communications have led to much wider variations in possibilities whether those be in terms of the variety of flavours, shapes, sizes and prices we can choose from, or the types of experiences we can have, be it Disneyland, Las Vegas or the Lake District. It may be that the range and nature of this consumption have been modelled by a fashion factor driven by producers such that what is new, different and significant this year loses its attraction when others have 'discovered' it or when something new beckons on the horizon (Lury, 1996). Whether knowingly or not, consumers are enlisted into this fashion cycle by producers. Consumers are, however, increasingly well informed with the iconography of their popular culture, they have become educated participants reading the signs and politics of celebrity, fashion, and novelty. This may have come about through engaging consumers to construct meaning in advertising, to become participants in what is being sold to them. Now young consumers 'read' advertising quicker than ever and they are becoming the producers themselves, creating their identities through consumption of esoteric labels and music such that the 'Cool Hunter' agencies are after their knowledge; the producer led by the consumer but only if these young, cynical, brand- and consumption-aware people let them. This take-up by the consumer of production responsibility and creativity will be further developed in Chapter 9.

So such conspicuous consumption is dynamic; it is the field on which the taste weapon is played out (Bourdieu, 1984). Moreover, as we compare, often we want to be like others as well as different to others. So we live in areas with people similar to ourselves, of the same social group and with similar tastes and even consumption patterns (Schor, 1998). The consumption may be conspicuous but it is also predictable. It is used as a form of social communication and distinction, to set us apart and to blend in. While we may not be able to change the houses we live in or the cars we drive easily, our clothing can give us a chameleon capacity, we know that we can change the way we look and even feel by the clothes we wear and how we wear them. And this ability has its functional uses. Lurie (1981), for example, describes how a journalist she knows changes his appearance, his clothes and accessories depending on the people he is interviewing. Others have found that clothes and appearances are readily decoded and assigned to different groupings (Bannister and Hogg, 2001). Consider, Lorimer Black, the hero of William Boyd's novel *Armadillo* who uses different costumes and accents to help him deal with the different people he meets in his job as a loss adjuster:

> The day before Lorimer had had his haircut and this morning had lightly gelled it flat. He was wearing a fawn leather blouson jacket, a pale blue shirt and striped knitted tie, black trousers and Italian loafers. He had removed his signet ring and had replaced it with a tooled gold band which he wore on his right middle finger. His briefcase was new, shiny brass and polished leather. All specialist loss adjusters had their own approach to

the job – some were aggressive, some cynically direct, a few bullied, or set out to inspire fear, others came in strong and hostile like hit-men, some were neutral apparatchiks emotionlessly executing orders – but Lorimer was different: he was much more interested in the absence of threat. He dressed this way not to disguise himself but – crucially, deliberately – to reassure: these were expensive clothes but they would not threaten the likes of Edmund or Rintoul, they did not hint at other worlds, strata of society alien or hostile or sitting in judgment – in theory they shouldn't even notice what he was wearing, which was, in fact their designed effect and the modus operandi of his personal and particular loss adjusting method. (Boyd, 1998: 61)

Here we see how the conspicuousness of consumption can be used as a facilitator but also as a disguise. So should we be careful about the short-hand inferences we make in regard to what goods mean and what their motive of communication is? Whether we like it or not it, we are probably making those connections and inferences all the time and for marketing of course the key is to connect the product with the message, 'Tiger Woods as a model to young people who want to play golf, as a symbol for the nation of an idealized vision of race relations based on merit and not prejudice, is appropriated to the selling not simply of golf shoes, but of a positive feeling about Nike and the Nike swoosh' (Waller and Robertson, 1998: 43). While we do associate different appearances with different motives and messages, we cannot assume that translation will always be correct; in this sense consumption does not even come close to language (Campbell, 1987a). And there are different types of messages being used by different people. Schor points out haute couture does not shout out what it is with labels and logos emblazoned over it, the nature, cut and sheer difference of it mark it out as worlds apart, but a Tommy Hilfiger shirt has the logo up front and clear for its own reasons and for those who wear it.

According to the designer Tommy Hilfiger: 'I can't sell a shirt without a logo. If I put a shirt without a logo on my selling floor next to a shirt with a logo – same shirt, same color, same price – the one with the logo will blow it out. It will sell 10 times over the one without the logo. It's a status thing as well. It really is.' And what does a Tommy Hilfiger logo symbolize?

> Interpreters of the Hilfiger craze have this to say: 'these clothes, traditionally associated with a white, upper middle class sporting set, lend kids from backgrounds other than that an air of traditional prestige'. (Schor, 1998: 47)

The Hilfiger example points to the use of clothes as part of a kind of social positioning. Here distinction is less the motivation, they do not proactively wish to distinguish themselves from others, but rather they find a way of blending in with social groups to which they aspire through camouflage. Fashion, of course, is peculiarly subject to the Simmel effect of a constant round of differentiation and conformity but clearly other items can be subject to the same fashion threat sometimes disguised as innovation. Electronic equipment such as mobile phones, cameras and laptop computers are constantly changing and being positioned as fashion statements. A recent BT Cellnet ad showed a young woman standing in the rain at a bus stop next to two men. She was covering herself with her hands as the rain made her blouse transparent. The line below read: 'Life contains enough embarrassments without your mobile being one: get the latest stylish mobiles on BT Cellnet Pay & Go^{TM}', clearly positioning the mobile phone as a fashion item which one needs to change as regularly as one might one's clothes. Cars, household equipment and furnishings have all in recent years been repositioned further and further away from their functional attributes and closer to fashion items. Once a good is perceived as subject to fashion, then it will need to be changed regularly. IKEA, the Swedish furniture store is expert at quirkily repositioning and changing people's ideas of what is appropriate in their homes.

> It's time to Live Unltd. Hey, it's 2002. It's time we put aside all the old ideas of how a home should work and came to some simpler, happier, smarter, freer answers. Why do you need a dining room if you never ever eat in it? Who says you can't have a garden just because you don't have an outdoor space? In the next few months, IKEA will be tackling such conundrums with a barrage of fresh Live Unltd ideas. Join us on our journey of interior possibilities and have a little giggle on the way. (IKEA promotional material, 2002)

We no longer need to live with the same tired furniture, the same old layout, IKEA will reform and remodel the twenty-first-century consumer's home and way of living and this call received a ready response from consumers as the home increasingly becomes part of the our extended selves (Belk, 1988).

When Our Consumption Becomes Us

Much has already been written about the role of consumption in the construction of selves; what our purchases say about us, and our identity, what we are and what we would like to be. While this may be crudely done at the level of the generalized attributes which people associate with brands and hence themselves, there are potentially deeper meanings which we could seek to comprehend related to understanding ourselves as consumers. We use goods, for example, to transform ourselves into other people, if only temporarily:

> Then I get back into my Porsche. It roars and tugs to get moving. It accelerates even going uphill at 80. It leadeth trashy women . . . to make pouting looks at me at stoplights. It makes me feel like a tomcat on the prowl . . .
>
> Nothing else in my life compares – except driving along Sunset at night in the 928, with the sodium-vapor lamps reflecting off the wine-red finish, with the air inside reeking of tan glove-leather upholstery and the . . . Blaupunkt playing the Shirelles so loud it makes my hair vibrate. And with the girls I will never see again pulling up next to me, giving the car a once-over, and looking at me as if I were a cool guy, not a worried, overextended 40-year-old schnook writer. (From Stein, 1985, quoted in Belk, 1988: 145)

Goods can also bring closeness to others. This is what Muniz and O'Guinn (2001) describe when they talk about a 'consciousness of kind' evident in the brand communities they investigated. The fact that others share their brand creates a sense of 'we-ness' (Bender, 1978), of knowing one another even if they have never met or are geographically distanced. Muniz and O'Guinn cite Cova (1997: 307) saying that 'the link is more important then the thing', but the link is essentially provided by the brand and its visibility to one another. Thus it acts as an aid, a facilitator to communication. Now while this may be interpreted as little more than a shallow form of social affiliation, it is perhaps one that is appropriate to the twenty-first century, where the means to communication may have become extensive, but people's ability and willingness to communicate with one another would appear to have become less active. Here goods, specifically brands, act as a bridge among and across people, to the extent, in some cases, that they feel strong moral responsibilities to those they see as members of their brand community. Here Muniz and O'Guinn describe what happens when one Saab driver saw another who had broken down.

> *Mark*: Yeah, we see another Saab on the side of the road, we pull over to help, no matter what it is.
>
> Mark adds that he does this sort of thing without even thinking; it just seems like the 'right thing to do.' That he does not stop to help drivers of all cars broken down on the side of the road, only those driving Saabs, suggests that he feels a strong moral responsibility to other Saab drivers. (2001: 425)

The downside to such communities is what Muniz and O'Guinn describe as Oppositional Brand Loyalty. If you belong to one community, you may well be in opposition to another. In other words, what you consume also helps to identify what you do not consume and what brand communities you do not belong to, the groups and people you wish to disassociate yourself from (Hogg and Savolainen, 1997). One of Muniz and O'Guinn's respondents succinctly categorizes people's political affinity by which computer they use, 'At that time, it was clear: IBM people were one way, wore suits and voted for Reagan, and Apple people were another, wore jeans and didn't vote for Reagan' (2001: 420). Similar comments were made by Saab owners of the Volvo, which was associated with safety but also dullness. Volvo also made tractors but Saab made airplanes and jet fighters; the Saab brand was fun, the Volvo wasn't. Thus in terms of social comparison, the use of goods may define us in terms of who we think we are, aspire to be, our relation to social positions, affinity with others and opposition to others. Goods therefore can and are used to present ourselves to the world and give order to this world. What we should be aware of is the possible implications this may have. It is one thing for a Volvo driver to be perceived as dull, another to have your political affiliation decided for you on the basis of what computer you use. Douglas and Isherwood (1996) has also shown how goods build the social system through which classifications are made and through which we order our worlds. But not only do goods act as markers of social status, they may help us to cling on to identities which are often frail and under threat.

When things are going badly we may use clothes or make-up to help us get through. We will 'treat' ourselves to chocolate or wine to help cheer ourselves up. We often cling to the possibility that in times of distress some goods can really make us feel better. Such compensatory consumption has been identified as a 'regular' part of consumer behaviour (Grunert, 1993) and may take the form of shopping to 'treat oneself' or comfort eating. Woodruffe's research (1997) found that compensatory consumption made up for deficiencies in people's lives that might not easily be filled, being depressed, tired, working too hard, having marital problems or just wanting more excitement in life.

Finally, conspicuous consumption can provide pleasure (Campbell, 1987b). Once distinguished from utility, the pleasure gained from objects can be about fantasies and illusions. The experience of shopping, the development of personal taste and style and the showing off of the style can give the individual pleasure. The importance and pleasure gained from such consumption should not be underestimated and some (Schaefer and Crane, 2001) have emphasized the importance of trying to understand that consumers, even in their guise as citizens, use consumption as a means by which social, emotional and other relationships are maintained in society. Maybe this is more prevalent in modern times because as Giddens puts it: 'the self is a somewhat amorphous phenomenon' (1991: 52). We are, he says, not given our self-identity, rather it is more the result of a prolonged creation and sustaining though our own reflexive actions and across our own biographies. Many of the choices we make with regard to our self-identity are done within a social context. The problem for people increasingly is that our social lives lack stability and things, products and brands, may hold a stability that people no longer can for us. Of course the fallacy of this argument is contained within the fashion cycle itself: the dress or sofa or car we held dear last year may no longer thrill us or reflect the current narrative of our self-identity.

Consumption Creating Ourselves

Goods may act as a substitute to our social selves or they may enrich them. The importance of goods to our sense of being and identity as a form of enrichment is well articulated in Russell Belk's work on the Extended Self (1988). Belk sets out the basic proposition that our possessions become parts of ourselves. Objects may remind and confirm our identities, but similar feelings may be conjured by ideas, experiences and places to which a person feels attached. Importantly, Belk reviews the contribution of Marx, Sartre and Fromm with regard to people's relationship with things. In essence this is an argument which revolves around the importance and relevance of 'having' versus 'doing'. The corollary of 'having' for Marx is 'commodity fetishism' where goods become the empty promise of happiness when for Marx real happiness is reached through work, which needs to be both meaningful and properly rewarded (Marx, 1967). The position that Marx takes with regard to 'having' and what it leads to in terms of how the commodity becomes fetishized will be considered further in the next chapter. For Sartre, the key defining moment of self stems from the notion that 'existence comes before essence' (1973: 26). Man therefore 'surges up in the world – and defines himself afterwards' (ibid.: 28). It is in the nature of this defining that possessions enlarge our sense of self; what we have helps identify what we are (1943). Finally, Fromm (1976) supports the being rather than owning mode of existence as preferable. For Fromm it is important 'to realize one's identity without the threat of losing it' (Belk, 1988: 146) and the problem with possessions is that one is always under threat of loss. This is summarized in Fromm's question, 'If I am what I have and if what I have is lost, who then am I?' (1976: 76). Belk concludes that possessions do create and maintain a sense of who we are and that the 'having, doing, and being are integrally related' (1988: 146). It seems, however, that a key difference between Sartre's view is that man cannot help but be defined by his possessions, whereas for Marx, a man may be alienated from the product of his labour by others, and for Fromm, man has fundamental choices and that the choice of having is ultimately unrewarding.

Having addressed the nature of the relationship between the self and possessions, we are in a better position to examine what the conspicuous consumer might be doing and feeling with the possessions he has. It is of critical importance to the innovation process we have been discussing. When McCracken refers to the Conspicuous Innovator (1998), he says that he both wants to be copied and be different. This paradox seems to come about because such people live in a constant state of flux, part of the innovator community but horrified when their innovation becomes taken up by contemporary culture. Once the adopters have appropriated the idea, it is time for the innovator to return to differentiation. So for such innovators differentiation becomes key. Differentiation is also of supreme importance for those who want to express themselves through their possessions but are not necessarily innovators. Then scarcity and price can act as barriers to entry and these in themselves produce differentiation. So if you are rich you can distinguish yourself through expensive designer goods. As Vittorio Radice of Selfridges makes clear, 'We choose a restaurant or a hotel or a shop because they give us a sense of excitement, of theatre. Creating this sense of arrival – Prada, for instance, does it brilliantly – is one of the few tools you have to make your environment stand out from the crowd' (van der Post, 2001: 9). This in turn becomes a process of comparison and distinction, as McCracken describes it in relation to Domains of Innovation:

> I know a New Yorker who gets an expensive, almost secret document by fax every week identifying the restaurants that have just broken or are about to break. This way he can be certain that he is out with people from Domain 2 and avoid those clueless bridge and tunnel has-beens from Domain 3. This is of course the nightmare of every restaurant owner. She knows her hippest patrons, the really fashionable ones are poised to move on. And once they do, it is only a matter of time before the Domain 3 crowd move on as well. (www.cultureby. com)

So the need to distinguish oneself affects both one's consumption and the production process as well. Such consumers are shifting, apparently promiscuous beings who will not be satisfied. Time and possessions go hand in hand, as one can only be distinguished by your possessions, or the places you go to until the others catch up.

Does it Matter What we Consume?

Conversely, perhaps, if consumption is about distinction, then being conspicuous may be less important to us than knowing whether we are consuming the 'right thing'. Look at all the fashion and style magazines, interior decorating, and even gardening and see how what was appropriate last year is no longer so. Swags and tails in curtains are replaced by roman blinds, wooden floors replace carpets and pink geraniums are replaced by white lilies. This is what Schor describes as the 'new differentiation' (1998: 52). The new differentiation is yet again about creating social distance. Ostensibly it may be about quality and style, authenticity and craftsmanship but it is also about distancing oneself from other consumers, avoiding too close a relationship with what might be perceived as part of the mass market. Giving another view on the IKEA phenomenon, she says:

> IKEA was great when it had one or two stores and was an innovating Scandinavian importer; now it's on the verge of

becoming McCouch. It's no fun to walk into someone else's living room and see your sofa. (Or as one interior decorator explained to me, when the pieces start appearing in the department stores, forget it. Couldn't possibly buy them.) (Schor, 1998: 58)

Now Schor has given a somewhat extreme take on this aspect of differentiation which hides perhaps a deeper-seated need to simply have something that is different to other people. But this behaviour leads people easily into a cycle of constantly changing decor to ensure differentiation, whether they like or indeed want the change. The problem is that whereas in the 1920s and 1930s it was relatively difficult for the 'average' consumer to emulate the tastes of their 'betters', now as Schor points out 'Upmarket tastes, just like downmarket ones, are predictable' (ibid.: 59). Schor presents this as a useless striving for individuality, of gaining in status of being different which ultimately is unsuccessful simply because eventually we are all going to look like everyone else. Certainly the goal may be a futile one but for many the journey could be worthwhile. Some people may well get a great feeling of completion and satisfaction from having things around them that they associate with style and even differentiation – we have to ask ourselves whether there is anything wrong with this. And of course there may be. We are after all consuming more and more and often getting new things with little thought of recycling, the environment or even whether we really want, let alone need, the latest, fridge, television or cooker. It is also quite possible that we are not making the best choices in relation to the functional appropriateness of our choices. For example, Schor bemoans the fact that people do not use aluminium siding because it is deemed not be aesthetically pleasing, although it is an excellent insulator, does not need painting and is durable. She interprets this as less about aesthetics but more about an association it may have of being low-class. Yet this seems somehow too simplistic an explanation. There are lots of areas where we do not necessarily choose the objectively best and indeed such a requirement would seem like a straitjacket that few of us would wish to inhabit. Consumption may on occasion be motivated by effectiveness and appropriateness but it is also about living with things which we like. We may choose cotton sheets over polyester because they have a classier image and feel nicer next to the skin, despite being difficult to iron – all these attributes can merge together as affecting our consumer choice.

Of course a problem with conspicuous consumption is that it is conspicuous. We see how some famous people are able to shop and consume and some of us want to do it too. Victoria Beckham can travel to Rodeo Drive and purchase a Louis Vuitton belt, so why can't we? This seems to be a question that many ask. Indeed, as noted earlier, they may not travel to California for it, but many can and do purchase Louis Vuitton. If you watch television and see people living in luxurious loft conversions, or in the country with tennis courts, swimming pools and driving Aston Martins, your perspective on the reality of people's lives may become a little distorted, to say the least (O'Guinn and Shrum, 1997).

The Downshifting Alternative

One solution to all the conspicuous consumption and the problems that it brings for consumers, whether they cannot afford it or because they find themselves on some hamster wheel of needless and pointless updating, is to find simplicity. Schor interviewed a number of people who had down-shifted either because they genuinely wanted to or, because of circum-stances, were forced to. She gives a frank and well-rounded view of the problems that downshifting can create such as not being able to go on holiday or to afford the branded clothes that children want to be part of the crowd. For some the choice to downshift comes from having had enough of demanding jobs and a stressful life, as Schor puts it: 'The most common reason cited for downshifting, by a wide margin, is "wanting more time, less stress, and more balance in life"' (1998: 114), but often as well as the stress and lack of time these people had in their past lives, they spent a lot of money and were not necessarily happy with their purchases or the consequences of their purchases. One respondent talked about weekends 'vegging' out and shopping after collapsing on a Friday night, of buying books and records that she would never read and even finding herself buying books she already owned. Another was weighed down by the responsibility of a prestige house. While an important element of their sense of being in relation to consumption now was to emphasize function over the symbolism of goods, Schor stressed that this was often a choice difficult to implement and in many cases required a moral commitment which represented commercialized culture as of little worth, morally bad with damaging effects on the environment and those people in devel-oping countries who have to work to support the Western lifestyle. Above all, these people now have to recognize whether or not they actually want the stuff that previously they would not have thought twice about buying. Take Jonathan, for example, at the time of Schor interviewing him he was only earning $12,000. He talked about his previous relationship with goods and how he deals with consuming now.

I was a thing junkie for a long time, so it's really hard. If there's something that I want, I ask myself what's motivating me, why do I really want this, what am I going to do with it? Just about anything. From a tool to a book to a piece of clothing or a chair, what is the life cycle of this thing going to be for me? How am going to deal with it? I'm not making a moral judgement, it's the reality of what am I getting by buying this, what am I adding to my life by having it? (Schor, 1998)

In order to overcome the problems of too much consumer spending Schor suggests that we need a new consumer consciousness and behaviour. She has developed nine principles to help people, as she puts it, 'get off the consumer escalator' (ibid.: 145). These principles include controlling desire, controlling ourselves, learning to share, and deconstructing the commercial system. While such principles may read like a well-intentioned self-help manual for consumers, there is little doubt that the sentiments are sincere. But to a certain extent the principles require us to live a life that is unrecognizable and potentially rather puritan in its objectives. For example, to control desire we have to stay away from shops, chuck catalogues in the recycle bin and avoid taking up new sports because of the inevitable desire for lessons and sports equipment that will go with it. The problem with such de-consumption is that it does not recognize the joy of consumption but only the negatives. It is as if we can either only be shopping addicts or self-righteous simplicity seekers.

Where Downshifting meets Reconsumption

Downshifting on the scale of Schor's interviewees is unnecessary and frankly unlikely for the majority of consumers. Consuming, buying, shopping, wearing, and even talking about the things we have bought and plan to buy are frankly too much fun for most people to want to abandon, especially when all around will continue to happily consume. It may be fine for some, but they are relatively few. This is not to say that Schor's message is not valid and important. It is, not least because it makes us reconsider what we are doing and why we are doing it. It is a mistake, however, as Miller (2001) pointed out, to demonize consumption but that does not mean that we should not be an educated consumer. Indeed, becoming an educated consumer is in fact part of one of Schor's nine principles. To become good consumers we need to understand more about ourselves and about the products and services we buy and ideally reconcile the two. We need to be able to deconstruct the advertising that we see everyday and laugh at it rather than admire it. We need to understand how and where things are produced and then make up our own minds as to what that means to us as consumers. It may mean we want to boycott some brands and not others, it may mean we consume less or downsize but it does not preclude us from continuing to consume if that is what we want. Veblen recognized that rising consumption levels were unlikely to raise people to a higher state of satisfaction about their material life and others too have recognized that our uncertainties of what and how to consume are manipulated and exploited by advertising (Leiss, 1976). Interestingly Veblen suggested that evidence of emulation was also to be found in conspicuous leisure as well as conspicuous consumption. Schor suggests that we downsize and take up gardening, reading, cooking, quilting, writing books, mountain biking, opening bed and breakfasts, socializing, playing music or learning a language. Perhaps we should consider whether however worthy and indeed interesting these activities might be to the educated middle classes, they are just another form of conspicuousness, noticeable by their apparent absence of consumption.

The more informed we are as consumers, the more likely we will be able to redefine our own consumption and our relationships with companies, products and brands. Such reconsumption needs to be built on a better understanding of what we are doing and what it is possible and even acceptable for us to do. Of course in order to do this, we do need to understand about our relationships with things at a deeper level than just as extensions of ourselves and our lives. Production as well as consumption needs to be considered in order to realign consumer relationships and understanding in a more realistic way. This is not just rhetoric; as noted in earlier chapters consumers are redefining the nature of relationships, their involvement and response to innovation require suppliers to understand consumers better and to explain to them more fully and equitably just what is going on. As such, the 'better' consumer may not be one who needs to downshift as such, but rather to make appropriate choices for themselves within a wider more 'democratic' arena, such that we at least get away from the question posed by Brown below:

> we have a system that is based upon the endless search for more wealth. We want more wealth because wealth has become the means to win the game of 'I am better than you.' We want to win this game because by winning it, we can achieve status. We need status because it is the means to achieving the respect of others. We need the respect of others

because this is how we obtain our self-esteem. We need self-esteem because this is how our natures are built. And what good is an economy that does not facilitate one of life's essentials: self-esteem? (1998: 210)

Conclusion

This chapter has further considered the nature of consumption as practised by individuals. It has examined some of the motives for consumption, in particular in relation to needs for differentiation and distinction. It has discussed how possessions can come to define our self-identities and questioned what effect this has upon individuals both as people and consumers. Consumption is a normal part of everyday life and some forms of association and distinction such as associating with others through the brands we buy may produce positive responses, but also the idea that we can become different or 'better' people through consumption is clearly limited and potentially unfulfilling. While conspicuous consumption has certain invidious connotations, it is suggested that this form of signing consumption is still only part of the consumer's repertoire and functional attributes will still be valued.

While at one end of the consumption continuum there is conspicuous consumption, at the other, there is downshifting that actively seeks to reduce consumption and find alternative ways to a fulfilling life. Downshifting effectively recognizes the dangers of continual consumption for people but the alternative it offers is fundamentally one of resisting consumption where marketing will be castigated and responses to existing and new brands and products will be oppositional. We suggest that this is a sign, however, that people are becoming more concerned and knowledgeable about consumption, reflecting on what they are doing and being critical of themselves and suppliers. Increasingly we see our role in the process of relationships and innovation and thus as consumers we question what they offer to us. Once this bridge has been crossed and the consumer's role moves in some way down the supply chain, it inevitably rekindles a desire to understand more about the process of production. It is early days yet in this process, but as the final chapter argues, what is happening increasingly is a repositioning of the consumer in line with production and consumption issues that concern them. It will be argued that understanding the consumer will be as much about understanding their take on production issues as it will on consumption issues.

So conspicuous consumption may be an attempt to achieve sign status but in so doing consumers can find themselves on a hamster wheel. The stability of the patterns imposed or reinforced by producers can be problematic for the function of marketing. In addition, a growing section of consumers are reacting against the wheel. While at one extreme we have the phenomenon of downshifting, more broadly, consumers are becoming aware of their role in consumption and production as a process. This poses issues of greater complexity of prediction for marketing in both theory and practice and also how we relate to the normative question of what 'good' consumers should do. These points are closely related as effective relationships with consumers may hinge on understanding both what the new involved consumer seeks or ought to seek. Marketing needs to use this understanding to lead to more effective relationships.

Chapter 9

Production and Consumption

To become good consumers we need to know more about how products are produced and what tax the manufacturing process levies on the planet, as well as about the health, safety, and environmental impacts of a product and its true long-term costs. (Schor, 1998: 155)

Introduction

The role of consumption and its relationship to production are undergoing fundamental change. A range of political, economic and social drivers is shifting the perspective of both consumer and supplier. The exercise of choice by consumers increasingly involves a range of considerations that go well beyond value for money and include environmental, ethical and social dimensions. As a consequence, twenty-first-century marketers face a growing number of issues that will require addressing; they can no longer maintain the comfortable position of supplier of new products, brands, ideas and communication. The imperative to be 'better consumers' and reactive suppliers, not only has implications for the marketers, but also marketing as a function and discipline will have to review its role in the chain of supply from production to consumption. The extent and manner in which they both engage will be dependent on the increased knowledge and information consumers have and what they decide to do with it. Some of these issues have developed out of social and economic structures that have grown up within the market society, others are about morality and what kinds of consumers we want to be but ultimately they all have some link with the production process.

While it is impossible to predict the ultimate consequences of a reorientation of the relationship to production, it has major implications for how we understand consumers and their changing priorities. For instance, it raises issues of how we might deal with the potential polarization of Western consumers into those who exercise choice based on production values and those who do not. At a practical level, this would be destructive of current marketing practice which is still largely applied across broad demographics. At a theoretical level we need a framework in which to analyse and comprehend so that we can deal with such questions as the role of product innovation or responses to GMOs effectively. This chapter draws on a range of perspectives to illuminate how we can approach such issues. From conventional marketing and economics it discusses the role of brands and production quality. This is extended to cover ethical and other attributes of the production process in terms of consumer values. Then, in order to understand the reorientation of consumption towards production, insights from Marxist analysis are developed so that this can be put in context in terms of an historical process with major economic and social implications. In order to set the scene for these perspectives we first consider how our tastes impact upon production. In the discussion of production and consumption, tastes may not at first seem like an issue worthy of inclusion, but tastes here mean not only what we may think is appropriate or prestigious or, indeed, invidious to us as consumers, but also the acquiring of tastes – the tastes that some of us now have for mangetout and kiwi fruit, for mobile phones and Internet shopping, for takeaway meals and foreign holidays. The tastes we have, including those for new and different things, inform the choices we make as consumers and citizens.

Tastes and Consumption Choices

When Appadurai (1986) acknowledged society as outlining the cultural and legally approved 'paths' for the circulation of objects, he also summarized the appropriate forms and types of exchange under different conditions, allowing goods to be traded through formal, economic and legal rules, such as market pricing, forms of credit, the quality of products, the appropriateness of selling second-hand goods or using them as gifts. But he also suggested that there are tendencies for interested parties to engineer 'diversions', to step off prescribed paths, so passages are dynamic and contextualized. In fact, the paths and circulation of goods are in essence as susceptible to innovative dynamics and change as they are to political, economic, technological and social drivers. These paths viewed historically may also have their own social lives. As such, we can view such paths from the production or consumption perspective and how the supplier or the consumer interacts and develops the processes. What is appropriate in terms of production could be of as much concern to us as how something is traded and how it is consumed. In some cases, the process of consumption and trading may dictate how and under what conditions production takes place. Multiple retailers, for example, may assert what is right in terms of milk or fruit production, thus dictating, changing and restricting the producers from whom they buy. But consumers have a stake in this process as well. For example, in a Food Standards Agency survey in the UK in September 2001, consumers were asked about what was important to them in buying food: 46 per cent said cost came first, 18 per cent taste, 17 per cent quality and 12 per cent health (www.kamcity.com). Therefore one could argue that multiple retailers are effectively supported by consumers to minimize costs. It is now widely known that sometimes for significant periods farmers are paid less than the cost of production for many of their goods. In economic terms one might argue that this is a normal feature of how markets work. While the current market power of multiple retailers may have no long-term effect on the supply of milk, it could alter the pattern of distribution permanently and reduce choice of outlet for many other products as well. Effectively, this is loss leading where the loss is borne elsewhere; in the short term by farmers and potentially in the longer term by consumers. Milk is probably the most widely quoted of these goods. In 2001 milk cost approximately 22p a litre to produce, but the farm-gate price at the beginning of March of that year was 17.6p per litre. In supermarkets milk was selling for about 35p. Increasingly supermarkets are also requiring farmers and suppliers to process and pack the food to their specifications. Farmers who cannot afford to purchase their own processing line may find their produce passed on to a supermarket own-brand supplier which makes the farmers' position less stable and easily expendable.[1] Effectively, the supermarkets are moving down the supply chain wielding the power they have to affect and control the production of many goods. As consumers we may want cheap milk, but we might also want to have more choice than what the four out of five multiple retailers who currently dominate the UK market have to offer. What we need to consider is that such production concerns often result from the consumption choices we make.

In some areas choice has declined. While there may be more products to buy in the supermarket, there are fewer different grocery stores to choose to do your shopping in. While there are more product ranges, these ranges are produced by relatively few companies. Such concentration will continue as supermarkets take on the additional roles as chemists, newsagents, clothes and petrol retailers. This is likely to have a huge effect on specialist retailers as consumers save on space and time in the 'one-stop' shop. At the same time consumers, it seems, have to be increasingly involved in the production of their own consumption. We pick up our fruit and vegetables and put it into trolleys, we pack our own bags, we serve ourselves tea and coffee, and if we shop at IKEA we pick up our furniture, put it in our cars and then take it home to assemble. We pay in and collect money from ATM machines and we issue our own books in university libraries. But while we may be more involved in some areas of production, in others we seem further and further away from the reality of our consumption. Partly this has arisen because of the difference between how time and space have been constructed for consumers in their everyday shopping lives. Time for the income-rich is valuable, and can be depicted easily as such with labour-saving devices, meals ready in minutes and admonitions to use our time wisely, constructively – to have laptops small enough so we can work on the train, or to have language tapes to listen to while we are driving to work. Ironically, the poor but time-rich consumers have nevertheless been socialized into also demanding time-saving products. Space is less valuable it would seem because it can be travelled across in an apparently timeless and indeed seamless continuum of exotic foods on our supermarket shelves. Consumers have rarely considered how long it has taken for goods to arrive on supermarket shelves from Ghana, or South Africa; they have been much more concerned with the sell-by and use-by dates as if these were some kind of mantra of suitability. These are symptoms of the traditional pressures towards considering only the direct capacity of commodities to meet our needs. Production has concerned us much less than consumption. But things are changing, a series of food scares, some of them linked with spatial issues, such as foot and mouth, although very much more to do with production issues, as in the case of BSE, have rekindled a desire and a need in consumers to understand the nature of production. Let us turn now to consider how consumers have moved through a cycle that is bringing the importance of understanding production processes and the implications of these processes closer to both the short- and longer-term interests of today's Western consumers. It is too early to say what the ultimate outcome of this movement will be at a time when our expectations are to see strawberries and kiwi fruit year round in our supermarkets, but a reorientation towards production is likely to have a major impact on marketing's understanding of consumers and their priorities in future years. It will affect what and how things are produced and the kind of relationships consumers will expect from suppliers.

The Production and Consumption Relationship

In relation to innovation, production and consumption are inextricably mixed. The more there is produced, the more potentially there is to consume. So while there is reduced choice in terms of the number of alternative grocery outlets, there is at the same time, many more brands on the supermarket shelves than five years ago. Schor (1998) sees the ever-increasing pace of product innovation as having a direct effect on over-purchasing. Lots of 'new' things are being marketed through a lifestyle approach, most of them only incrementally different. Often there is a drive to have what is appropriate, so if you move into a house with a 'fifties' kitchen it is presumed that it will be replaced by something more modern and 'better'. If you don't have a dishwasher, you will be intending to get one at some point; if your current car doesn't have air conditioning, your next one will. 'Gourmet cereal, a luxurious latte, or bathroom fixtures that make a statement, the right statement, are offered to people almost everywhere on the economic spectrum' (Schor, 1998: 5). If it has been produced it can be consumed, and if a new version of a product has been produced, then sooner or later some or all of us will trade up. This 'trading up' is less to do with the choice available and much more to do with what is considered appropriate, fashionable, and also can be used as a means of social distinction. Clearly, the responsibility for such a cycle of production and consumption cannot all be placed at the door of the innovators or lifestyle creators. As consumers we have the choice of whether to spend money changing perfectly serviceable goods such as kitchen units. We may have functional motives for getting a car with air conditioning. It is easy to slight consuming more or different things as only more lifestyle choices yet even when we are aware of the reasons and motivations behind them we are still essentially making value judge-ments. Tim Edwards implies that many goods are primarily produced, marketed and consumed in a sign value rather than use value sense with only passing concern with regard to technical or functional improvement:

> The systems of provision involved in fashion or clothing, cars or many electrical goods, demonstrate significant similarities, as they are all increasingly invested with a strong sense of sign value as opposed to use value, involve similar motives in marketing or purchase centred on the desire to replace often perfectly functional existing products and, in particular are caught up in increasingly international and fast-paced modes of production, with some underlying sense of technological transformation. (2000: 42)

While the importance of sign value need not be underestimated, what is also significantly implied here is the range of motivations and needs that may imbue consumption, some of which are clearly linked to the pro-duction process. Why does a consumer buy a Sony TV, an AEG washing machine or a BMW? Certainly the lifestyle connotations of these items may be motivational factors. The consumer may wish to identify with and be seen to identify with Sony's reputation for technical excellence. However, for many, the brands also offer an implicit guarantee of quality in terms of the nature of their manufacturing. The brand acts as a reputational warranty of quality which forms an attribute for choice, and a functional one at that. I do not believe that I am alone in knowing people who have owned an AEG washing machine for over ten or fifteen years. Understanding these distinctions will be increasingly critical to analysis of emerging trends. We need to clearly distinguish a traditional focus on consumption quality attributes from other motivational impingements on the production process, as the symptom of preoccupation with brands is the same but the analytic and practical consequences are vastly different. They express themselves first in how consumers exercise choice in relation to production.

Consumers, Choice and Production

As consumers we do have some choice in terms of whether we face up to how the things we consume are produced. We can walk up and down the high street and into shops that use children on poor wages and never think of this as we buy our clothes. We can zoom round the supermarket with no consideration as to how the chocolate or bananas arrived on the shelves and we can cook salmon steaks with little wonder as to what chemicals might be part of the bright pink flesh in our frying pans. To paraphrase Slater, the central issue is how in modern life we relate to things (1997). When we lose the connection and the control of that connection, we move into a state of alienation and distance (Slater, 1997). Many see this at its most intense in the increasing differentiation and refinement in tastes and needs. We are so caught up in consumption that we do not have time for concern over production; we can do little to change the production mechanisms, so why should we bother?

While it may appear that we have become less and less connected to the production of things over the years, interestingly motivation research tended to show that the consumer psyche certainly used to strive for maintaining some link to production. Take the case of instant coffee, for example (Haire, 1950). Over 50 years old, this simple case was developed around a projective technique to try to better understand people's responses to a relatively new product at the time, instant coffee. To a standard question such as 'do you use instant coffee?' when a respondent said no and was then asked why, a reply frequently given was 'I don't like the flavour'. The researchers felt that this was a simple answer to what was really quite a complex question, such that it allowed the respondent to give the interviewer an answer but might well conceal other motives. The researchers decided to use an indirect approach. Two shopping lists were prepared, identical except that one specified Nescafé instant coffee and the other Maxwell House ground coffee. One hundred people each had one list only and were asked to read the shopping list and to try to characterize the kind of woman who bought the groceries. As a result a clear picture emerged showing that the instant coffee represented a departure from making the coffee yourself. The Nescafé housewife was more often described as lazy and failing to plan for her household, she was less often described as a good wife or thrifty. Essentially it was the making, the producing of the coffee that was deemed important. The researchers described this aspect of coffee as being of real importance to the consumer's life such that they were effectively motivating purchase and non-purchase, 'Coffee has a peculiar role in relation to the household and the home-and-family character. We may well have a picture, in the background, of a big black range that is always hot with baking and cooking, and has a big enamelled pot of coffee warming at the back' (Haire, 1950: 653). Similarly when cake mixes were first introduced as only needing to be mixed with water, they were largely rejected. It was not until they were replaced by mixes which required adding an egg that they began to gain popularity. The need to retain some connection with production was contained within the addition of an egg. Today these examples may appear little more than amusing, but it reveals the real connection people did need to feel to that production process and may indicate that stepping back into a closer relationship with production in respect of other less tangible attributes is not so far-fetched. Consider, for example, the proliferation of cooking and home-making programmes now on the television. It is often suggested that people watch the celebrity chefs but buy ready-made-meals, but even so, if all they are searching for is some kind of reconnection, it is still a reorientation towards production.

There is actually an increased amount of information available to us as consumers about how our goods are produced and for the prosperous among us we may well have the ability to choose, dependent on our ethical and political motivations. I say the prosperous among us because some consumers really do not have the same choices as others. I can visit my local Tesco and choose to buy their own label brands; I can choose Tesco Finest, Tesco's standard own label goods or the cheapest of the line-up, Tesco's Value items. I can choose to buy organic salmon, free-range eggs and home-produced bacon. I live in an area, and have an income that gives me these choices. But there are many places in Europe and the USA where such choices would not be in the shops to begin with, supermarkets that only stock white sliced bread, sausages with low meat content and pies with high fat content. Some consumers in some locations have no choices about how their goods are produced because they do not have the income to make those choices. If you live on a low income in the North East of England you may not be in a position to consider shopping at the Metro Centre which claims to offer free 'shopertainment' all year round.

Offering the Best in Retail Therapy

MetroCentre offers a unique shopping experience and whether your choice is serious shopping or a family day out, there's always a treat in store for all the family.

MetroCentre offers the very best in 'Retail Therapy'. Famous names – Marks and Spencer, BhS, Littlewoods, House of Fraser, Argos, Gap and Next contrast with smaller special shops in unique themed areas.

The Forum, Garden Court and The Village offer everything from Indian art to collectables and Victorian jewellery.

Open seven days a week, late every weekday, with many restaurants and leisure attractions open even longer. More and more visitors are coming after work in the evening to enjoy an hour or two of shopping and a meal in one of the many restaurants and cafés.

Longer opening hours also means easy access during the weekend, making MetroCentre a relaxed shopping experience for everyone, every day.

MetroCentre is more than just a shopping experience. No longer do children dread the thought of shopping with mum and dad! Leisure attractions include the Centre's unique theme park, The New MetroLand, complete with the New Rollercoaster and Wonderful Waveswinger; UCI eleven-screen Cinema; Crèche; Megabowl Entertainment Centre (offering 20 lanes of computerized ten-pin bowling) and Quasar, a state-of-the-art laser game for all the family.

MetroCentre provide a programme of Shoppertainment throughout the year, which is free fun for all the family.

Whether it is a snack, a meal or a well-deserved drink, you're spoilt for choice with over 50 restaurants, bars and cafés, including a 650-seater Food Court.

If you do not have the money to get there, you have no other choice than to consume what is available in the local shops. Department stores close down, up-market supermarkets see no point in opening in your area; you can't buy the named brands even though you would love to. In the USA small towns such as Hearne in Texas have suffered from the Wal-Mart phenomenon; Wal-Mart went in to the area with low-priced goods, small local shops closed and then eventually Wal-Mart moved out, leaving the town bereft of any shops at all (*Food Junkies*, BBC2 TV, 3 May, 2002). It can be claimed that really there is little new about this. It can also be argued that there is an increasing polarization between those consumers who can afford to be concerned about how goods are produced and those who cannot. As the above makes clear, the relationship between consumption and production is becoming more complex. To begin to develop a framework at a theoretical level, in which to analyse and comprehend the implications, we now look at the extent to which the nature of the production process can be characterized as attributes sought by consumers in the choice of the brands they buy.

Production as an Attribute

Despite what has been said so far, there is little doubt that recent years have seen a growing concern by consumers with the process of production itself as an attribute of the product or service being purchased. Consumers seek to buy goods which come with a guarantee that certain production values have been followed. One of the best known examples is of course the BodyShop which appeals to three key values: the non-exploitation of animals in product testing; the payment of fair wages with provision of good working conditions in manufacture; and environmental responsibility through recycling packaging. The BodyShop example makes clear that the focus is on attributes of production that reflect ethical considerations. It is important in each case to separate these ethically based attributes related to the production process from attributes related to the consumption values of the product. For example, the growing market for organic produce and opposition to genetically modified foods has at least two sets of drivers. On the one hand, there is a traditional concern with the consumption qualities of the food in terms of taste and product safety. The arguments here tend to be based on future risks to health. On the other, there are quite distinct concerns about the side effects on the production side. The arguments here are about the risks to the planet's genetic diversity from unintended gene flow from modified organisms with the prospect of whole eco-systems being destroyed by super-weeds. There are also concerns that in attaching property rights to the building blocks of life a redistribution of the wealth of mankind in its natural endowment is taking place and that the imperatives of our Western economic system are driving a form of neo-colonialism.

Producers are only too aware of new attributes that can be used to enhance their brands and if they have identified that consumers are concerned with production attributes they will build this into the profile of their brands. Klein remarks how Reebok capitalized on the attention being paid to Nike's labour practices by positioning itself as the 'ethical shoe alternative' (2000: 422). Klein quotes the Vice President of Reebok, Jo Harlow, as saying that consumers were looking for what companies stood for, in other words a positively presented ethical position could become a brand attribute. Reebok responded by developing Reebok Human Rights Awards given to activists battling against injustices such as child labour and repressive governments. Klein is not impressed by such a response saying, 'This is all rather sanctimonious, coming from a company that produces many of its shoes in the very same factories as Nike, and that has seen more than its own share of human-rights violations, though with less attendant publicity' (ibid.: 422). Klein also extrapolates one potential route of following the ethical attributes of production as becoming little more than ethical shopping guides helping us make personal lifestyle choices, 'Are your sneakers "No Sweat"? Your rugs "Rugmark"? Your soccerballs "Child Free"? Is your moisturizer "Cruelty-Free"? Your coffee "Fair Trade"? Some of these initiatives have genuine merit, but the challenges of a global labor market are too vast to be defined-or limited- by our interests as consumers' (ibid.: 428). Too easily consumers can be reassured by a label or symbol implying safety or fairness, but as Klein points out, rights cannot be assured by symbols on the labels of well-known brands. Similarly, codes of conduct espoused by producers and made publicly available are also criticized as, unlike laws, they cannot be enforced, have not been drafted together with employee cooperation, but rather have been put together by public relations firms after the companies they represented had been through some kind of embarrassing media revelation.

It could be argued that the rise of ethical considerations in purchasing represents a fundamental re-orientation in the relationship between the buyer and supplier from a system of production of commodities orientation to one focused on the choices of consumers in terms of their sets of preferred attributes. Already in earlier chapters the shortcomings of such a view have been highlighted from the consumption choices perspective, we can also view this from a production perspective. Consider the environmental consequences of productivist agriculture; food is largely sold to consumers on the basis of attributes of appearance, keeping quality, taste and, almost always a poor last, nutritional value. It is produced under conditions of intense world-wide competition. Producers face a given price which does not set a value on any other attribute and in particular does not capture the side-effect consequences of intensive monocultural production, pollution and over-use of unpriced natural resources such as water. The further implications of this process are well described by Schlosser:

In the early 1970s, the farm activist Jim Hightower warned of 'the McDonalidization of America.' He viewed the emerging fast food industry as a threat to independent businesses, as a step toward a food economy dominated by giant corporations, and as a homogenizing influence on American life. In *Eat Your Heart Out* (1975), he argued that 'bigger is not better.' Much of what Hightower feared has come to pass. The centralized purchasing decisions of the large restaurant chains and their demand for standardized products have given a handful of corporations an unprecedented degree of power over the nation's food supply. Moreover, the tremendous success of the fast food industry has encouraged other industries to adopt similar business methods. The basic thinking behind fast food has become the operating system of today's retail economy, wiping out small businesses, obliterating regional differences, and spreading identical stores throughout the country like a self-replicating code. (2001: 5)

Schlosser describes in detail what the foregoing may mean for the small producer. One example he uses is the poultry industry in the USA. Schlosser writes of how the poultry industry was revolutionized by just one innovation; the chicken McNugget which 'turned a bird that once had to be carved at a table into something that could easily be eaten behind the wheel of a car. It turned a bulk agricultural commodity into a manufactured, value-added product' (ibid.: 139). Chicken no longer has to be sold whole, indeed, according to Schlosser, 90 per cent today is sold as 'pieces, cutlets or nuggets' (ibid.: 140). But what is really interesting is the way the chicken processors have developed their production process. There are eight chicken processors controlling around two-thirds of the market. They moved their production to the poor rural south where they entered into a relationship with chicken growers which would appear to advantage only the processor. Often the grower does not own the birds but has them supplied by the processor as day-old chicks. They live on the grower's property but the processing company supplies the feed and technical support. It is a controlling relationship with the power all on the side of the processor, with the result that the grower makes little money and indeed often goes out of business. In some ways this story seems prescient of the current relationship between milk farmers and the supermarkets in the UK and it also indicates the impact that popular forms of consumption, such as processed food, can have on the ultimate producers.

Schlosser's work details many other examples of relationships between large commercial organizations, producers, growers and workers which draw attention to the problems and power relationships which develop in the production and consumption dialectic. That as consumers we have become removed from the production process is well documented; we eat increasingly large amounts of processed food, children have to be taken to special farms where they can see where milk and eggs really come from and they have to be taught at school rather than home what different vegetables look like. But the very recognition of this divorce between production and consumption in the twenty-first century has at least brought with it a rethinking and concern in terms of the implications for local and global consumption. It is important that this is not over-emphasized, the majority of consumers probably have not moved far beyond certain concerns with regard to production in terms such as those espoused by the BodyShop. Nevertheless, there is an increasingly strong trend in academic and media interest in the implications of production on consumption and consumption on production to suggest that sometime in the near future dominant Western consumers may see production processes as integral to their consumption choices, representing a synthesis of the currently clashing and contradictory drivers of consumption and production.

Of course consumption and production have always been linked, however, during the long historical evolution of the relationship, very different forces have been at work. For instance, in the nineteenth century consumers attached value to the very fact that a product was factory-produced and those who made their own at home endeavoured to imitate the manufactured product. The pullovers or 'fisher ganseys' worn in Frank Sutcliffe's photographs of Whitby were hand-knitted in the round but given false side seams so that they looked more manufactured. What we are witnessing in the twenty-first century, however, differs fundamentally in kind; the new focus is on production attributes which potentially impinge widely on our entire social and political structure. While it is possible to analyse both earlier and new concerns in terms of signing values, we must not let this obscure the critical change. Irrespective of whether it is driven by concern or ignorance, how consumers exercise choice with respect to this new set of production attributes as part of their consumption will become increasingly important in terms of understanding consumers for marketers and for those disciplines concerned with consumption. Whether consumers grow up with little understanding of how their food arrives in the shops, let alone how it is grown, or whether they assiduously check the origin and contents of everything they buy, these positions affect marketing. Marketers will increasingly find themselves being held to account ethically and morally, and under pressure from consumers and others with vested interests in how goods are produced. In turn, this has to have an impact on the nature of the goods stocked, how marketers communicate with their customers, and the manner of distribution and pricing; in other words, the marketing mix. It is with this in mind that I suggest the importance of also understanding the historical context of this rebirth of a production orientation.

The Rebirth of the Production Orientation

In the light of what might seem like an overwhelming desire to understand and explore consumption in a postmodern world, production has sometimes become relegated to the backseat, the means to and for consumption but little else. This is perhaps unsurprising given the dominance of neo-liberalist ideology and its stress on consumer sovereignty. In this picture of the world, as depicted in conventional textbooks on economics, well-informed consumers acting rationally express their tastes in purchases. Tastes and attitudes are taken as a given. The role of production and supply is one of a competitive process to satisfy consumers. Others, notably sociologists and anthropologists, despite being primarily concerned with issues of consumption and consumer culture, have explored within the broader context of production and consumption (Miller, 1987, 1998; Lee, 1993; Slater, 1997; Edwards, 2000). In order to accomplish their explorations, they have returned to an analysis of Marx and in particular his belief that production was more than a means to life but rather contained the potential for self-realization and advancement (Lee, 1993). The centrality of production to the human condition for Marx is reflected in the following quotation, 'As individuals express their life, so they are, what they are, therefore, coincides with their production, both with *what* they produce and with *how* they produce' (Marx and Engels, 1974: 42). As Lee expresses this, production is not just a reflection of functional utility but rather it has a 'metaphysical kernel' an essence of its creation and its social and historical context (1993: 5). Central to Marx's view of production under capitalism is the objectification of value which results in an impoverished realization of human activity. 'The object that labour produces, its product, stands opposed to it as *something alien*, as a *power independent* of the producer. The product of labour is labour embodied and made material in an object, it is the *objectification* of labour' (Marx, 1975: 324).

However, as Edwards (2000) makes clear, for Marx consumption was fundamentally inseparable from production, as Marx unmistakably acknowledged that consumption is required for production to exist. A

Marxist understanding of consumption is generally predicated upon a description of the differences in the notions of value. Use value could be described as the functions of commodities, a car is a means of transport, bread is a form of food, while exchange value required the commodities to be products of monetary exchange, with workers part of this process of commodified exchange. Consumers, in the West, have, of course, long existed in a world where the use-values for consumption have been replaced with exchange values. The Western consumer is alienated from all aspects of the metaphysical kernel of production, just as much as the producer is separated from the product of labour. Exchange values fail to signal any of the ethically and culturally relevant attributes which may inform true use value. The objectification of value as exchange value alienates the consumer from these attributes.

It is worth considering what the separation of the production and consumption process might mean to thinkers, activists and consumers. Marx is again the obvious informant here, as central to his analysis of modern capitalism is this development of the separation of production and consumption and the implications for attitudes and tastes. The essence of the Marxist perspective is that we must look underneath the surface phenomena of market exchange and apparently new conceptions of what is desirable to understand them. New attitudes do not drive the system, they are a product of the system. Marx developed his materialist conception of history to explain the process of historical change. The substructure, or productive conditions of the society taken as a whole, drives the superstructure of religion, laws, ethics, institutions and general attitudes. The superstructure should be seen as self-justifying in terms of the interests of the dominant class. Significant changes in how society views issues do not occur because new ideas emerge on what would be better. They occur because changes in the productive forces of society occur and these come into conflict with the existing realities of production and in particular with the prevailing property system. These relations of production serve the self-interest of the dominant class. However, they now act as a fetter on productive change which would favour a rising class. Hence the process of change to a new and more productive economy of necessity involves class struggle. This would clearly involve major changes in social attitudes as the rising class adopts attitudes sympathetic to its own role and self-identification and these come in time to dominate the society. This is of course not to say that the previous attitudes disappear entirely. They are relegated to the margins of society. Central to Marx's work was the need for an environment where production and consumption were integrally and transparently related. But the production of commodities in capitalist society meant that a product was made for sale in the market rather than for direct consumption. The wage earner is not only alienated from his product but the production itself is fragmented through the division of labour which furthers the separation. Importantly, the consumer is also alienated from production. Industrial capitalism means that people are estranged from one another and from the creation of goods. Of course it is this very process which unleashes the productive force of capitalism, something which Marx well recognized as his description of capitalism in *The Communist Manifesto* (Marx and Engels, 1983) attests.

From a managerial perspective the publication of Taylor's (1911) *Principles of Scientific Management* sealed the division between production and consumption in terms of the ideology of capitalist practice. Taylorism, as it became known, aimed to rationalize production through developing principles that would create increased industrial efficiency and productivity. The resulting mechanization, division of labour and rationalization of processes led, of course to the automated assembly line often employing unskilled or semi-skilled labour in highly routinized jobs. It was this system and the dominant role of manufacturing in Western countries which determined the dominant productivist ideology and associated attitudes to consumption which were engendered in all classes. Productivism emphasizes the growing application of technology and the achievement of economies of scale in production. Efficiency and production at the lowest cost are lauded as virtues and failure to be internationally competitive is ascribed to cultural or institutional barriers to the adoption of new technology. Its dialectical twin is consumerism. Consumers adopt a value system of aspiring to a continued supply of new commodities, their palates constantly titillated by advertising to create the market for burgeoning production. Consumers are driven by an imperative to desire new attributes and to constantly upgrade with the focus on consumption values alone, putting aside the issue of whether the commodity is in the first place socially useful. Use values are entirely subsumed by exchange values.

These joint elements have posed and continue to pose major contradictions in modern capitalism. The productivist stress on constantly lowering manufacturing costs made itself felt in the first wave of globalization as successive GATT rounds pursued free trade in manufacture. It was a relatively short step from here to the movement of capital to the Third World. Following years of labour unrest and economic crises in the 1960s and 1970s, manufacturers in a West dominated at the time by a Reagan/Thatcherite view of neoliberal trade saw the prospect of cheap labour with little or no union organization, often in countries with no social security or welfare support for the unemployed, as very attractive. Additionally, in such countries time was an increasingly flexible commodity for producers with the imposition of long working days and no union representation to fight such exploitation. The 'innocent' time–space equation, seen as immensely positive, hid some of the deeper political tensions. Consumerism alienated consumers from the effects on the production chain in their own location. The sporadic attempts to get consumers to buy locally made but more expensive goods were tokenistic and doomed to failure as they defied the basic logic of the system. So the spatial and temporal expansion of capital was underway and with it the production of cheaper goods across space and time which has continued throughout the late twentieth century and into the twenty-first century. The globalization process has imposed major structural change on Western economies. It has also been associated with fundamental change in productive relations through the application of information technology. De-industrialization and a structural shift to services, especially financial services, have involved major changes in the attitudes and tastes which drive consumer behaviour.

The workers in the new dominant sector see themselves as individual agents in a new economy. This rising class does not identify with nationally or locally based productivist relations. They are more likely to identify with their peers in other countries than with other classes in their region. The rising class is income-rich but time-poor and their interests are opposite to those caught in low income and the enforced leisure of unemployment of 'rust-belt' regions. These changes in productive forces favour the expression of new values. The rising class identifies with intangible attributes which, after all, is what they 'produce'. They are more likely to therefore identify with the intangible attributes of commodity production, both traditional service attributes and elements such as environmental or ethical aspects of the production process.

Many of us are members of this rising class or we are influenced nevertheless by its values. What is particularly interesting is that there is a reflection between product and consumption in terms of this temporal and spatial flexibility as if each one is feeding and growing off the other. Lee points to the ability to use and consume goods in a variety of places and at different times which have become so much a feature of modern consumption. Much of this has been due to labour-saving devices and technology including the videocassette, the computer and the mobile phone. Products do not need to be tied to a physical space and television programmes can be watched at any time. We consume more than one thing at a time, eat our meals while watching TV or read a book while listening to music. This has implications for labour again in terms of flexibility of time. Consider the supermarkets and telephone banks open 24 hours, shops open on Sundays – all this is now normal. Some of it is provided by technology, such as ATMs and interactive Internet sites, but other products and services still have to involve labour at the point of sale. Spatially, as well, we expect to consume with increased flexibility, we can use our laptops whenever we travel, we can order food from supermarkets without visiting a store, order airline tickets without going to a travel agent and buy books without ever entering a book shop. We need to understand these changes in the context of the insights into social change discussed from a Marxist perspective above. People do, however, have the ability to operate in a cooperative manner, thus making them a creative species. Importantly, Marx suggested that alienation is not the only route for humans but that it is the result of the economic, social and political institutions which are part of capitalism (Bocock, 1993). While the alienation of modern consumer capitalism has been well documented, we should also consider ways in which such alienation might change or lessen in light of consumers' responses to the experience of such estrangement.

In the past few years there have been a number of commentators who have investigated the production processes of modern consumption and their implications for people, the environment and our futures. Writers such as Klein (2000), Schlosser (2001) and Humphreys (2002) have examined in detail likely futures for consumers and producers and how the way a good is produced directly affects our consumption. In purely material terms we might think about the technological innovations in production and the creative thinking involved in producing new things. Goods have become smaller, TVs and music systems take up less room, compound commodities allow for 'easy' consumption; we can buy ready-made gin and tonics to go with our ready-made 'meat and two veg'. We 'experience' galleries, theme parks and garden centres. But along with the creative side of production we need also to address the other issues related to how, where and under what conditions goods are produced. In what follows we look at these issues using the insights developed on how the production reorientation can be explained. We first trace the implications of space and time constraints before looking at the dark side of productivist extension to the Third World and the dilemmas it poses for both practitioner and analyst before finally addressing the issues and dilemmas posed for innovation, consumption and the role of marketing.

Paths of Production: Space and Time

In the Introduction to their 1996 edition of *The World of Goods* Douglas and Isherwood recount a conversation with the economist Wassily Leontieff:

> 'Where do tastes come from?' he asked, in his direct and searching way.
> 'Well, from the social structure.'
> 'Yes, but what does that mean?'
> 'Well, you could describe the distribution of tastes according to the time and space constraints imposed by occupations.'
> (Douglas and Isherwood, 1996: xxvii)

This response in effect picks up the Marxist insights on the relationship of the economic mode of production to the resultant social structure and ensuing attitudes and tastes. Douglas and Isherwood proceed to develop a pragmatic approach to describing tastes using the time and space constraints the structure imposes. This allows us to draw practical inferences within the relevant historical and cultural reference frame. As socially determined constraints, time and space are fundamental factors in looking at taste and consumption, especially when linked with production and technology. For Douglas and Ishherwood this meant the potential for an apparently neat model which started with consumers whose cultural preferences would drive their choice of goods. In turn, this demand would drive production, and the two together drive technology whose outcomes ultimately affect people. In particular, the outcomes shape consumer space in that people will be crowded together either in tidy or untidy forms or people might escape and live separated from each other. As they say, 'Each social environment permits only certain kinds of control, and this allows the dominant cultural bias to develop' (ibid.: xxvi).

Cultural preferences do drive the production and consumption of goods and technology has allowed a greater range of preferences and this, in turn, has created further outcomes. An example and one that is highly pertinent to the key issue of inclusion of production values may make this clear. Following their line of thinking, it could be plausibly argued that the shift away from being an economy based on manufacturing to one based on services, especially financial services, caused major shifts in productive relations which in turn involve major changes in tastes where space and time constraints have played a major role. The growing service sector has been characterized by a much reduced role for trade unions and the emergence of a new class of workers who identify with individualist work practices. They are relatively income-rich but time-poor. Spatially they identify themselves as agents in a new economy without spatial boundaries other than those set by limitations on access to the Internet. They value what they and their recognized peers produce which are intangible service values. In contrast to the productivist values of value for money in commodities, they are likely to exhibit tastes for similar values in their consumption decisions since in doing so this asserts or signs their own values. This may well account for some consumers asserting ethical attributes of the production process in the expression of their tastes. At the other end of this widening spectrum one could contrast those marginalized by the shift in production relations, unemployed former manufacturing employees who are left income-poor but time-rich and who as a consequence express traditional value for money tastes but in a highly spatially circumscribed environment. There is also the interesting question of if and when the view of the rising class might become dominant and start to seriously influence tastes of other groups. How else might we explain the rising consumption of convenience foods by the income-poor and time-rich?

Nevertheless, some consumers do now reflect on these outcomes in which time and space play crucial roles. The debate about the wrongs and rights of production in a global marketplace is played out in many spheres but nowhere has this been more significant that in the arena of food production and consumption. As an area where all consumers have experience, an examination of our knowledge of food and its production, our purchasing and preferences provides useful insights to understanding. Cook et al. (1998) suggest that debate in this area largely revolves around differences in opinion as to consumer understandings of food provision. So, on the one hand, there are those who believe that consumer knowledge and power will drive the behaviour of retailers and those who regulate them (Kahn and McAllister, 1997), while others question the extent of consumer knowledge and power (Fine and Leopold, 1993), and the nature of the information on food in terms of how it is supplied in such areas as labelling information (Lang, 1996). Cook et al. reject what they call the 'blunt dichotomy between either a knowledgeable, and hence powerful, or ignorant, and hence manipulated, consumer' (1998: 166). Rather, they argue that there is some evidence for both positions, but that consumer knowledge, however extensive it may be, may well be a significant factor in food choices in terms of an increase in concern with the production process of foods, highlighted, for example, in choices made in favour of Fairtrade goods. It is important to remember that many of these concerned consumers are time-poor. Rather than invest time in gathering information, they wish to exercise their consumption choice to create an imperative to provide the information or guarantee the production attribute. Perhaps more important than the extent of any knowledge with regard to production is what the consumer does with what knowledge they have. For example, Cooke et al.'s research on 12 north London households found that consumers established 'thresholds' in which they placed some reliance. So a household might source vegetables from local suppliers thus avoiding the distanciated geography of mainstream foods but on the other hand people could reject the very notion of knowing everything about the origin of their food, not only because it was physically impossible but also, they suggest, because the household may be expressing 'an impulse for food consumption to involve some autonomy from concerns with the public world of provision' (1998: 164). While Cooke et al. reject the notion that consumer cultures that are ignorant or reject their connections to production are amoral (Sack, 1993), they indicate that there is a deep need for individuals and institutions to recognize and take responsibility for the two-way relations between producers and consumers.

More often than not this relationship involves another axis which is built around local and global choice. Purchasing, preparation and consumption of food are time-consuming, such that it is difficult to expect consumers to be involved with the production process other than on the basis of how it might affect their health and economic welfare. Involvement is something that consumers often have little truck with until there is some particular motivation, often personal or risk-induced to change. That people have become concerned is evidenced by responses to issues like genetic modification, but this is an issue that might directly affect our health through consumption, just as BSE in the UK has done. Concerns about the production and distribution of food are in some ways more difficult to respond to and also may involve subtle trade-offs. For example, take the matter of how far food travels before it reaches us; if nothing else, this has an environmental effect. We may prefer to eat organic food because we think it is better for us or the environment but as the chef Anthony Worrall Thompson has pointed out, the calculations and trade-offs we should be making in our choice for organic food may not be so straightforward, 'Why buy organic food which has travelled 10,000 miles when you can buy British and even buy locally and help the environment that way?' (quoted in Mackenzie, 2001: 21). Some foods that we have come to expect and enjoy cannot be grown in the UK but as Mackenzie (2001) says, that does not mean we should not be aware that a kiwi fruit may use five times its own weight in fuel to reach the UK. Over the past 20 years the distance travelled by food in Britain before being purchased has risen by 50 per cent with as much as 70 per cent of the organic market being imported in the UK (Aslet, 2002). So there are a range of existing and potential 'externalities' from health to environmental effects that may be driven by the way food is currently produced and distributed. Add to this, the growth in demand for certain goods and the impact it has on the country where the food is grown and we can see that the implications of not ensuring and understanding the transparency between production and consumption may be huge.

This lack of transparency may be particularly important in the context of sign values. Consuming organic food only sends the correct sign if the information context is supportive, but if organic goods are set within a context of other kinds of exploitation or environmental damage, then such value is lost, but this can only become clear once the consumer is reconnected to the production process and its implications.

> Brazil has one of the worst child malnutrition rates in the world, but devotes millions of acres to growing soya for use in European animal feed. A German study has shown that 80 per cent of Brazil's oranges go into making orange juice that is drunk in Europe. If German rates of drinking orange juice became standard around the world, 32 m acres would be needed just for growing oranges. (Aslet, 2002: i)

One response has been to refocus upon localizing food, but with the best will in the world, as a consumption alternative, this is currently limited to a restricted group of the socially and economically privileged. Aslet points to the development of farmers' markets from the first in Bath in 1997 to the current count of over 300. He continues, perhaps unwittingly highlighting the elitist nature of the distribution: 'Once, farmhouse ice-cream, home-cured bacon and British goat's cheese would have been rarities; now the internet is awash with them' (ibid.: i). The UK government commissioned a report on the future of farming and food in 2001. The central theme of the report issued at the beginning of 2002 was the idea of 'reconnection', including reconnecting consumers with their food and where it has come from. Among their recommendations the Commission suggests the following routes to achieving this particular reconnection:

> Honest, straightforward food labelling to empower consumers and help them make their consciences count at the checkout.
>
> A new national champion for 'local' food, to assist this exciting new market expand. (Policy Commission on the Future of Farming and Food, press release, 2002)

We of course have yet to see what such suggestions will entail and whether the consciences of the multiple retailers will be made accountable. The chief executive of one was on the Commission. The trouble is that as consumers we have come to expect kiwi fruit and mangetout in the farm shop as well as the supermarket. It really would take a huge reconnection with the nature of what is possible locally for such a philosophy to make real inroads into the psyche of most consumers.

We have seen how understanding the relationship between the productive conditions of society and the social determination of time and space constraints can inform analysis. An understanding of the social context is critical for both practice and theory. Like symptoms can have very different causes and we need to be able to make informed judgements about trends, ethical issues and major social, political and economic implications. Using the related concept of commodity fetishism we can further illuminate the critical issues posed by an example which goes to the heart of the operation of the information economy and extends the foregoing to a consideration of the whole value chain.

The grubby chrysalis of production

> The ways in which commodities converge and collect in the market, their untarnished appearance as they emerge butterfly-like from the grubby chrysalis of production, the fact that they appear to speak only about themselves as objects and not about the social labour of their production is ultimately what constitutes the fetishisms of commodities. The sphere of production is thus the night-time of the commodity: the mysterious economic dark side of social exploitation which is so effectively concealed in the dazzling glare of the market-place. (Lee, 1993: 15)

Let us consider one butterfly-like commodity which has emerged from a grubby chrysalis of production – coltan.[2]. Coltan is a dull metallic ore: it is a substance three times heavier than iron and abundantly found in the eastern Congo of Africa, Rwanda and Uganda. Once refined, it becomes tantalum, a high quality conductor of electricity which is highly resistant to heat. This heat-resistant tantalum powder is an essential ingredient in the capacitors needed for laptop computers, cell phones and pagers. The consumption path of the mobile phone is a curious one. It has moved from being a highly functional item used almost exclusively by business people, to fashion object and now it is progressing onwards into being a technically innovative products, with a range of different features and uses. In one domain we can see how its attributes make it a cost-effective tool for those whose work involved issues of mobility and time management. Top executives shared this in common with plumbers and electricians.

However, its adoption by top executives created sign values expressive of aspiration rather than its initial use values. Further change has come about through its miniaturization and its price fell and the mode of purchase changed. For example, the introduction of pay-to-use phones shifted the path immediately from those with existing home telephones to a wider and younger market. Now that the mobile phone has become seemingly ubiquitous, however, the suppliers persuade us that we need to upgrade, and buy newer smaller models with more features. They have also had to face a decline in sign value. However, this rapid take-up has meant that, up until relatively recently, the market for coltan has been buoyant.

Although the Congo is full of natural resources, this 'failed state' has by World Health Organization estimates, 72,800 monthly avoidable deaths from a range of treatable diseases and malnutrition. Its history is one of exploitation from colonial powers; in the nineteenth century when it was a profitable source of ivory and rubber for Belgium, interference from the USA and selfish dictators. Now it is in the grip of a terrifying and complex civil war that has caused the deaths of literally millions of people. In the middle of all of this another battle is being played out, one which links an almost stone age form of production where the labourers barely know what they are mining for and few know how it will be used, with some of the more sophisticated and fashionable elements of Western consumption in the form of mobile phones and laptop computers. Coltan is painstakingly collected through mining with shovels and then panned to separate the dark grit which is coltan from the mud. Many of the miners do not know what they are mining other than it can make them some money, more money than they could possibly earn doing anything else in the Congo. Coltan effectively has become a unit of currency such that people would trade a spoon or a tin of it for food or sexual favours. The gold rush mentality meant that thousands of men left their families, children and crops and the incidence of sexually transmitted diseases including AIDS soared.

The UN Security Council has recently outlined the alleged exploitation of natural resources, including coltan, from the Congo by countries such as Rwanda, Uganda and Burundi involved in the current war. The coltan is smuggled out of the Congo and the revenue raised used to continue the war effort. The Rwandan army may have made as much as $250 million in less than two years through selling coltan although it is not mined in Rwanda and the Rwandan government deny exploiting the Congo's natural resources.

Mining is affecting the lives of all the people and even the animals in the rainforest of the Congo. For example, miners strip off large pieces of the bark of the giant eko tree and use it to make a trough into which they put the mud that bears the coltan which is then flushed with water. This stripping bark has killed thousands of such trees and has directly affected the local pygmies who rely on the eko for supplies of honey which bees make from its flowers. Lots of other people are concerned with the effect mining has on areas such as Kahuz-Biega, a world heritage site and home to the eastern lowland gorilla. When the price of tantalum on the world market soared, thousands of fortune seekers moved into the Congo's national parks in search of coltan. Hunters moved into the park and shot the wildlife to sell to miners for food. While there are many other issues involved in the mining of coltan, not least how it is fuelling the civil war in the Congo, critical to this discussion is the link between the nature and effects of its production and the vagaries of consumption. In the spring of 2000 the price of Coltan crashed, falling to just 8 dollars a kilo in June from the March price of 80 dollars. The demand for coltan from the mobile phone companies fell as their phone sales slumped. This, of course, had an immediate effect on the miners, and they found it increasingly difficult to afford food. There is an ironic twist to the fate of these Congolese producers which has largely come about because of the attention that has been paid to them by the world's media and other concerned bodies. The pictures showing the ruin of the Congo's national parks have led to embargos and companies pulling out of Congolese coltan altogether. Nokia and Motorola, for example, have publicly demanded that their suppliers do not use ore mined illegally in Congo. While coltan has made a great deal of money for the unscrupulous people who have taken advantage of the poor miners, it is these miners who will be the real losers as in this 'failed state' there will not be any constructive Western intervention. 'For local people who are trying to make a bit of money out of coltan, how can an embargo possibly help?' is the question posed by Aloys Tegera, who directs the Pole Institute, a non-governmental social research institute in Coma, in eastern Congo. Tegera is no apologist for coltan, having written a study which examined the social impact of the mining including how teenage girls turned to prostitution to service the miners and how even teachers were lured to mining, leaving schools bereft.

For our purposes it is not the complexity of the moral dilemmas raised over the roles of private enterprise, governments and consumers which is important. Even if the moral issues were clear and consumers knew the implications of what they were buying in terms of the people who had produced it, would it make any difference? Do consumers receive the information, translate it into knowledge on which they take action? This is a bit like asking, what effect does advertising have on sales? The answer is usually something like, we know it does have some impact but we are never sure how much, with whom and what other factors might have had a bearing. In the West we love chocolate but many of us know that countries like the Ivory Coast have had to produce cocoa as a cash crop to repay international loans. Now the Ivory Coast plantations are largely worked by young people who are effectively slaves.

At a public town meeting in April 2000, the people of Garstang declared themselves the first Fairtrade Town. When you visit Garstang, you do not notice any great difference between it and other market towns in the north of England. Many of the shops do try to stock Fairtrade products, but they are on the shelves with all the other goods, all the other varieties of chocolate, and there are far more brands of chocolates than those with the Fairtrade logo. When I asked a local café owner why they stocked both Fairtrade and other brands of chocolate, he replied that they had to as that was what the consumer expected and if they didn't stock it, other shops did and they would lose potential business. As consumers many of us are concerned with how things are produced and with the hardship of those producing the goods, but we are also fickle, we forget and we are wound up with our everyday concerns, we can only realistic-ally expect the understanding of the importance of production to consumption to seep into consumers' consciousness over time, and as has been noted earlier, there are many consumers who quite simply cannot afford to be concerned or even aware of production.

Some (Strong 1997) have highlighted how difficult it is to develop 'equitable' trading relationships between First and Third World countries, and have pointed to the consumers' lack of commitment in this area. Another point that Strong makes is that much of the consumer agenda is defined by the media. For example, Marks and Spencer received mass media coverage when it was alleged that they had indirectly been responsible for the employment of child labour in North Africa; this was an issue that the media took up and for which Marks and Spencer suffered moral outrage. In reality this may have more to do with the combination of a sustained media interest and the high profile of the company. Unfortunately, Strong suggests even Fairtrade consumers are not ethically consistent.

> For example, those who buy Café Direct may pay for the product from a wallet or purse produced by a workforce in a Third World location under conditions of extreme exploita-tion. The consumer who buys BodyShop products because of their fair trade value may dine on fruit picked by people forcibly removed from their land by a company which then employs them for starvation wages. (Strong, 1997: 36)

Perhaps to some extent the answer to the dilemma lies in the response endorsed by Klein. That we live in an 'Age of Shopping' is a reality and stopping people from shopping will not necessarily help, rather it may create a backlash. At another level, anti-shopping protests are arguably too focused on the consumption issues anyway. If the issues end up being only about what we should or should not consume and less about changing the nature of production, will anything ultimately be different? Activists, says Klein, are less bothered about the consumption rights or wrong to the extent that they wear and use the products that might be considered unethical by others, However, she continues:

> They are young men and women in Hong Kong and Jakarta who wear Nikes and eat at McDonald's, and tell me they are too busy organizing factory workers to bother with Western lifestyle politics. And while Westerners sweat over what kinds of shoes and shirts are most ethical to buy, the people sweating in the factories line their dorm rooms with McDonald's advertisements, paint 'NBA Homeboy' murals on their doors and love anything with Meeckey. (Klein, 2000: 429)

As more Fairtrade products come on the market, it is possible that more people will buy them, just as organic goods have greatly increased over recent years, even if at present this is essentially a middle-class phenomenon. As there is more news coverage on items such as chocolate, slavery and prostitution in the Congo, more people will at least be aware and as more books like Naomi Klein's *NoLogo* hit the best-seller lists, then we at least know that this awareness is becoming more widely spread. But just as I have argued that organic food consumption may bring its own unexpected dilemmas in terms of production, the involved consumer needs to be wary about the ultimate implications of their choices.

Innovation and Production

While any discussion of the relationship between production and consumption inevitably focuses on issues of how global consumption may affect Third World production and the implications thereof, we must also look closer to home to see other outcomes of the production–consumption relationship. The fair trade issue shows consumers recognizing that there are ethical production concerns associated with the rights of workers in Third World countries which can be impounded in consumption decisions. Nearer home there is the issue of the intellectual property created by 'street' innovators. Why, for example, are the producers of fashion ideas from the street so often left out of the profits? Agencies employ 'cool-hunters' to seek out what is happening or about to happen on the street, but how are the innovators recompensed if at all? Sometimes McCracken says, citing the West Coast inventors of the Beat and hippie movements, the creators of inventions are so far beyond the mainstream that they would always be alienated from it, but today the mainstream linkage between production and consumption may in one sense be closer, such that the creators of fashion innovations are being culled for their production usefulness without being compensated. McCracken says that those people who are the inventors of contemporary culture should be rewarded but are not:

> as it stands, Nike's chief designer, Tinker Hatfield, goes to the ghetto to see how kids are customizing their sneakers. It is not clear Nike returns profit to the source. It is one thing to hire middle class Afro-Americans and Afro-Canadians to staff stores. Putting educational resources into the community at the point of stylistic origin is quite another. Nike has drawn from the cultural infrastructure here. Isn't this one of the obvious places to make a repayment? (www.cultureby.com)

The need to assess implications such as those suggested by McCracken so far seem to have passed suppliers by. There is an enormous contradiction here. The very existence of patent law and copyright are basic to incentives to invest in innovation in modern capitalism. Research and development budgets have to be justified on the basis that the innovator will have protection from other businesses simply copying the idea when it comes out, without having to bear any of the development costs. We live in a time of unparalleled attention being given to these intellectual property rights, their enforcement and protection, which is hardly surprising given that the value of a company such as Microsoft resides in little else. We have seen that the issue of intellectual property rights has been a major focus of national policy especially in the USA. For instance, resolution of these issues played a key role in US foreign policy support for Chinese accession to the WTO. The very multinationals who vigorously monitor world markets for any infringement of their trademarks or intellectual property and who routinely use the courts to enforce, treat ideas and innovations from the street as a free resource. This is not to suggest that what they do is illegal. However, a black letter law defence of practice is surely unsustainable given the moral outrage often vented over, for instance, illegal copying of software or music. Given in many cases the impracticality of widespread enforcement in this area, the protection of intellectual property depends on the quality of the cultural and moral response and multinationals have not been backward in making this point. Unless one is prepared to denigrate or deny the creativity of the street, the ethical issue would appear to be the same. This sort of contradiction is an emerging risk just as the use of Third World sweatshops was a decade ago, though that is not to suggest it is of the same proportion. Nevertheless we are confronted in marketing from both a practical and theoretical point of view with how we adapt our approaches to embrace this sort of complex challenge. How should the boundary between appropriate and inappropriate use of cultural infrastructure be drawn?

Conclusion

In Fine's (1984) review of Marx's *Das Capital*, he makes clear that Marx viewed the need to produce and consume as integral to human nature. This is still very much the case and as such there is nothing 'wrong' with either production or consumption. But what Marx wanted was the exposure and explanation of social relations and organization of production and, as Fine puts it, 'To distinguish people's possible relations with the physical world from those induced with it and other people' (ibid.: 18). A renewed interest and understanding of existing and potential relations within production processes and their impact on labour value and consumer value are as necessary now as they were in the nineteenth century; more so even as the impact of structures, relations and choices are affecting people across continents, within their own lands and across generations. In this chapter we have looked at issues at the frontier of change in marketing theory and practice. These issues are complex in postmodern Western society as our earlier discussion of paths of involvement made clear. We have drawn on conventional economics and marketing, Marxist analysis and a wide range of other approaches and authors. We have seen how disparate fields can illuminate our understanding of context and issues. In so doing we are again seeing the importance of the central theme of this book. To understand the challenges of marketing in the complexity of the postmodern world we need to be prepared to recognize that this demands an eclectic approach to the knowledge and skills from different disciplines. It is only by bringing these effectively to bear as a team enterprise that we can understand and react appropriately to the challenges posed.

Notes

1   The information in this section owes much to Corporate Watch: Whats wrong with supermarkets? http://www.corporatewatch.org.uk/pages/whats_wrong_suprmkts.htm

2   This discussion on the mining and use of Coltan is based on the following: Harden (2001) and the transcript from BBC Radio 4, *File on Four*, Tuesday, 10 July 2001 (www.bbc.co.uk/radio4).

Chapter 10

Conclusion

This book began by suggesting that marketing needed to reflect upon how it had positioned itself in relation to consumption in advanced Western society. The functional rubrics of segmentation, target marketing and continued innovation practised for so long lack the subtlety to deal with the postmodern world. The current modes of operation exemplified by relationship marketing do little better. Too often marketing has been found wanting and on a number of fronts. Supposedly consumer-centric, it still falls back on power relations and tactics for more consumption rather than better or more appropriate consumption. It innovates in ways that suit suppliers but does not respond readily to consumers who either want something different to what is on offer, or initiate new ways of doing things with existing offerings.

Above all, companies have not been successful at conceptualizing consumer behaviour. There is increasing resistance to marketing although as, Holt (2002) points out, the resistance strategies might be seen as at the extremes of a distribution curve. At one end we may find 'ravenous chameleon-like consumers' (ibid.: 87) who engage and create from the existing brand, using materials to produce different outcomes for their own creative purposes. These might be compared to the use-initiators of this book, the Internet surfers, credit card savers, condom football players and text messaging teenagers who create from existing or new goods benefits and uses not envisaged or sanctioned by marketing. They may also be the cool-hunters, street kids or ageing yuppies who create, develop and discard products as signs of self-identity. So in our argument such creative consumers use products and brands both functionally and symbolically. At the other end of the curve are those consumers who Holt suggests 'get semiotic vertigo from so much cultural fragmentation and dynamism' (ibid.: 87). These may be our downshifters and resisters, they may find reassurance in brand communities or remove themselves from consumption situations. However, this group may well also include consumers as citizens who see alternatives whether through speaking out at annual general meetings, questioning corporate decision-making, or forming new alliances to head off what they may see as inappropriate corporate behaviour. What both these extremes have in common is an increased desire and willingness to understand and be part of production and consumption.

If we consider the path of production to consumption in the twenty-first century it is less prescribed and more dynamic and contextualized than ever before. One of the first lessons that students of marketing learn is that any marketing action is seen within the context of technological, political, environmental, economic and social factors. One can only produce and market products within the limitations of the setting, a motorbike designed for urban driving will not be suitable for use in rugged desert areas, cigarettes will be consumed by children if the culture and legislation approve or ignore the implications. While in the past such factors have been seen as a backdrop to marketing and consumption, increasingly they form the paths on which production and consumption decisions are made. But whereas the opportunities and limitations have been largely in the hands of marketers, the balance of power is shifting. With its shift consumers are becoming increasingly concerned about the entire path from production to consumption and how it impacts upon them. They are interacting and developing the process. Now it may be, as Holt implies, that there is a vast middle of the distribution curve where consumers respond to brands and use them in the development of their self-identity but have too little time or energy to actively develop the dialogue or, to use his terminology, become 'consumer-artists' (ibid.: 87). Nevertheless, the movement at either end of a curve is ultimately likely to have some effect on the less active middle band. We already have examples of this effect in areas such as genetically modified organisms and organic food. The drive against one and for the other by the peripheral consumers has had an impact on the large supermarkets. They are responding with provision of organic goods for all consumers if they choose to buy, and putting up notices saying that their food has not been genetically engineered. The same may happen with FairTrade goods. Increasingly, consumers acting on knowledge of the conditions of production for tea, coffee and chocolate may drive a response from producers. Building on Holt's argument though, one must be aware that the vast middle band includes consumers who are unable to make any choices with regard to consuming appropriately produced goods because they cannot afford or are unable to do so. This of course has an ethical dimension, from a marketing viewpoint. Why do firms market goods they know to be inferior or damaging to health to consumers who do not have the choice or information to resist? Why do financial service companies close branches when they know pensioners will be disadvantaged? Why do supermarkets support charities and schools while wielding power over small producers? Maybe this is about a drive for increased profits that is more important than treating consumers fairly. It may be about power, as Monbiot says, what does it matter if one consumer decides to take their business elsewhere? The supermarkets know there are plenty more out there, one consumer makes no difference to them. There is a counter-argument to this which says that consumers are the final arbiters and if they don't like the company or the brand, it will go out of business (*The Economist*, 2001). This is far too simple an idea; brands are not about a one-to-one relationship of equal parity, they are still about mass marketing and whether consumers can be bothered or able to investigate, discriminate or resist. If some companies are suffering as *The Economist* suggests, it is a long time coming. As Foot suggests in relation to banks in the UK:

> The idea that there is competition between the banks or that competition leads to freedom of choice is laughable. All the banks effectively charge the same rate of interest. The only free choice is to switch banks, if you can find another branch in your neighbourhood and be overcharged and exploited every bit as much. All banks close down branches whenever they can make a profit out of it. What Barclays does today, Lloyds/TSB did yesterday and Natwest will do tomorrow. (2000)

The real point with banks is that scale is important, and with significant barriers to entry there are few producers, and thus there is great potential for tacit collusion and extensive power in terms of the relationship with the end consumer.

The apologists for marketing companies suggest that the arguments of Klein and Schlosser detailed in this book suggest either that the reality is more complicated and that consumers are fickle and companies are vulnerable (*The Economist*, 2001) or that the argument is essentially a political and social one whereby marketing is caught in the crossfire (Holt, 2002). However, *The Economist* also notes that Naomi Klein was ranked as one of the world's most influential people under 35 in *The Times*. It concedes that, published in seven languages, *NoLogo* has touched a universal nerve. If as *The Economist* would have us believe, brand building is becoming trickier, more complex, that consumers are 'seeing through' advertising because they are so adept at reading messages and that marketing and business behaviour are entwined so that greed and hypocrisy are punished, what is marketing's response? According to *The Economist*, the next big thing is social responsibility, and they quote the branding expert Wolf Olins who says 'it will be clever to say there is nothing different about our product or price, but we behave well'. And as if on cue, Barclays bank published an advertisement in *The Financial Times* entitled 'Barclays Awards for people making a real difference',

> Devdass Konaherkanaidu (Dev to his friends), who normally works on the switchboard at Barclays Mauritius, was in London last week at the bank's building at Docklands. But he wasn't answering phones. He was picking up one of the 11 Chairman's Awards for outstanding community and diversity action by bank employees. Mr Konaherkanaidu was recognised for his work in helping to empower disabled people in the south of Mauritius, which has included creating an Association for disabled people, and helping to set up a day centre that provides care, education and social facilities. Incidentally, Mr Konaherkanaidu has been blind since birth. (Barclays advertisement in *Weekend FT*, 22 June 2002: 31)

These are just the first few lines of a lengthy two-page advertisement highlighting what Barclays is doing for communities over the world. This is from a bank who previously told us that the best thing was to be 'Big' and who pay huge salaries to executives while their employees raise small sums for charity. Their pensioners plead for their pensions to rise and their customers see their local banks closing. The failure is that such social responsibility tokenism is just another fad, similar to those outlined by Klein and Schlosser. From a marketing point of view, it will be seen as at best an irrelevance by consumers who have fundamentally shifted their response and are much more likely to respond cynically to such declarations of social responsibility.

The foregoing may look like another diatribe of the Klein, Schlosser variety and at one level it is, but it is also a plea for companies and marketing to understand that now more than ever is the time to rethink their relations with their customers and then the vulnerability that beckons may actually be turned into something useful and beneficial. What might this mean? Above all, it requires trying to understand consumers and to treat them fairly and respond appropriately to them. Real relationships are essential to the health of suppliers and real relationships have to be with real, thinking, active customers whose trust has been earned by treating them fairly and intelligently. It requires serious second thoughts on marketing's approach both as a discipline and function.

Below are highlighted some potentially key issues for reconceptualizing the consumer–marketing relationship.

1 *Consider what having a relationship really means*

First, marketing needs to abandon its hitherto assumed onward and upwards viewpoint and take time to reflect on how the future may be influenced by consumers and then developed by marketers and consumers in tandem rather than conflict. On this issue Holt recognizes just such a dilemma for academic marketing, 'Academic marketing theorizes away conflicts between marketing and consumers. Such conflicts result only when firms attend to their internal interests rather than seek to meet consumer wants and needs. The marketing concept declares that, with the marketing perspective as their guide, the interests of firms and consumers align' (2002: 70). Therefore the rhetoric of techniques such as relationship marketing need to be replaced by an attempt to build tangible relationships whether those be through the creativity of the brand or through functional advantages that the consumer wants and responds to. Assumptions that relationships can be developed through proxies such as loyalty cards are mistakes, what is needed is a real relationship of meaning that the consumer responds to. This may of course require the company to move out of mass marketing mode and assign investment towards significantly different groups, who will change and develop in time and across boundaries. While costly, it may produce real efficiencies as well as profitable relationships that will need maintenance.

2 *Understand the paradoxes of consumption*

Accepting that consumption is important to consumers on a number of different levels both functional and symbolic and that consumers change and are fickle. That we source meaning from our possessions is a normal and natural process but postmodern marketing cannot rely on this alone. Clever, witty advertising and manipulation of fashion cycles are not enough, functional values will also be important. We should not delude ourselves that there is a coming marketing utopia in which people will develop social and cerebral worlds where consumption is a sideline activity. Marketing should and could respond to this subtly by identifying the symbolic and functional needs of consumers better. In particular segmentation variables, rather than just pigeon-holing people, might develop by returning to them truly tailored offerings. Crowding similar people into segments is defensive marketing but identifying key needs and opportunities and then making an offering on that basis is simple, costly perhaps, but likely to achieve a very positive response. What again needs to be addressed is what the relationship and the product or brand mean to the consumer? Meaning to the customer in terms of something really worthwhile, valuable and equitable and for the supplier one that involves commitment such that it is maintained and positive consumer-centric changes are made as and when necessary. Above all, segmentation needs to better reflect consumer behaviour rather than marketing imperatives. This offers the prospect of reducing surprise. As we have seen, traditional techniques are failing to capture the shifting basis of consumer choice.

3   *Accept that the marketplace belongs to the consumer*

Consumers want to use the marketplace. They do not want to be told what to do. They do not want services removed at a moment's notice. They have in the past believed that companies are working for them and not just shareholders and the board of directors, but they learn fast. Technology has given them above all a means to compare notes and to whip up agitation if they feel they have been unfairly treated. The tools are there to undermine the information asymmetry which suppliers have exploited. This is just the beginning. Consumers do have more power now, not as much as some would have us believe, but the power is growing and the knowledge passed from one consumer to another is increasing. Marketing needs to respond by always answering questions and responding to consumer's questions and concerns, if they do not, this will be interpreted as having something to hide. Similarly, companies need to be consistent. Consumers will not be fooled by a nod to charity by overpaid executives. The days of lip service to a consumer-centric approach based on trust are over.

4   *Innovation is for consumers as much as for companies*

Consumers developing new and better ways of doing things need to be embraced pro-actively as a real opportunity to firms rather than seen as a threat. If in the process consumers find they save money or do not necessarily need all the company would like to offer, then so be it, but this is still a marketing opportunity. Strategies which are essentially defensive, and aim at mitigating the risks from the perceived threat, undermine the essence of long-term relationships of trust with consumers. Firms need to look more carefully at how consumers respond to new and old products and brands and learn from it rather than setting themselves up in a fortress with walls which inhibit or stop consumer innovation and use-initiation practices. If a system has been set up that does not work or that the consumers can manipulate to their advantage, then change it but do not penalize your consumer in the process. The short-term gains are likely to be at the expense of hollowing out the long-term advantages of deep investment in relationships.

5 *Innovation and resistance are two parts of a continuum*

Innovation and resistance are not positioned at two ends of this continuum, rather, they are placed on it. As McCracken has shown, innovation can be a shifting, moveable process where resistance is as much part of it as acceptance. Companies need to understand and watch how new things are accepted and rejected in the marketplace and learn from it. They must not assume that consumer resistance is more about the consumer than the product. They need to examine both the functional and, crucially in a postmodern setting, symbolic benefits of the timing of the introduction into the existing market-place to contextualize what they are placing in the market against what is happening and will happen.

6 *Consumption is about production*

Increasingly people are concerned about the production of what they consume. Whether it is the safety of the food we eat, control of the food chain by supermarkets, or the conditions in which our clothes are produced, we are more concerned with revealing and explaining the production process. Partly this is as a direct result of globalization. Initially such globalization divorced consumers from production issues. We may have noted where our clothes were made or that more exotic fruit was on the supermarket shelves but we were too involved in the process of consumption to go beyond the veneer of more choice. This globalization of consumption has become politicized through investigative journalism and health scares. The result is that consumers are better informed. Now they have another choice to make, whether to continue to consume knowing what they know or not? As has been highlighted, the information avail-able to consumers is unlikely to be perfect and some of the choices made may appear contradictory but there is an increasing emanci-patory action going on where consumers respond in some way to a deeper and better knowledge of how their goods arrive in the stores. Holt's distribution curve of consumers may continue with little change coming to the mass in the middle or its shape may transform and the impact of consumers' concern and increased knowledge be felt.

Understanding consumers is the critical first step to marketing reconceptualizing what it is about and what it should be about. This is not in the first instance a question of tactics and strategy but more fundamentally about role and function in today's rather than yesterday's society. There is a need to reflect on the range of choices available to consumers and what this really means to the companies supplying the new and the old products and services to the marketplace. If companies were to use the old marketing technique of SWOT analysis they might find that the opportunities and threats are equally weighted, but the balance could shift, and while the twentieth century was primarily one of opportunities, the twenty-first may not be so kind to them.

It has been the essence of this book that an holistic understanding of the context of consumer behaviour is critical to finding a new relevance for marketing in both theory and practice. Much of what has been outlined and discussed has been about synthesizing material drawn from a range of disciplines. As such, some of it has an inevitably contingent status as part of an exciting dialogue between theorist and practitioner, producer and consumer. Nevertheless, if the new kid on the block in our business schools is to grow up to meet the challenges of postmodern complexity, marketing must throw off the temptations of the false security of the tried and true techniques of avoidance and instead embrace and understand today's consumer. Hopefully, this book is a small step forward on that path.

Bibliography

Adam, B. (1995) *Timewatch* Cambridge: Polity Press.

Appadurai, A. (1986) *The Social Life of Things* Cambridge: Cambridge University Press.

Armitage, S. (2002) 'A tree full of monkeys', http://www.bbc.co.uk/radio3drama/dram3_monkeys.shtml

Aslet, C. (2002) 'Clocking up food miles', *FT Weekend*, 23–4 February: i.

Assael, H. (1987) *Consumer Behavior and Marketing Action*, 3rd edn. Boston: Kent Publishing Company.

Ajzen, I. and Fishbein, M. (1980) *Understanding Attributes and Predicting Social Behavior*. Englewood Cliffs, NJ: Prentice-Hall.

Bannister, E.N. and Hogg, M.K. (2001) 'Mapping the negative self: from "so not me" . . . to "just not me"', *Advances in Consumer Research*, 28. Valdosta, GA: Association for Consumer Research, pp. 242–8.

Barak, B. (1998) 'Inner-ages of middle-aged prime-lifers', *International Journal of Ageing and Human Development*, 46 (3): 189–228.

Barnet, H.G. (1953) *Innovation: The Basis of Cultural Change*. New York: McGraw-Hill.

Bartram, P. (2001) 'Child's play', *Director*, February: 64–7.

Baudrillard, J. ([1970] 1998) *The Consumer Society: Myths and Structures*. London: Sage.

Baudrillard, J. (1981) *For a Critique of the Political Economy of the Sign*. St Louis, MO: Telos.

Bauman, Z. (2001) 'Consuming life', *Journal of Consumer Culture*, 1 (1): 9–29.

Belk, R.W. (1975) 'Situational variables in consumer behavior', *Journal of Consumer Research*, 2: 157–64.

Belk, R.W. (1978) 'Assessing the effects of visible consumption on impression formation', in K.H. Hunt (ed.), *Advances in Consumer Research*, Vol. 5, Ann Arbor, MI: Association for Consumer Research, pp. 39–47.

Belk, R.W. (1980) 'Effects of consistency of visible consumption patterns on impression formation', in J. Olson (ed.), *Advances in Consumer Research*, Vol. 7, Ann Arbor, MI: Association for Consumer Research, pp. 365–71.

Belk, R.W. (1986) 'Art versus science as ways of generating knowledge about materialism', in D. Brinberg and R.J. Lutz (eds), *Perspective on Methodology in Consumer Research*. New York: Springer, pp. 3–35.

Belk, R.W. (1988) 'Possessions and the extended self', *Journal of Consumer Research*, 15: 139–68.

Bender, T. (1978) *Community and Social Change in America*. New Brunswick, NJ: Rutgers University Press.

Benson, J. (1997) *Prime Time: A History of the Middle Aged in the Twentieth Century*. London: Longman.

Berger, J., Blomberg, S., Fox, C., Dibb, M. and Hollis, R. (1972) *Ways of Seeing*. London: British Broadcasting Corporation.

Blair, T. (2001) 'We made progress, despite the violence', *The Sunday Times*, 22 July: 2.

Bloch, P.H. (1981) 'An exploration into the scaling of consumers' involvement with a product class', in K.B. Monroe (ed.), *Advances in Consumer Research*, Vol. 8, Ann Arbor, MI: Association for Consumer Research, pp. 61–5.

Bloch, P.H. and Richins, M.L. (1983) 'A theoretical model for the study of product importance perceptions', *Journal of Marketing*, 47 (3): 69–81.

Bocock, R. (1993) *Consumption*. London: Routledge.

Bourdieu, P. (1984) *Distinction: A Social Critique of the Judgement of Taste*. (trans. Richard Nice). Cambridge, MA: Harvard University Press.

Bowlby, R. (2000) *Carried Away: The Invention of Modern Shopping*. London: Faber and Faber.

Boyd, W. (1998) *Armadillo*. London: Hamish Hamilton.

Brown, D. (1998) 'Conclusion', in D. Brown (ed.), *Thorstein Veblen in the Twenty-first Century: A Commemoration of The Theory of the Leisure Class, 1899–1999*. Massachusetts: Edward Elgar Publishing Inc, pp. 208–11.

Burton, D. (1994) *Financial Services and the Consumer*. London: Routledge.

Campbell, C. (1987a) *The Romantic Ethic and the Spirit of Modern Consumerism*. Oxford: Macmillan.

Campbell, C. (1987b) 'The meaning of objects and the meaning of actions: a critical note on the sociology of consumption and theories of clothing', *Journal of Material Culture*, 1 (1): 93–105.

Castells, M. (2000) *The Rise of the Network Society*. Oxford: Blackwell.

Cook, I., Crang, P. and Thorpe, M. (1998) 'Biographies and geographies: consumer understanding of the origins of foods', *British Food Journal*, 100 (3): 162–7.

Corlett, J. (1999) 'Shattering the stereotypes of the fifty plus shopper', *Vital Speeches of the Day*, 64 (5): 478–80.

Cova, B. (1997) 'Community and consumption: towards a definition of the linking value of product or services', *European Journal of Marketing*, 31 (Fall/Winter): 297–316.

Cova, B. (1999) 'From marketing to societing: when the link is more important than the thing', in D. Brownlie, M. Saren, R. Wensley and R. Whittington (eds), *Rethinking Marketing*. London: Sage, pp. 64–83.

Demby, E.H. (1994) 'Psychographics revisted: the birth of a technique', *Marketing Research*, 6 (2): 26–30.

Dichter, E. (1964) *Handbook of Consumer Motivations*. New York: McGraw-Hill.

Dittmar, H. (1992) *The Social Psychology of Material Possessions*. Hemel Hempstead: Harvester Wheatsheaf.

Douglas, M. and Isherwood, B. (1996) *The World of Goods: Towards an Anthropology of Consumption* revised edn. London: Routledge.

Dover, P.A (1994) 'Why home banking bombed in Britain', *Journal of Retailing*, XV (40): 30–8.

Eco, U. (1977) 'Does the audience have bad effects on television?', *Apocalypse Postponed*. Bloomington: University of Indiana Press, pp. 87–102.

Edwards, T. (2000) *Contradictions of Consumption: Concepts, Practices and Politics in Consumer Society*. Buckingham: Open University Press.

Elliott, R. (1999) 'Symbolic meaning and postmodern consumer culture', in D. Brownlie, M. Saren, R. Wensley and R. Whittington (eds), *Rethinking Marketing*. London: Sage, pp. 112–25.

Engel, J.F. and Blackwell, R.D. (1982) *Consumer Behavior*, 4th edn. London: Dryden Press.

Featherstone, M. (1991) *Consumer Culture and Postmodernism*. London: Sage.

Fine, B. (1984) *Marx's Capital*, 2nd edn. London: Macmillan.

Fine, B. and Leopold, E. (1993) *The World of Consumption*. London: Routledge.

Fletcher, R. and Mills, L. (2001) 'The price is wrong', *The Sunday Telegraph Business*, 7 October, 8.

Fletcher, W. (2000) 'Decisions, decisions', *The Business FT Weekend Magazine*, 29 Jaunary: 34–40.

Foot, P. (2000) 'Close down, cash in', *The Guardian*, 18 April. (http://www.guardian.co.uk/columnists/column.html)

Ford, J. (2001) 'Evolution versus extinction', *The Business FT Weekend Magazine*, 8 December: 12–16.

Fournier, S., Dobscha, S. and Mick, D.G. (1998) 'Preventing the premature death of relationship marketing', *Harvard Business Review*, 76, January/February: 42–51.

Foxall, G.R. (1983) *Consumer Choice*. London: The Macmillan Press Ltd.

Foxall, G.R. (1984) *Corporate Innovation: Marketing and Strategy*. London: Croom Helm.

Foxall, G.R. (1988) 'Consumer innovativeness: novelty-seeking, creativity and cognitive style', in E.C. Hirschman and J.N. Sheth (eds), *Research in Consumer Behavior*, Vol. 3. Greenwich, CT: JAI Press, pp. 79–113.

Foxall, G.R. (1989) 'Adaptive-innovative cognitive styles of market initiators', in M.J. Kirton (ed.), *Adaptors and Innovators: Styles of Creativity and Problem Solving*. London: Routledge, pp. 125–57.

Foxall, G.R. (1994) 'Consumer initiators: both innovators and adaptors!', in M.J. Kirton (ed.), *Adaptors and Innovators: Styles of Creativity and Problem Solving*, 2nd edn. London: Routledge, pp. 114–36.

Foxall, G.R., Goldsmith, R.E. and Brown, S. (1998) *Consumer Psychology for Marketing*, 2nd edn. London: Routledge.

Friends of the Earth(2001) www.foe.co.uk/campaigns/corporates/success_stories/balfour_beatty_give_up.html

Fromm, E. (1976) *To Have or To Be*. New York: Harper and Row.

Gabriel, Y. and Lang, T. (1998) *The Unmangeable Consumer*. London: Sage.

Game, A. and Pringle, R. (1984) *Gender at Work*. London: Pluto Press.

Gatignon, H. and Robertson, T.S. (1985) 'A propositional inventory for new diffusion research', *Journal of Consumer Research*, 11: 849–67.

Gatignon, H. and Robertson, T.S. (1989) 'Technology diffusion: an empirical test of competitive effects', *Journal of Marketing*, 53 (1): 35–49.

Gatignon, H. and Robertson, T.S. (1991) 'Innovative decision processes', in T.S. Roberton and H. Kassarjian (eds), *Handbook of Consumer Behavior*. Englewood Cliffs, NJ: Prentice-Hall, pp. 316–46.

Giddens, A. (1991) *Modernity and Self-Identity*. Stanford, CA: Stanford University Press.

Gold, B. (1981) 'Technological diffusion in industry: research needs and shortcomings', *Journal of Industrial Economics*, 29 (March): 247–69.

Goldsmith, R.E. (1987) 'Self-monitoring and innovativeness', *Psychological Reports*, 60: 1017–18.

Goldsmith, R.E. and Hofacker, C.F. (1991) 'Measuring consumer innovativeness', *Journal of the Academy of Marketing Science*, 19 (3): 209–21.

Graham, G. (1996) 'Debit card transactions top 1 billion', *The Financial Times*, 17 August: 1.

Graham, R.J. (1981) 'The role of perception of time in consumer research', *Journal of Consumer Research* 7, March: 335–42.

Gramsci, A. (1971) *Selections from the Prison Notebooks*. ed. Q. Hoare and G. Nowell Smith. London: Lawrence and Wishart.

Gross, B.L. (1987) 'Time scarcity: interdisciplinary perspectives and implications for consumer behavior', in J.N. Sheth and E.C. Hirschman (eds), *Research in Consumer Behavior* 2. Greenwich, CT: JAI Press, pp. 1–54.

Grunert, S. (1993) 'On gender differences in eating behaviour as compensatory consumption', in J.A. Costa (ed.), *Proceedings of the 2nd Conference on Gender and Consumer Behavior*. Utah: University of Utah, pp. 74–86.

Haire, M. (1950) 'Projective techniques in marketing research', *Journal of Marketing*, 14: 649–56.

Hall, S. (1992) 'Our mongrel selves', *New Statesmen and Society*, June 19, London: 56–58.

Hand-Boniakowski, J. (2001) 'Greed capitalism and dysfunction, methaphoria', 8 (11) http://www.sover.net/~jozef/ac4t0107.html

Harden, B. (2001) 'The dirt in the New Machine', *The New York Times Magazine*, 12 August: 35–9.

Hastorf, A.H. and Cantril, H. (1954) 'They saw a game: a case study', *Journal of Abnormal and Social Psychology*, 49: 129–34.

Hebdige, D. (1979) *Subculture: The Meaning of Style*. London: Methuen.

Hebdige, D. (1988) *Hiding in the Light: On Images and Things*. London: Routledge.

Hesser, A. (2001) 'Spooning up a cloud', *The New York Times*, Dining Out, 15 August: D1.

Hightower, J. (1975) *Eat Your heart Out: Food Profiteering in America*. New York: Crown Publishers.

Hirschman, E.C. (1980) 'Innovativeness, novelty seeking and consumer creativity', *Journal of Consumer Research*, 7: 283–95.

Hirschman, E.C. (1981) 'Technology and symbolism as sources for the generation of innovations', *Advances in Consumer Research*, Vol. 9, Association for Consumer Research, pp. 537–41.

Hirschman, E.C. (1987) 'Adoption of an incredibly complex innovation: propositions from a humanistic vantage point', in M. Wallendorf and P. Anderson (eds), *Advances in Consumer Research*, Vol. 14. Provo, UT: Association for Consumer Research, pp. 57–60.

Hogg, M.K. and Savolainen, M. (1997) 'The role of aversion in product/brand choice', paper presented at the Association for Consumer Research conference, Denver.

Hoggan, K. (1990) 'Whatever happened to Spangles? It needs more than mere nostalgia to persuade companies to keep their often famous brands alive', *Marketing*, 15 February: 22–4.

Holt, D. (2002) 'Why do brands cause trouble?', *Journal of Consumer Research*, 29, June: 70–90.

Horkheimer, M. and Adorno, T.W. ([1944] 1996) *Dialectic of Enlightenment*. New York: Continuum.

Horton, R.L. (1979) 'Some relationships between personality and consumer decision making', *Journal of Marketing Research*, 16: 233–46.

Houston, F.S. (1986) 'The marketing concept: what it is and what it is not', *Journal of Marketing*, 50: 81–7.

Humphreys, J. (2002) *The Great Food Gamble*. London: Coronet.

Hunt, S.D. and Morgan, R.M. (1995) 'Relationship marketing in the era of network competition', *Marketing Management*, 32 (2): 19–28.

Janowitz, T. (1999) *A Certain Age*. London: Bloomsbury.

Jobber, D. (1998) *Principles and Practice of Marketing*, 2nd edn. Maidenhead: McGraw-Hill.

Kahn, B.E. and McAllister, L. (1997) *Grocery Revolution: The New Focus on the Consumer*. Reading, MA: Addison-Wesley.

Kapuściński, R. (2001) *The Shadow of the Sun: My African Life*. London: Allen Lane.

Kassarjian, H.H. and Sheffet, M.J. (1991) 'Personality and consumer behavior: an update', in *Perspectives in Consumer Behavior*. Englewood Cliffs, NJ: Prentice-Hall, pp. 281–303.

Klein, N. (2000) *NoLogo*. London: Flamingo.

Knox, S. and Denison, T. (2000) 'Store loyalty: its impact on retail revenue. An empirical study of purchasing behaviour in the UK', *Journal of Retailing and Consumer Service*, 7: 33–45.

La Ferla, R. (2001) 'Travel to exotic places and buy, buy, buy', *The New York Times*: Sunday Styles, 12 August, (9): 1.

Lang, T. (1996) 'Power to the people', *BBC Good Food Vegetarian*, April: 34–7.

Larréché, N.J.-C., Lovelock, C.H., Parmenter, D. (1997) 'First Direct: branchless banking', in C. Lovelock, S. Vandermerwe and B. Lewis (1999), *Services Marketing: A European Perspective*. Harlow: Prentice-Hall Europe.

Lawson, H. (2001) *Closure: A Story of Everything*. London: Routledge.

Leclerc, F. and Schmitt, B.H. (1999) 'The value of time in the context of waiting and delays', in M.B. Holbrook (ed.), *Consumer Value: A Framework for Analysis and Research*. London: Routledge, pp. 29–42.

Lee, M. (1993) *Consumer Culture Reborn; The Cultural Politics of Consumption*. London: Routledge.

Lee, R.A. (1997) 'The youth bias in advertising', *American Demographics*, 19 (1): 46–50.

Leiss, W. (1976) *The Limits to Satisfaction: An Essay on the Problems of Needs and Commodities*. Toronto: University of Toronto Press.

Leiss, W., Kline, S. and Jhally, S. (1990) *Social Communication in Advertising:*

Persons, Products and Images of Well-Being, 2nd edn. Scarborough, ONT: Nelson.

Levine, R. (2000) 'Talk is cheap', in R. Levine, C. Locke, D. Searls and D. Weinberger (eds), *The Cluetrain Manifesto: The End of Business as Usual*. London: Financial Times, pp. 47–72.

Levine, R., Locke, C., Searls, D. and Weinberger, D. (2000) *The Cluetrain Manifesto: The End of Business as Usual*. London: Financial Times.

Levitt, T. (1983) *The Marketing Imagination*. New York: Free Press.

Lewis, D. and Bridger, D. (2000) *The Soul of the New Consumer*. London: Nicholas Brealey.

Lewis, M. (2001) *The Future Just Happened*. London: Hodder and Stoughton.

Lovelock, C., Vandermerwe, S. and Lewis, B. (1999) *Services Marketing: A European Perspective*. Prentice-Hall Europe.

Lurie, A. (1981) *The Language of Clothes*. London: Random House.

Lury, C. (1996) *Consumer Culture*. Cambridge: Polity Press.

MacKenzie, J. (2001) 'Follow that tomato', *The Big Issue*, 425, 12–25 February: 20–21.

Marcuse, H. (1986) *One-Dimensional Man*. London: Ark.

Martin, J. (1995) 'Ignore your customer', *Fortune*, 1 May, 131, 8: 121–4.

Marx, K. ([1842] 1967) 'The centralization question', *Writings of the Young Marx on Philosophy and Society*, trans. L.D. Easton and K. Guddort. Garden City, NY: Anchor.

Marx, K. (1975) *Early Writings*. Harmondsworth: Penguin.

Marx, K. and Engels, F. (1974) *The German Ideology*. London: Lawrence and Wishart.

Marx, K. and Engels, F. (1983) *The Communist Manifesto*. London: Lawrence and Wishart.

McCracken, G. (1986) 'Culture and consumption: a theoretical account of the structure and movement of the cultural meaning of consumer goods', *Journal of Consumer Research*, 13: 71–83.

McCracken, G. (1988) *Culture and Consumption: New Approaches to the Symbolic Character of Consumer Goods and Activities*. Bloomington and Indianapolis: Indiana University Press.

McCracken, G. (1998) http://www.cultureby.com.

McKibbin, R. (1998) *Classes and Cultures: England 1918–1951*. Oxford: Oxford University Press.

Midgley, D.F. (1977) *Innovation and New Product Marketing*. London: Routledge.

Midgley, D.F. and Dowling, G.R. (1978) 'Innovativeness: the concept and its measurement', *Journal of Consumer Research*, 4: 229–42.

Midgley, D.F. and Dowling, G.R. (1993) 'A longitudinal study of product innovation: the interaction between predispositions and social messages', *Journal of Consumer Research*, 19: 611–25.

Mikkelson, B. (1999) http://www.snopes2.com/coklore/newcoke.htm.

Miller, D. (1987) *Material Culture and Mass Consumption.*. Oxford: Blackwell.

Miller, D. (1998) *A Theory of Shopping*. Cambridge: Polity Press.

Miller, D. (2001) 'The poverty of morality', *Journal of Consumer Culture*, 1 (2): 225–43.

Mitchell, V.-W. and Boustani, P. (1993) 'Marketing development using new products and new customers: a role for perceived risk', *European Journal of Marketing*, 27 (2): 17–32.

Mitchell, V.-W. and Boustani, P. (1994) 'A preliminary investigation into pre- and post-purchase risk perception and reduction', *European Journal of Marketing*, 28 (1): 56–71.

Mittelstaedt, R.A., Grossbart, S.L., Curtis, W.W. and DeVere, S.P. (1976) 'Optimal stimulation level and the adoption decision process', *Journal of Consumer Research*, 3: 84–94.

Monbiot, G. (2000) *Captive State: The Corporate Takeover of Britain*. London: Pan Books.

Moschis, G.P., Lee, E., Mathur, A. and Strautman, J. (2000) *The Maturing Marketplace:Buying Habits of Baby Boomers and their Parents*. Connecticut: Quorum Books.

Mudd, S.A. (1990) 'The place of innovativeness in models of the adoption process; an integrative review', *Technovation*, 11: 119–36.

Muniz, A.M. and O'Guinn, T.C. (2001) 'Brand community', *Journal of Consumer Research*, 27: 412–32.

Nunes, P.F. and Kambil, A. (2001) 'Personalization? No thanks', *Harvard Business Review*, 79 (4): 32–3.

O'Brien, S. and Ford, R. (1998) 'Can we at last say goodbye to social class?', *Journal of the Market Research Society*, 30 (3): 289–332.

O'Guinn, T.C. and Shrum, L.J. (1997) 'The role of television in the construction of consumer reality', *Journal of Consumer Research*, 24: 278–94.

O'Malley, L. and Tynan, C. (1999) 'The utility of the relationship metaphor in consumer markets: a critical evaluation', *Journal of Marketing Management*, 15 (7): 587–602.

O'Shaughnessy, J. (1995) *Competitive Marketing: A Strategic Approach*, 3rd edn. London: Routledge.

Passingham, J. (1998) 'Grocery retailing and the loyalty card', *Journal of the Market Research Society*, 40 (1): 55–63.

Peck, H., Payne, M. Christopher, M. and Clarke, M. (1997) *Relationship Marketing: Strategy and Implementation*. London: Chartered Institute of Marketing and Butterworth-Heinemann.

Peppers, D. and Rogers, M. (1993) *The One-to-One Future*. London: Piatkus.

Peterson, R.A. (1995) 'Relationship marketing and the consumer', *Journal of the Academy of Marketing Science*, 23 (4): 278–81.

Pettie, A. (2001) 'Pick of the day', *The Daily Telegraph*, Television and Radio Seven Day Guide, 10 April: 21–27.

Piirto Heath, R. (1995) 'Psychographics: qu'est-ce que c'est?', *Marketing Tools*, Nov.–Dec. http://www.demographics.com/publications/mt95_mt/9511_mt/MT388.htm.

Pinson, C. (1987) *Swatch*. Fontainebleau: Insead-Cedep.

Price, L. and Ridgway, N.M. (1983) 'Development of a scale to measure use innovativeness', in R.P. Bagozzi and A.M. Tybout (eds), *Advances in Consumer Research*, Vol. 10. Ann Arbor, MI: Association for Consumer Research, pp. 679–84.

Prisig, R.M. (1976) *Zen and the Art of Motorcycle Maintenance*, London: Corgi.

Radley, A. (1996) 'Relationships in detail: the study of social interaction', in D.

Miell and R. Dallos (eds), *Social Interaction and Personal Relationships*. London: Sage and the Open University.

Ram, S. (1987) 'A model of innovation resistance', in M. Wallendorf and P. Anderson (eds), *Advances in Consumer Research*, Vol. 14. Provo, UT: Association for Consumer Research.

Ram, S. and Sheth, J.S. (1989) 'Consumer resistance to innovations: the marketing problem and its solutions', *Journal of Consumer Marketing*, 6 (2): 5–14.

Ramstad, Y. (1998) 'Veblen's propensity for emulations: is it passé?', in D. Brown (ed.), *Thorstein Veblen in the Twenty-first Century: A Commemoration of The Theory of the Leisure Class, 1899–1999*. Massachusetts: Edward Elgar Publishing Inc, pp. 3–27.

Ray, M.L. (1973) 'Marketing communications and the hierarchy of effects', in P. Clarke (ed.), *New Models for the Mass Communication Research*. Beverly Hills, CA: Sage Publications, pp. 147–76.

Reece, D. (2001) 'No one likes us. Do we care?', *The Sunday Telegraph/Business*, 6 May: 5.

Riley, M.W. and Riley, J.W. Jr. (1994) 'Structural lag: past and future', In M. Riley, R. Kahn and A. Foner (eds), *Age and Structural Lag: Society's Failure to Provide Meaningful Opportunities in Work, Family and Leisure*. New York: John Wiley & Sons Inc, pp. 15–36.

Robertson, T.S. (1967) 'The process of innovation and the diffusion of innovation', *Journal of Marketing*, 31, January: 14–19.

Robertson, T.S. (1971) *Innovative Behavior and Communication*. New York: Holt, Rinehart and Winston.

Robertson, T.S., Zielinski, J. and Ward, S. (1984) *Consumer Behavior*. Glenview, IL: Scott Foresman.

Rogers, E.M. (1962) *The Diffusion of Innovations*. New York: The Free Press.

Rogers, E.M. (1983) *The Diffusion of Innovations*, 2nd edn. New York: The Free Press.

Rogers, E.M. (1995) *The Diffusion of Innovations*, 3rd edn. New York: The Free Press.

Rogers, E.M. and Shoemaker, F.F. (1971) *Communication of Innovations: A Cross-Cultural Approach*, 2nd edn. New York: The Free Press.

Rogers, M.F. (1999) *Barbie Culture*. London: Sage.

Rook, D.W. (1985) 'The ritual dimension of consumer behavior', *Journal of Consumer Research*, 12: 251–64.

Sack, R. (1993) *Place, Modernity and the Consumer's World*. Baltimore: Johns Hopkins University Press.

Sahlins, M. (1976) *Culture and Practical Reason*. Chicago: University of Chicago Press.

Sartre, J.-P. (1943) *Being and Nothingness: A Phenomenological Essay on Ontology*. New York: Philosophical Library.

Sartre, J.-P. ([1948] 1973) *Existentialism and Humanism*. London: Methuen.

Schaefer, A. and Crane, A. (2001) 'Rethinking green consumption', in D.R. Rahtz and P. McDonagh (eds), *Globalization and Equity: The Proceedings of the 26th Annual Macromarketing Conference*. Williamsburg, VA: The College of William and Mary, pp. 178–95.

Schlosser, E. (2001) *Fast Food Nation*. London: Allen Lane.

Schor, J. (1998) *The Overspent American: Upscaling, Downshifting, and the New Consumer*. New York: Basic Books.

Schroeder, J.E. (2000) 'The consumer in society: utopian visions revisited', *Marketing Intelligence and Planning*, 18 (6/7): 381–7.

Seybold, P.B., Marshak, R.T. and Lewis, J.M. (2001) *The Customer Revolution*. London: Random House.

Sheth, J.N. (1981) 'Psychology of innovation resistance: the less developed concept (LDC) in diffusion research', *Research in Marketing*, 4: 273–82.

Sheth, J.N. (2001) 'The future of marketing', presentation given at the 10th AMS Congress, Cardiff, July.

Sheth, J.N. and Parvatiyar, A. (1995) 'Relationship marketing in consumer markets: antecedents and consequences', *Journal of the Academy of Marketing Science*, 23 (4): 255–71.

Sheth, J.N., Sisodia, R.S. and Sharma, A. (2000) 'Customer-centric marketing', *Journal of the Academy of Marketing Science*, 28 (1): 55–66.

Shiffman, L.G. and Kanuk, L.L. (1991) *Consumer Behavior*, 4th edn. Englewood Cliffs, NJ: Prentice-Hall.

Shih, C.-F. (1998) 'Consumer experiences in cyberspace', *European Journal of Marketing*, 32 (7/8): 655–63.

Shoemaker, R.W. and Shoaf, F.R. (1975) 'Behavioral changes in the trial of new products', *Journal of Consumer Research*, 2: 104–9.

Sims, J. (2000) 'Stuck on you', *The Business FT Weekend Magazine*, 2 December: 18–21.

Simon, E. (2001) 'Barclaycard drops its annual fee', *The Sunday Telegraph*. Money, 1 July.

Simon, H. (1947) *Administrative Behavior*. New York: Macmillan.

Slater, D. (1997) *Consumer Culture and Modernity*. Cambridge: Polity Press.

Smith, A. (1976) *An Inquiry into the Nature and Causes of the Wealth of Nations*. ed. R.H. Campbell, A.S. Skinner and W.B. Todd. Oxford: Clarendon Press.

Strong, C. (1997) 'The problems of translating fair trade principles into consumer purchase behaviour', *Marketing Intelligence and Planning*, 15 (1): 32–7.

Taylor, F.W. (1911) *The Principles of Scientific Management*. New York: Harper Bros.

The Economist (2001) 'Who's wearing the trousers?', www.economist.co.uk. 6 Sep.

The Financial Times (1990a) 'Access loses Lloyds 375,000 cardholders', 1 February.

The Financial Times (1990b) 'Barclays £8 fee aims to halt decline in profits', 25 April.

The Sun (2000) 'Is it right to ban this ad?', 20 December: 17.

The Times (1998) 'Am I more loyal?', 9 January.

Thibaut, J.W. and Kelley, H.H. (1959) *The Social Psychology of Groups*. New York: John Wiley and Sons.

Tuck, M. (1977) *How Do We Choose? A Study in Consumer Behaviour*. London: Methuen Essential Psychology.

Turckle, S. (1991) 'If the computer is a tool, is it more like a hammer or more like a harpsichord?', *National Forum*, Summer, 71 (3): 8–11.

Tynan, C. (1997) 'A review of the marriage analogy in relationship marketing', *Journal of Marketing Management*, 13: 695–703.

van der Post, L. (2001) 'I am not merely well-heeled, I am also cultivated, sophisticated and knowledgable', *Weekend FT*, How to spend it, (67) April: 8–10.

Veblen, T. ([1899] 1970) *The Theory of the Leisure Class*. London: Unwin Books.

Venkatraman, M.P. (1991) 'The impact of innovativeness and innovation type on adoption', *Journal of Retailing*, 67 (1): 51–68.

Vine, S. (2001) 'Naked ambition', *Times 2*, 28 February: 5.

Waller, W. and Robertson, L. (1998) 'The politics of consumption and desire', in D. Brown (ed.), *Thorstein Veblen in the Twenty-first Century: A Commemoration of The Theory of the Leisure Class, 1899–1999*. Massachusetts: Edward Elgar Publishing Inc, pp. 28–48.

Wasson, C.R. (1971) *Product Management: Product Life Cycles and Competitive Marketing Strategy*. St Charles, IL: Challenge Books.

Weinberger, D. (2000) 'The longing', in R. Levine, C. Locke, D. Searls and D. Weinberger (eds), *The Cluetrain Manifesto: The End of Business as Usual*. London: Financial Times, pp. 39–45.

Wells, W.D. (1975) 'Psychographics: a critical review', *Journal of the Marketing Research*, 12, May: 196–213.

Wensley, R. (1998) 'Falling in love with a marketing myth: the story of segmentation and the issue of relevance', in S. Brown, A.-M. Doherty and B. Clarke (eds), *Romancing the Marketing*. London: Routledge, pp. 74–84.

Winnett, R. and Toyne, S. (2001) 'Switching accounts to be made easier', *Sunday Times*, Money: 1.

Woodruffe, H.R. (1997) 'Compensatory consumption: why women go shopping when they're fed up and other stories', *Marketing Intelligence and Planning*, 15 (6/7): 325–35.

Worthington, S. (1988) 'Credit cards in the United Kindom – where the power lies in the battle between the banks and the retailers', *Journal of Marketing Management*, 4 (1): 61–70.

Worthington, S. (1995) 'The cashless society', *International Journal of retail and Distribution Management*, 23 (7): 31–41.

Worthington, S. (2001) 'M&S finally get a break', (http://uk.news.yahoo.com/010309/27/barhy.html).

Ziliani, C. (2000) 'Retail micro-marketing: strategic advance or gimmick?', *The International Review of Retail, Distribution and Consumer Research*, 10 (4): 355–68.

Index